CW01022783

THE STORY OF YUSUF عليه السلام

A MODERN ANALYSIS OF YUSUF'S عليه السلام RISE FROM THE DEPTHS OF DARKNESS TO THE HIGHEST OF STATIONS

SHAYKH DR. SAJID UMAR

QUILLSPIRE

QUILLSPIRE

The Story of Yusuf ﷺ

A modern analysis of Yusuf's ﷺ rise from the depths of darkness to the highest of stations.

For more information or permission requests, contact:

Quillspire Ltd

Email: contact@quillspire.com

Website: www.quillspire.com

ISBN: 9781739521509

First Edition

Honorifics Key

For the Divine

Symbol	Arabic	Translation
	سُبْحَانَهُ وَتَعَالَىٰ	Hallowed and exalted be He
	تَبَارَكَ وَتَعَالَىٰ	Blessed and exalted be He
	جَلَّ وَعَلَا	Majestic and exalted be He
	عَزَّ وَجَلَّ	Mighty and majestic be He
	جَلَّ جَلَالُهُ	Awesome be His majesty

Prayers of *Salām*

Symbol	Arabic	Translation
	صَلَّىٰ ٱللّٰهُ عَلَيْهِ وَسَلَّمَ	Allah confer blessing and peace upon him
	عَلَيْهِ ٱلصَّلَاةُ وَٱلسَّلَامُ	Upon him be blessing and peace
	عَلَيْهِ ٱلسَّلَامُ	Upon him be peace
	عَلَيْهَا ٱلسَّلَامُ	Upon her be peace
	عَلَيْهِمَا ٱلسَّلَامُ	Upon them (dual) be peace
	عَلَيْهِمُ ٱلسَّلَامُ	Upon them be peace

Prayers of *Riḍā*

Symbol	Arabic	Translation
رضي الله عنه	رَضِيَ ٱللَّهُ عَنْهُ	Allah be pleased with him
رضي الله عنها	رَضِيَ ٱللَّهُ عَنْهَا	Allah be pleased with her
رضي الله عنهما	رَضِيَ ٱللَّهُ عَنْهُمَا	Allah be pleased with them (dual)
رضي الله عنهم	رَضِيَ ٱللَّهُ عَنْهُمْ	Allah be pleased with them
رضي الله عنهن	رَضِيَ ٱللَّهُ عَنْهُنَّ	Allah be pleased with them (fem)

Prayers of *Raḥmah*

Symbol	Arabic	Translation
رحمه الله	رَحِمَهُ ٱللَّهُ	Allah have mercy on him
رحمها الله	رَحِمَهَا ٱللَّهُ	Allah have mercy on her
رحمهما الله	رَحِمَهُمَا ٱللَّهُ	Allah have mercy on them (dual)
رحمهم الله	رَحِمَهُمُ ٱللَّهُ	Allah have mercy on them
رحمهن الله	رَحِمَهُنَّ ٱللَّهُ	Allah have mercy on them (fem)

ACKNOWLEDGEMENTS

From the teachings of the Man of Praise ﷺ is his saying, "He who does not thank the people does not thank Allah." It is in that vein that I eulogise those many individuals who have contributed to my scholastic journey and to the release of this work.

All praise ultimately belongs to Allah, alone. His sovereignty is uppermost and He has no partner. It is through the blessings of Allah that I have been able to bring this book to the world, a book dedicated to studying a story taught to us by Allah Himself. May Allah be pleased with my efforts.

With that in mind, I would like to express gratitude for my parents. Their labours of unconditional love throughout the years have helped me reach a position in which I am able to produce a work such as this. Yaʿqūb's love for Yūsuf ﵇ exemplifies a parental bond that transcends the ages. I only hope that I am able to repay their kindnesses with enough kindnesses of my own so that Allah counts me among those who are excellent to their parents.

Academia comes with its strains and unpredictability. Sharing the burden of all this—with unflinching warmth, patience, and majesty—is my wife, Umm ʿAbdillāh, whom I cherish dearly. Both her and our children, who bring joy to our hearts, deserve acknowledgement and gratitude for their contributions and support. Likewise my two beloved sisters—Allah honour and bless them. Their selfless sacrifices and their unabating encouragement will never be forgotten.

Beyond that, my teachers, colleagues, and students fill the halls of campuses, libraries, and mosques with earnest zeal. My teachers have long stressed the need for independent thought, for a break from blind dogmatism, and for being exceptional in all our endeavours. My students have helped me with logistics, with motivation, and with their fantastic contributions along the way. Their passion and intelligence draws great optimism for the future of this ummah. I would like to take this opportunity to thank all of them.

Shaykh Yusuf Ja'far Idris, Usman Ali, Mohammed Mughal, Mohammed Arshad Ali, Aadil Ali, Azhar Safwan, and the Bhaijee family were instrumental in bringing this work to fruition. I would like to express my warm thanks and gratitude to them. Coupled with their efforts are those of the many institutions that support my vision of a world of ignited communities that benefit humanity. In particular, AlKauthar Institute, Mercy Mission World, Knowledge International University, New Muslim Academy, Muslim Research and Development Foundation (MRDF), The Islamic Council, Islamic Finance Advisory, and Family Events.

I would like to thank the team at Quillspire for their support throughout this project. Their handling of the administrative and logistical aspects of publishing allowed me to complete this work which I had hoped to complete many years ago. Their attention to detail coupled with their fervour for authenticity makes them a welcome addition to our scholastic legacy. This project marks the inaugural launch of Quillspire Ltd as a publishing house. Based on my interactions with the team, I cannot help but feel that Quillspire will soon be a household name synonymous with publishing excellence.

Finally, I would like to thank the esteemed reader and all students of the Glorious Qur'an. As our teachers taught us: *al-Qur'ānu raḥmun bayna ahlih*—"The Qur'an is a fraternity full of compassion among its members." It is an honour to share this book with you. I hope that you pray for me, that you find benefit in this work, and that you forgive me for any mistakes you find in it—exalted be He who never errs. May Allah make us all among His specially chosen folk: the Folk of the Qur'an. *Āmīn*.

Shaykh Dr. Sajid Umar

CONTENTS

PREFACE

The Book of Allah is the greatest blessing that He ﷻ bestowed upon the ummah. The Qur'an is the uncreated speech of Allah ﷻ, and it is His final direct communiqué to the world. It is a mercy, a cure, and a guidance to all of mankind until Allah inherits the earth and all upon it. As such, it is incumbent upon us as the best nation sent forth to humanity to continually renew the qur'anic discourse by delivering its timeless morals to modern audiences.

The story of Prophet Yūsuf عليه السلام is one of the most captivating narratives in the Qur'an. It is a tale of courage, patience, and hope. It is one of overcoming adversity with unyielding faith. The wisdom imbued within *Sūrah Yūsuf* is universal. In this work, we endeavour to demonstrate this universality via engaging and accessible stylistic additions. There are diagrams, tables, and figures throughout the book to break the visual dullness of prose. The use of three unique prompts to engage readers is another innovative approach in our presentation.

These are:

TRANSFORMATIVE WISDOM

REFLECT...

DID YOU KNOW?

The first prompt, 'Transformative Wisdom', is a call to action. It brings an important lesson to the reader's attention which, if applied in their personal life, will undoubtedly transform them for the better. The 'Reflect...' prompt is an invitation to pause and wonder at the profundities found in the story. Finally, the 'Did You Know?' prompt offers readers fascinating factoids and interesting information relating to the *sūrah*.

Imam Ibn Qayyim al-Jawziyyah said that there are more than one thousand benefits in this blessed *sūrah*. Sadly, he did not go on to list them. Though an order of magnitude lower, there are more than one hundred reader prompts—or 'benefits'—across this book. These are not randomly placed, but instead draw directly from the context wherein they are found.

The book is designed to appeal both to the general masses as well as serious students of knowledge. Consequently, the main narrative is discussed in the body of the text, while rigorous linguistic and exegetical analyses are provided in the footnotes. Giants of *Tafsīr* and their works are cited whenever there is room for interpretation. The words of the luminaries in qur'anic commentary perfume the academic references in this work; including figures like Shaykh al-Mufassirīn Ibn Jarīr al-Ṭabarī, Imam Muḥammad al-Qurṭubī, and al-Ḥāfiẓ Ibn Kathīr—as well as many more. Where there are multiple possible understandings, the different views are discussed, and a decision as to the most accurate understanding is tacitly offered.

The book explores and draws upon many relevant qur'anic and Islamic sciences, including prophetic *sīrah*, Arabic syntax and morphology, dream interpretation, and the variant modes of recitation. To aid readers in their personal qur'anic journeys, a set of principles is offered to employ whenever they approach the Qur'an with the intention of reflecting over its message. Throughout the commentary, the Beautiful Divine Names are constantly invoked—in the native Arabic as well as an English rendition—enticing readers to utilise them in their private and public supplications.

In terms of the structure of the book, each chapter begins with an aphorism. The relevant passage from the *sūrah* is then quoted in its original Arabic with an appropriate translation given thereafter. No single published translation was wholly relied upon or copied from, though many were nonetheless consulted. Thereafter, a commentary is given on the quoted passage. It should be noted that, in discussing said passage, it is no longer a 'translation' that is used in the main body of the text, but an expansive interpretation which builds upon the original English translation given.

Qur'anic verses and Hadith reports are all duly referenced. Any scholarly works cited are likewise mentioned accordingly. With *Tafsīr* works, it was deemed sufficient to quote the statement of a given exegete as part of their commentary on the passage in question. This was due to the abundance of commentaries referenced and the frequency with which they were cited. For example, a single verse may yield three references, then the next another two, and the third four references, and so on. As such, the quotations are of the following nature: "Commenting on this verse, Qurṭubī ﵀ said, ... Ibn ʿĀshūr ﵀ said, ... Saʿdī ﵀ said, ..."

It should be noted that the first four chapters discuss preliminary subjects related to the Qur'an, its revelation, and its miraculous nature. These chapters act as a thematic and logical progression which leads readers steadily onto the narrative at hand. The story of Yūsuf ﵇ begins from Part V.

By the grace of Allah, I have delivered lecture series on *Sūrah Yūsuf* numerous times for over a decade now. The first of these was delivered live on air with Radio Islam International spanning fourteen one-hour live broadcasts in 1427 AH/2006 CE. Subsequently, the broadcast evolved into a formal course for AlKauthar Institute that included 120 pages of detailed notes, taught across many countries and reaching the four corners of the globe. Notwithstanding this, every time I share this magnificent story with others, Allah ﷻ allows me to see what I previously had not, and gives me understanding which I previously did not hold. What you have before you is the final iteration of many years' worth of distilled research and reflection.

I pray that readers find as much joy going through this book as I have had authoring it. May it be an edifying and educational experience. May Allah ﷻ allow us, through this work, to come closer to Him, and come closer to emulating His slave and messenger Yūsuf ﷺ.

I ask Allah to accept my meagre efforts as sincere and well-placed. I ask Him to forgive my shortcomings and errors. I ask Him to excuse my inadequacies and flaws. I ask Him to pardon my blunders and oversights. I ask Him to, instead, allow this work to impact the hearts of Muslims across the globe, to allow it to inspire our ummah, and to allow it to guide those searching for a model to follow.

O Allah, You revealed to us the best of stories, here is my attempt to explain it to the people. Accept it from me—I have no haven other than with You. *Āmīn*.

May peace, blessings, and prayers be showered upon our Prophet Muhammad ﷺ.

Praise be to Allah, Lord of the Worlds.

PART

I

INTRODUCTION

There is nothing like the Book of Allah ﷻ.

As a senior among the idolators of Quraysh, al-Walīd ibn al-Mughīrah was encouraged to speak disparagingly about the Qur'an. His response became a timeless testament to its indescribable beauty: "By Allah, the speech which he (the Prophet ﷺ) utters (i.e. the Qur'an) is sweet and graceful. It is fruitful at the top, copious at the bottom. It rises and nothing rises over it, and it obliterates all that is beneath it."[1] If this is what hearing the Qur'an did to a stubborn, arrogant heart, then what of a humble, attentive one?!

In even more moving words, Allah's Messenger ﷺ described the Qur'an with compendious precision: "The Book of Allah! In it are the accounts of those before you, the news of those to come after you, and judgement to rule among you. It is the decisive word, not one taken lightly. Any tyrant that leaves it, Allah breaks him; and whoever seeks guidance from other than it, Allah leads him astray. It is the mighty rope of Allah, the wise reminder, and the straight path. Intentions are set right through it, and opinions are made sound by it. Tongues do not mistake it, and it does not diminish from repetition. Its wonders never end, and the knowledgeable can never have enough of it. Whoever speaks with it speaks the truth. Whoever rules by it judges fairly. Whoever acts upon it is rewarded. Whoever calls to it is guided to a straight path."[2]

1 The full and lengthy account is reported by Ḥākim in his *Mustadrak* (2/507) on the authority of Ibn ʿAbbās ؓ. He graded it as authentic, and Dhahabī supported him on this.

2 Reported by Tirmidhī (2906) and Dārimī (3374) in their *Sunan* on the authority of ʿAlī ibn Abī Ṭālib ؓ. Ibn Taymiyyah ؒ quotes the report in his *Dar' Taʿāruḍ al-ʿAql wa al-Naql* and says: "It has many routes of transmission (*lahū ṭuruq*)", indicating he deems it acceptable.

One of the major themes of the Glorious Qur'an is the account of the prophets عليهم السلام. These accounts serve as a powerful source of guidance and admonishment. Allah ﷻ says: "All what We relate to you of the stories of the messengers is to strengthen your heart therewith. In this there has come to you the truth, a good counsel, and a reminder to the believers."[3] The story of Yūsuf عليه السلام is an excellent example of this. Allah ﷻ says in its conclusion: "This is one of the stories that was beyond your knowledge which we now reveal to you."[4] It is unique among all other qur'anic narratives in that it is the only story of a prophet which has a whole *sūrah* dedicated to it. Other accounts are usually split-up and oft-repeated throughout the Qur'an. For example, various parts of the narrative of Mūsā عليه السلام are recounted separately from one another.[5] All of the story of Yūsuf عليه السلام, from beginning to end, is found in the *sūrah* named after him.

The *sūrah* gives an incredibly comprehensive and detailed account of Yūsuf عليه السلام and his tests. From when he was a young boy who saw an awesome dream until he was finally reunited with his family as one of the most powerful men in the world, there is so much that happens in this prophetic epic. There are so many lessons to learn and morals to internalise. So much of the human experience is expressed in this deeply moving and dramatic narrative. There is something to learn for the weak and oppressed just as much as for the strong and powerful. We can find a masterclass in prophetic parenting in the *sūrah*, as well as a lesson in chastity and fidelity. We are taught grace and moral excellence, as Yūsuf عليه السلام is recognised as

3 *Hūd*, 120.

4 *Yūsuf*, 102.

5 Among all prophets, the story of Mūsā عليه السلام is mentioned most often in the Qur'an. The most extensive passages may be found in *al-Aʿrāf*, *Ṭā-Hā*, *al-Shuʿarāʾ*, and *al-Qaṣaṣ*.

an upright man both in prison as well as when he was the minister of Egypt. Through his experiences, we are also given a stellar example of how to invite to truth with wisdom and eloquence. From this story, we learn patience and foresight. Above all, we learn to always put Allah first and that we must fight to trust His plan.

Further to the narrative itself, there will also be benefits drawn from related qur'anic sciences. Ultimately, this is a book that invites us to instil within ourselves the transformative wisdom of the Qur'an. So bring a sharp mind and an open heart for a unique, engaging, and interactive experience, by the grace of Allah!

PART II

REVELATION

The Qur'an is the best of statements.[1]

Allah ﷻ revealed the Final Testament as a guidance for all mankind until the end of times. On that fateful night in Cave Ḥirā', Archangel Jibrīl ﷺ relayed Allah's words directly to the Prophet ﷺ, commanding him:

اقْرَأْ

❝ Recite! ❞[2]

Over the next twenty-three years,[3] the full Qur'an was revealed to the Prophet ﷺ.

Allah ﷻ says: "The month of Ramadan in which the Qur'an was revealed."[4] He ﷻ also says: "Indeed, We have sent it down on the Night of Destiny"[5]; "Indeed, We have revealed it on a blessed night."[6] In various reports relayed from him, Ibn ʿAbbās ؓ describes the revelation of the Qur'an as being twofold: first from Allah ﷻ to the lowest heaven (*al-samā' al-dunyā*), then from there to the Prophet ﷺ in its appointed time and place.[7]

1 *al-Zumar*, 23.

2 *al-ʿAlaq*, 1. The first five verses of this *sūrah* were the first to be revealed upon the Prophet ﷺ.

3 More precisely, it is just over twenty-three years. The Prophet ﷺ passed away in Rabīʿ al-Awwal, the third month of the Hijrī calendar.

4 *al-Baqarah*, 185.

5 *al-Qadr*, 1.

6 *al-Dukhān*, 3.

7 Reported by Ḥākim in his *Mustadrak* (2879), Ibn ʿAbbās ؓ said: "The Qur'an was sent down altogether to the lowest heaven on the Night of Destiny, then it was sent down

DID YOU KNOW?

Some disbelievers objected to the Qur'an being revealed gradually (*munajjaman*), demanding that it come down altogether in one go (*jumlatan wāḥidah*). Their qualm and the response to it are recorded in the Qur'an:

"Those who disbelieve say, 'If only the Qur'an was sent down to him all at once!' It is such that We may strengthen your heart thereby—We arranged it in precise order—and they do not come to you with an example except that We bring you the truth and the best explanation." Q 25:32-33

MAKKAH AND MADINAH

The call of the Prophet ﷺ is divided into two distinct periods. He ﷺ was born and raised in Makkah. At the age of forty years, it was there that he received the first revelation. For thirteen years he invited to Islam and propagated pure monotheism in the Mother of Cities[8].

[upon the Prophet ﷺ] over twenty years." Ḥākim grades the report as authentic. It is also reported by Bayhaqī in *al-Asmā' wa al-Ṣifāt* (497). Another narration quotes Ibn ʿAbbās as saying: "The Qur'an was taken from *al-Dhikr* (i.e. *al-Lawḥ al-Maḥfūẓ*—the Preserved Tablet) and was placed in the House of Honour (*Bayt al-ʿIzzah*) in the lowest heaven." This is reported by Nasā'ī in *al-Sunan al-Kubrā* (7937) as well as others. As it is a matter of the Unseen, and since a companion is a reliable narrator, this knowledge must have come from the Prophet ﷺ. It is one possible way to reconcile the Qur'an being sent down on a specific night and it being revealed over twenty-three years.

8 Makkah is also known as *Umm al-Qurā*; literally 'the mother of towns.' See Q 6:92, and Q 42:7.

When Allah ﷻ gave him permission to migrate with the Muslims, he ﷺ chose Madinah as the newfound settlement for the believers. The Supporters (*Anṣār*) wholeheartedly welcomed the Migrants (*Muhājirūn*), and the call of the Messenger ﷺ continued for another ten years until he left this world and returned to his Lord.

It is important to note that in the context of revelation, 'Makkan' and 'Madinan' are temporal as opposed to geographical classifications. In other words, Qur'an revealed before the migration to Madinah is referred to as 'Makkan' even if it was revealed in other than Makkah, and Qur'an revealed after the migration is referred to as 'Madinan' even if revealed in other than Madinah.[9]

The nature of the message was undoubtedly different during each period. During the initial phase of the call, it was secretive. It became a public call after the third year from the advent of prophecy. There was immense persecution against the early Muslim community. Naturally, the Qur'an came to strengthen the believers, remind them of what is most important, and grant them solace in a testing time. In Madinah, the believers finally had an independent state and the liberty to act at the command of their leader, the Prophet ﷺ. Thus, the Qur'an came down to regulate their interactions, unite their forces against the enemies of Allah, and admonish the sedition of the hypocrites.

We further notice that the style of Makkan revelation is distinct from the Madinan. Makkan Qur'an is usually comprised of short, succinct,

9 An example of this is the third verse of *al-Mā'idah*: "... Today I have perfected for you your religion, completed over you my blessing, and approved for you Islam as a religion..." It was revealed during the Hajj of the Prophet ﷺ towards the end of his life, and was among the final passages to be revealed upon him. Nonetheless, it is still considered Madinan.

striking verses. Each *āyah* hits hard and penetrates deep. The listener is helplessly disarmed as powerful verse after powerful verse comes down heavy on his ears and heavier on his heart. One cannot help but be left humbled and awestruck at the unrelenting spiritual blows. For example, Allah ﷻ says:

"The Calamity!
What is the Calamity?
What will make you realise what the Calamity is?!
A day when mankind become like scattered moths,
And the mountains become like carded wool."[10]

He ﷻ also says:

"By the morning light,
And the night as it settles,
Your Lord has neither forsaken you nor does He despise you,
And that which is to come is better than what has passed,
And your Lord shall surely give you until you are pleased."[11]

Contrastingly, Madinan verses are usually quite long. They are often formed of many sentences with many clauses. The injunctions therein are detailed and multi-layered, some taking as long as a full page to complete.[12] Allah ﷻ says:

"You who believe, when you contract a debt for a stated term, put it down in writing: have a scribe write it down justly between you.

10 *al-Qāriʿah*, 1-5.

11 *al-Ḍuḥā*, 1-5.

12 In the modern King Fahd copy of the *muṣḥaf*, *Āyat al-Dayn* in *al-Baqarah* takes exactly one side. In it, Allah speaks about loans and contracts. It is the 282nd verse of the *sūrah*, and completely fills page 48 from top to bottom.

No scribe should refuse to write: let him write as Allah has taught him, let the debtor dictate, and let him fear Allah, his Lord, and not diminish anything from it. If the debtor is feeble-minded, weak, or unable to dictate, then let his guardian dictate justly. Call in two men as witnesses. If two men are not there, then call one man and two women out of those you approve as witnesses, so that if one of the two women should forget the other can remind her. Let the witnesses not refuse when they are summoned. Do not disdain to write the debt down, be it small or large, along with the time it falls due: this way is more equitable in Allah's estimation, more reliable as testimony, and more likely to prevent doubts arising between you. But if the merchandise is there and you hand it over, there is no blame on you if you do not write it down. Have witnesses present whenever you trade with one another, and let no harm be done to either scribe or witness, for if you did cause them harm, it would be a crime on your part. Be mindful of Allah, and He will teach you. Allah has full knowledge of everything."[13]

13 *al-Baqarah*, 282.

CLASSIFICATION OF REVELATION

MAKKĪ AND MADANĪ

The scholars have categorised qur'anic verses as being either Makkī or Madanī

Makkī āyāt	*Madanī āyāt*
Those revealed before the Hijrah (migration) of Prophet ﷺ from Makkah to Madīnah.	Those revealed after the Hijrah of the Prophet ﷺ.

General Attributes

Makkī	Madanī
Strong wording and a severe and stern form of address	Gentle style of address
Shorter *āyāt*	Longer *āyāt*
Powerful impact with strong 'proofs' and arguments	Mention of rulings without many proofs and reasoning

General Themes

Makkī	Madanī
1. *Tawḥīd* and the correct Islamic *ʿaqīdah* (creed, in particular that which is related to the worship of Allah ﷻ alone and belief in the Last Day).	1. Detailed rulings regarding *ʿibādāt* (acts of worship).
2. The stories of previous prophets and messengers and their peoples.	2. Detailed ruling on *muʿāmalāt* (social dealings and transactions among people and groups of people).
3. Instilling good character and moral virtue.	3. The theme of Jews and Christians and their religions.
	4. The theme of the *munāfiqūn* (hypocrites), their plots, their plight, and their eventual fate.

FIṬRAH

Allah ﷻ created Ādam ﷺ with His own two hands.[14] After He ﷻ fashioned his form, He blew into him from His own spirit[15] and taught him the Names[16]. Among all of Allah's creation, Ādam ﷺ is unique, and his progeny are honoured.[17] Before we came into this world, we were all made to stand before Allah ﷻ and we bore witness to His lordship.[18] We have been given the trust[19] which the heavens, earth, and mountains saw too great to carry: moral accountability (*taklīf*).

Allah ﷻ says: "Set your face upright to the religion. This is the disposition (*fiṭrah*[20]) of Allah upon which He originated mankind. There is no altering Allah's creation. This is the correct religion, but most people do not know."[21] On the authority of Abū Hurayrah ؓ, the Prophet ﷺ said: "Every child is born upon the *fiṭrah*, then his parents turn him Jew, Christian, or Zoroastrian. It is as a farm animal gives birth to its new-born—do you find it marked by a fault (i.e. severed ear, nose, or

14 See Q 38:75.

15 See Q 15:29, 38:72.

16 See Q 2:31.

17 See Q 17:70.

18 See Q 7:172.

19 See Q 33:72.

20 The trilateral root *f-ṭ-r* (فطر) refers to causing something to come about for the first time, usually breaking or splitting something open in doing so. If one says: *faṭara al-nabāt*, then one means that plants have split the earth and sprouted. The statement: *faṭara nābu al-ba'īr*, refers to a beast's sharp teeth breaking the gums and protruding. This is why the root also has connotations of creation. Allah ﷻ is *al-Fāṭir*—the Originator, the Initiator, and the Creator. Therefore, the *fiṭrah* of a thing is its initial, unadulterated state. It is its 'nature', and the disposition it has been created upon. The *fiṭrah* of mankind is pure monotheism.

21 *al-Rūm*, 30.

lip)?"[22] Abū Hurayrah 🙏 would often recite the forementioned *āyah* after narrating this report.

> ## REFLECT...
>
> Acknowledging the *fiṭrah* instils an attitude of positivity and optimism. Regardless of how corrupt they may be, any person has the potential for transformation. Some of the best companions of the Messenger 🙏 practised idolatry and other heinous deeds before Islam. Yet, when we mention their names now, we honour them by saying, 'May Allah be pleased with them'!

Every human being has the capacity for goodness. It simply has to be ignited. The Arab idolators were no different. They inherited polytheistic practices from their forefathers who changed the pure religion of Ibrāhīm 🙏. They ignorantly associated false deities with Allah 🙏. However, they still believed in Him as God and they honoured the Ka'bah as His House. They needed to be shaken up. They needed a reminder of something they already knew deep within them. A trigger to awaken their conscience. What better reminder than the Reminder, and who better as its carrier than al-Ṣādiq al-Amīn—the True One 🙏?!

Consequently, the aim of revelation sent down during the Makkan period was to do just that. Its focus was on four main themes:

1. Allah 🙏 as the one and only God, and that He alone is worthy of worship.

---

22 Reported by Bukhārī (1358) and Muslim (2658).

2. The Last Day, its cataclysmic events, the resurrection, and the reckoning.
3. The Prophet ﷺ as Allah's true messenger.
4. Upright moral character.[23]

Imagine a large block of ice from which a sculpture is to be formed. An intelligent sculptor is deliberate and precise. He uses sharp, firm, and consistent knocks with his chisel. A clumsy sculptor would smash the block with big swings. Even if he is done in a shorter amount of time, he risks breaking the whole block apart. And even if he manages to have a sculpture at the end, it will not be smooth and detailed. Not only will it lack beauty, but it will likely disintegrate quicker due to internal fractures.

REFLECT...

Another analogy is to think of the *fiṭrah* as the native human programme. Polytheism is the virus, and the Message from Allah ﷻ is the antivirus. Can you think of other analogies to help understand this concept?

To Allah ﷻ belongs the loftiest parable. Makkan Qur'an aimed to chisel away at pagan Quraysh with potent and poignant passages. Allah ﷻ wished to expose their *fiṭrah*, getting rid of the polytheistic filth that had accumulated over their hearts. Had Allah ﷻ revealed rulings and legal injunctions to start with, it would not have impacted them nor moved their hearts. In fact, it would have likely repelled them away from the truth. ʿĀʾishah ﵂ said: "The earliest passage to

23 An example of this is where Allah ﷻ says: "Your Lord ordained that you worship none but Him and that you show excellence to your parents." Q 17:23. This is a Makkan passage.

be revealed was a *sūrah* from the *mufaṣṣal.*[24] In it was the mention of the Garden and the Fire. Once the people returned to Islam, the lawful and unlawful came down. Had the command to not drink alcohol come down from the onset, they would have said, 'We will never leave alcohol'; and had the command to not fornicate come down, they would have said, 'We will never leave fornication.'"[25]

When Allah's Messenger ﷺ sent Muʿādh ibn Jabal ؓ to Yemen, he said to him: "You are going to a people of scripture. When you reach them, call them to bear witness that there is no god but Allah and that Muhammad is the Messenger of Allah. If they obey you in this regard, then inform them that Allah has obligated upon them five prayers every day and night. If they obey you in this regard, then inform them that Allah has obligated upon them a charity that is to be taken from the wealthy among them and given to the poor. Do not take from their most treasured wealth. Beware the supplication of the oppressed, for there is no barrier between it and Allah."[26]

TRANSFORMATIVE WISDOM

We must prioritise *tawḥīd* in our revivalist projects and endeavours. The integral part of daʿwah is calling to Allah ﷻ. It is counterproductive to emphasise external religious practice to someone who has not fully submitted to Allah. Firstly, we must create a bond with Allah founded on worship, adoration, and love. Then we must invite others to do the same. If this is established, adherence to revealed law will take place naturally.

24 The *mufaṣṣal* is everything from *Qāf* to *al-Nās*. The chapters here are shorter and predominantly Makkan (the 28th *juz'* is a notable exception).

25 Reported by Bukhārī (4707) in his *Ṣaḥīḥ* as part of a longer account.

26 Reported by Bukhārī (1496) and Muslim (19) on the authority of Ibn ʿAbbās ؓ.

A SIMPLE MESSAGE

The call of the prophets ﷺ was straightforward. Over and over again, Allah quotes them as exhorting their people: "Worship Allah, you have no other god except Him!"[27] This is the mission that unites the greatest men to walk the earth.[28]

'Alī ibn Abī Ṭālib ؓ said: "Speak to people according to what they know. Do you like that Allah and His messenger be denied?!"[29] There is a time and place for technical theology. There is a context where, to defend Islam, scholars of the ummah have used the enemies' jargon against them and defeated them at their own game. However, disciplines like ontology, epistemology, and dialectic philosophy are beneath revelation. The Book of Allah and the Sunnah of His messenger ﷺ are much higher than any manmade fields of enquiry. The Qur'an is wisdom, guidance, and counsel. It is a cure for sick hearts and a light to eliminate darkness. The legacy of the Prophet ﷺ is to show us how to embody qur'anic values and properly live by them. 'Āʾishah ؓ describes the character of Allah's Messenger ﷺ by saying: "His morality was the Qur'an."[30] He ﷺ was the paragon of virtue.

---

27 *al-Aʿrāf*, 59, 65, 73, 85.

28 There are many chapters in the Qur'an which have a rhetorical seam that runs across the stories of the prophets. In narrating the story of each prophet, Allah uses a similar style or a repeated passage to highlight the universality of pure monotheism. These include *al-Aʿrāf, Hūd, al-Shuʿarāʾ, al-Ṣāffāt,* and *al-Qamar*.

29 Reported by Bukhārī (127) in his *Ṣaḥīḥ*.

30 Reported by Aḥmad (25813) and others.

TRANSFORMATIVE WISDOM

Knowing who your target audience is allows you to gauge the tone you should strike when addressing them. At times, it is necessary to soften people's hearts through moving, emotional sermons. At other times, one must remain objective and level-headed. Appreciating others' temperaments helps inform one's approach in calling them to truth.

SŪRAH YŪSUF

DID YOU KNOW?

The name of Prophet Yūsuf ﷺ is mentioned only twice outside of *Sūrah Yūsuf*: in the 84th *āyah* of *al-An'ām* and the 34th *āyah* of *Ghāfir*. Additionally, it is one of six qur'anic chapters to be named after a prophet. The others are: *Yūnus, Hūd, Ibrāhīm, Muḥammad,* and *Nūḥ*. May Allah confer blessings of exaltation and peace upon all His prophets.

The Makkan period is characterised by patience and perseverance. The hostility of the Quraysh against the believers was great. The early Muslims suffered terrible torture and oppression at the hands of the polytheists. For the most part, it was a time filled with anguish and grief.

The Muslims were socially ostracised with strict sanctions against them, lasting for almost three years.[31]

Following this came the Year of Sorrow: the tenth year after the advent of prophecy, and the third year before Hijrah. The Prophet ﷺ lost his uncle Abū Ṭālib as well as his beloved wife Khadījah ؓ in the same year. Consequently, the idolators' persecution of the Prophet ﷺ was uninhibited. Before his death, Abū Ṭālib's status as chieftain of Quraysh deterred other seniors of the clan from harming Allah's Messenger ﷺ. When he passed away, their tyranny knew no bounds.

Furthermore, the Prophet ﷺ was seeking political alliances during this time. He ﷺ travelled to Ṭāʾif in order to invite its leaders to Islam. However, they denied him and sought to humiliate him in the worst of ways. They sent their children to pelt stones at him, chasing him out of their town.[32]

It was in this context, and as solace during dreadful difficulties, that the Companions ؓ requested from the Prophet ﷺ: "Would that you

---

31 The whole ordeal is referred to as *Shiʿb Abī Ṭālib*, and took place from the 7th year to the 10th year from the advent of prophecy. The *Shiʿb* is the area in Makkah where the Muslims were surrounded and not allowed to trade. There was an agreement among the Quraysh that the Muslims were not to be married into nor dealt with in commerce, and it was hung upon the Kaʿbah—the Arabs venerated covenants this way and honoured their word. This led to severe poverty and loss among the believers. When Allah willed for it to end, the parchment detailing the pact was destroyed by bugs overnight. It is said that everything but the name of Allah was destroyed.

32 The Prophet ﷺ described this as one of the worst days he ever experienced, coupling it with Uḥud. On the authority of ʿĀʾishah ؓ, she asked Allah's Messenger ﷺ: "Did you ever encounter a day worse than that of Uḥud?" He ﷺ replied: "I suffered—how I suffered!—at the hands of your people. The worst of it came on the day of ʿAqabah (i.e. his journey to Ṭāʾif)." Reported by Bukhārī (3231) and Muslim (1795).

narrate to us [stories to console us]."[33] Thus, Allah ﷻ revealed: "We narrate to you the best of stories..."[34]

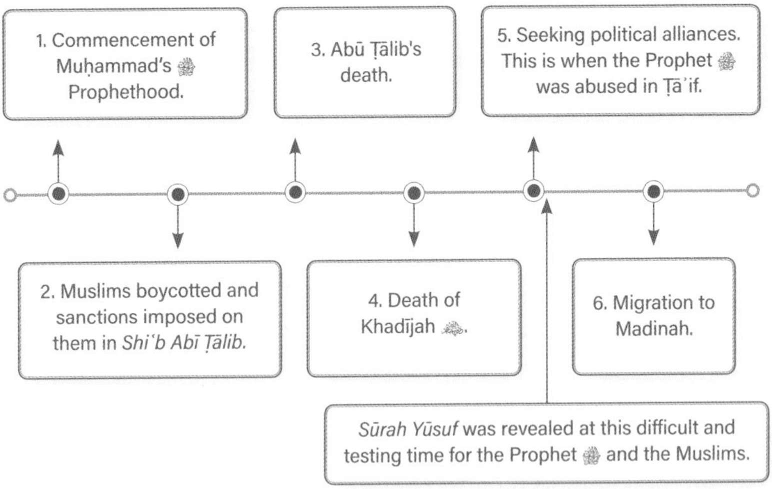
1. Commencement of Muḥammad's ﷺ Prophethood.
3. Abū Ṭālib's death.
5. Seeking political alliances. This is when the Prophet ﷺ was abused in Ṭā'if.
2. Muslims boycotted and sanctions imposed on them in *Shi'b Abī Ṭālib.*
4. Death of Khadījah.
6. Migration to Madinah.
Sūrah Yūsuf was revealed at this difficult and testing time for the Prophet ﷺ and the Muslims.

A message of reassurance is very strongly felt throughout the *sūrah*. Unlike the Muslims during the Makkan period, Yūsuf did not suffer for a decade, but for at least four until Allah ﷻ finally changed his affairs. In this beautiful chapter, we read: "Despair not from Allah's mercy!"[35] It is also here that the adage *ṣabrun jamīl*—'a beautiful patience'—is found.[36] The whole *sūrah* is about having hope in Allah and placing our trust in Him, the Knowing, the Wise.

33 See Wāḥidī's *Asbāb al-Nuzūl* (1/141), commenting on Q 12:3. This is one view with regards to the reason of the *sūrah*'s revelation. Another is that it came as a response to a test from the People of the Book, the Jews among them specifically. The Prophet ﷺ is from the lineage of Ibrāhīm, so they wished to question him about Yūsuf to test his prophethood.

34 *Yūsuf*, 3.

35 *Yūsuf*, 87.

36 *Yūsuf*, 18, 83.

REFLECT...

Does this chapter fit the general pattern of the Qur'an revealed before Hijrah? If not, why do you think that is? It is ultimately a story, and as such requires its own medium of expression with descriptive passages and detailed narration. Short and terse verses would not have accomplished this motif as effectively.

PART

III

‘IN THE NAME OF ALLAH’

Allah ﷻ introduces Himself to us with mercy.

At the beginning of every *sūrah* in the Qur'an, we recite what is known as the *basmalah*:

بِسْمِ ٱللَّهِ ٱلرَّحْمَٰنِ ٱلرَّحِيمِ

❝ In the name of Allah, the Merciful, the Mercifier[1] ❞

The only exception is *Sūrat al-Tawbah*, which was revealed with firmness against the hypocrites and disavowal from the idolaters.[2]

REFLECT...

Among all the Beautiful Names, Allah chose that He be known to us via not just one name of mercy, but two! What better highlights His benevolence for the Children of Adam ﷺ than this?!

1 The names of Allah *al-Raḥmān* and *al-Raḥīm* are both derived from the trilateral root *r-ḥ-m* (رحم), which has connotations of mercy and compassion. The name *Raḥmān* is of the morphological setup *fa'lān*, which implies an internal state. The name *Raḥīm* is of the morphological setup *fa'īl*, which implies an externalised action. That is to say: We recognise Allah ﷻ as *al-Raḥīm* when we perceive that which is merciful and compassionate. When we witness mercy in creation, we witness *al-Raḥīm*. However, Allah ﷻ is *al-Raḥmān* regardless—it is who He is! The latter is the only name used interchangeably with the name 'Allah', and some scholars hold it to be *Ism Allah al-A'ẓam*—the Greatest Name of God.

2 The Prophet ﷺ did not recite the *basmalah* at the beginning of this *sūrah*. This is the bottom line, and any reflections as to the reason thereafter are beneficial though not essential. Nonetheless, it is certainly the case that the themes of the *sūrah* are overtly incommensurate with mercy. It begins with Allah proclaiming: "A repeal from Allah and His messenger from those you have covenanted from the polytheists." Q 9:1.

THE BASMALAH

The Arabic language is a generative one—it allows for the production of new words by manipulating their form.[3] The *basmalah* has no linguistic meaning but for the fact that it is a reference to the statement: *Bismillāhi al-Raḥmāni al-Raḥīm*.[4] Other examples include the *ḥawqalah*[5] and the *ḥay'alah*[6].

It is the motto of the faithful as they embark on any venture, be it banal or grand. It is an invocation of Allah's name and its blessings, a supplication that Allah aids us and places goodness in our endeavours. One possible understanding of the *bā* in *bism*, is that it is one of *isti'ānah*—seeking help. In other words, it is as if one is saying, "I seek help from Allah over this matter and I begin in His name." Thus, before we eat, enter the mosque, or recite the Qur'an, and as we commence any noble deed, we say the *basmalah* to bless our efforts and bring about Allah's grace.

3 This is known as *Ishtiqāq* in the Arabic language. It is to derive words from existing roots (sg. *jidhr*; pl. *judhūr*), words, or sentences to generate new meaning. As explained here, one may use *basmala* and *yubasmilu* as a verb to refer to a person uttering the *basmalah*. Such a person may be referred to as a *mubasmil*. All these are words derived from the utterance: *bismillāh*—'In the Name of Allah.'

4 It is worthy to note that the same is not true for the word *isti'ādhah*. It linguistically refers to seeking refuge and protection. It also refers to the statement: *A'ūdhu billāhi min al-shayṭāni al-rajīm*—'I seek refuge in Allah from the accursed devil.'

5 Referring to the invocation: *lā ḥawla wa lā quwwata illā billāh*—'There is no might nor strength except through Allah.'

6 Referring to the section of the Islamic call to prayer where the muezzin says: *ḥayya 'alā al-ṣalāh; ḥāyya 'alā al-falāḥ*—'Hasten to the prayer; hasten to success.'

QUR'ANICITY

The *basmalah* comes up as part of *Sūrat al-Naml* in the narrative of Sulaymān ﷺ. Quoting how Sulaymān's message to Sheba was received, Allah ﷻ says: "It is from Sulaymān, and it is in the name of Allah, the Merciful, the Mercifier."[7]

As for *Sūrat al-Fātiḥah* specifically, and the beginning of every *sūrah* generally, there are various scholarly positions[8] in terms of the status of the *basmalah*. These are:

1. The *basmalah* is a means of blessings and earning reward but is not an *āyah* of the Qur'an.
2. The *basmalah* is the first *āyah* of every *sūrah*, including *al-Fātiḥah.*
3. The *basmalah* is the first *āyah* of *Sūrat al-Fātiḥah*, but is an independent *āyah* at the beginning of every other *sūrah*.
4. The *basmalah* is an independent *āyah* revealed at the beginning of every *sūrah* of the Qur'an.

The position which accounts for all the available evidence and thus

7 *al-Naml*, 30.

8 The scholars exercise judicious discretion and vast expertise in deducing their verdicts. The process includes authenticating traditions and critiquing their validity, interpreting them holistically, and finally reaching the most proper conclusion given the evidence. On top of that, polymaths and multi-disciplinarians draw upon various fields of knowledge as opposed to just one or two. For example, the science of the *qirā'āt* is one that has some bearing on this matter, since some *qurrā'* recite the *basmalah* between each *sūrah*, others do so as an option, and others omit it altogether except when they initiate their recitation from the beginning of a *sūrah*.

seems most accurate is the fourth, and Allah knows best. The narration which describes the revelation of *Sūrat al-Kawthar* indicates that the *basmalah* was revealed unto the Prophet ﷺ to be recited at the beginning of the *sūrah*.[9] The narration where the Prophet ﷺ speaks about the virtue of *Sūrat al-Mulk* indicates that the *basmalah* is nonetheless independent from the main body of the *sūrah*.[10] There are various other reports used as proof for this position, but these two accounts showcase that the *basmalah* is a unit of revelation, but not one that is part of the *sūrah* in question.

Consequently, the immense reward which the Prophet ﷺ promised the reciter of the Qur'an applies for the *basmalah* as much as the *sūrah* itself. On the authority of the Ibn Masʿūd ؓ, the Prophet ﷺ said: "Whosoever recites a letter of the Qur'an will be rewarded with a good deed (*ḥasanah*), and a good deed is multiplied tenfold. I do not say that *Alif-Lām-Mīm*[11] is a letter. Rather, *alif* is a letter, *lām* is a letter, and *mīm* is a letter."[12] This is one of the many spiritual fruits of this discussion.

---

9 Reported by Muslim (400) on the authority of Anas ibn Mālik ؓ: "While the Messenger of Allah was among us, he dozed then came to, smiling as he did. We asked, 'What makes you laugh, Messenger of Allah?' He said, 'A *sūrah* was just revealed to me.' He then recited, 'In the Name of Allah, the Merciful, the Mercifier...'" The Prophet ﷺ recited the *basmalah* as part of what has been revealed to him before reciting the *sūrah*.

10 Reported by Abū Dāwūd (1400), Tirmidhī (2891), Nasāʾī (10546), Ibn Mājah (3786), and Aḥmad (7975). On the authority of Abū Hurayrah ؓ, the Prophet ﷺ said: "There is a *sūrah* that intercedes for the one who recites it. It is thirty *āyāt*. Verily, it is: 'Blessed be He in whose hand is dominion...' [Q 67:1]" On this occasion, the Prophet ﷺ did not recite the *basmalah* before reciting the beginning of the *sūrah*.

11 Part of *al-Ḥurūf al-Muqaṭṭaʿah*. See next chapter.

12 Reported by Tirmidhī (2910) and others.

PART IV

THE MIRACULOUS QUR'AN

The Qur'an is accessible yet inimitable.

Allah ﷻ revealed it in a clear Arab tongue.[1] He ﷻ chose this language to be the medium for His final revelation. There is immense wisdom behind this. One element of it is that the pre-Islamic Arabs reached a level of eloquence and rhetoric that was unmatched by any other people.[2] Their linguistic heritage was a source of great pride, and it was an integral part of their identity. It was such a powerful tool that a whole tribe may be either elevated or disgraced through a single couplet of poetry.[3]

---

1 *al-Shuʿarāʾ*, 195.

2 The Arabic language has the capacity for immense literary expression. Phonetically, sonorous consonants like the *ʿayn*, *ḥā*, and *ḍād* yield a rich and pleasant cacophony of vocalisations. In terms of semantics, Arabic's subtle morphology (*ṣarf*), intricate syntax (*naḥw*), and vast lexicon (*mufradāt*) give its user the necessary linguistic tools to produce the inimitable.

3 The tribe of Banū Anf al-Nāqah—'the Camelnoses' if converted to English parlance—were so named due to an incident where a man arrived late to a camel-meat banquet held by his brothers. He was only left with the nose. He and his progeny were thence referred to as the Camelnoses. Understandably, they were ashamed of their family name. This was until a poet struck the following parable and it became prevalent among the Arabs:

قَوْمٌ هُمُ الْأَنْفُ وَالْأَذْنَابُ غَيْرُهُمُ .:. وَمَنْ يُسَوِّى بِأَنْفِ النَّاقَةِ الذَّنَبَا

"A people: they are the nose where the rest are tails.
Who is it that equates the camel's nose to its tail?"

The nose is a symbol of haughtiness and the tail one of lowliness. Thus, the label became a source of honour as opposed to shame. Conversely, Numayr were one of the noblest tribes of the Arabs. This was until the well-known poet Jarīr infamously lampooned one of their tribesmen. The heaviest couplet on them was:

فَغُضَّ الطَّرْفَ إِنَّكَ مِنْ نُمَيْرٍ .:. فَلَا كَعْبَاً بَلَغْتَ وَلَا كِلَابَاً

"So lower your head, for you are from Numayr;
Neither Kaʿb nor Kilāb did your people reach."

Numayrīs, once boasting of their lineage to all Arabs, ascribed themselves to ʿĀmir ibn Ṣaʿṣaʿah—Numayr's father and grandfather—after Jarīr humiliated them. If a Numayrī

Allah revealed the Qur'an and challenged the Arabs to produce ten chapters like it. He ﷻ says: "Or do they say, 'He has fabricated it?' Say, 'Then produce ten *sūrahs* like it, fabricated, and call upon whomever you can apart from Allah if you are truthful.'"[4] He ﷻ even challenged them to come with a single *sūrah* like it, the shortest being comprised of three *āyāt*. He ﷻ says: "If you are in doubt about what We have sent down upon Our slave, then bring a single *sūrah* of its like, and call your witnesses apart from Allah if you are truthful."[5] History testifies to their failure. The Qur'an leaves its listeners incapacitated to produce anything like it. Even the staunch disbelievers of Quraysh were mesmerised by it.[6]

REFLECT...

Our capacity to perceive and generate meaning is what makes us distinct from the rest of creation. The timeless miracle of the Qur'an is its language. Unlike other miracles, we are able to enjoy this divine gift until the end of time.

---

was asked of his lineage, he would say he is ʿĀmirī in order to avoid the newfound stigma Jarīr inflicted upon him and his tribe. See Ibn Rashīq's *ʿUmdah* (1/11) and Yūsī's *Muḥāḍarāt fī al-Lughah wa al-Adab* (1/16).

4 *Hūd*, 13.

5 *al-Baqarah*, 23.

6 Ibn Hishām reports in his *Sīrah* that Abū Sufyān, Abū Jahl, and al-Akhnas went out to listen to the Prophet ﷺ reciting Qur'an one night, each unaware of the other's presence. At first light, they left their places and headed back, only for each one to meet the other two on the way. They promised to not return lest false news spreads that they believe in it. The night after, all three went out again, and again the same thing happened—they promised they would not return. On the third night, when they met each other on the way back from listening to the Qur'an for the third time, they took stringent oaths to never return and never did. Such is the Qur'an's beauty and its effect even on the disbelievers. See also al-Walīd ibn al-Mughīrah's description of the Qur'an reported in Part I.

THE DISCRETE LETTERS

There are a number of *sūrahs* which Allah ﷻ opens with discrete, disjointed letters from the Arabic language. They are known as *al-Ḥurūf al-Muqaṭṭaʿah.*[7] The exact significance of the letters used and their combinations is discussed in great length among scholars and commentators on the Qur'an.

DID YOU KNOW?

There are **29** letters in the Arabic language. There are also **29** *sūrahs* which begin with discrete letters. There are **14** letters used disjointedly in the Qur'an:

(ا ح ر س ص ط ع ق ك ل م ن ه ي)

Remembered via the mnemonic:

نص حكيم قطعا له سر

Which aptly means: "A text with wisdom which undoubtedly has a secret."

There are also **14** combinations used as *sūrah* openings:

الم - المص - الر - المر - كهيعص - طه - طسم - طس - يس - ص - حم - عسق - ق - ن

One noticeable pattern is that when Allah ﷻ opens a *sūrah* with such letters, He mentions the Qur'an thereafter. For example, Allah ﷻ says: "*Alif-Lām-Mīm*. This is the Book wherein is no doubt, a guid-

7 Also referred to as *al-Ḥurūf al-Muqaṭṭaʿāt*, *Fawātiḥ al-Suwar*, and *al-Fawātiḥ*.

ance for the God-conscious"[8]; "*Ṭā-Hā*. We have not sent down the Qur'an to you so that you become distressed"[9]; "*Yā-Sīn*. By the Wise Qur'an, you are certainly among the messengers, sent on a straight path."[10]

The same is true for *Sūrah Yūsuf*. Allah ﷻ begins the *sūrah* by saying:

بِسْمِ ٱللَّهِ ٱلرَّحْمَٰنِ ٱلرَّحِيمِ

الٓر تِلْكَ آيَاتُ ٱلْكِتَابِ ٱلْمُبِينِ ﴿١﴾

إِنَّا أَنْزَلْنَاهُ قُرْآنًا عَرَبِيًّا لَعَلَّكُمْ تَعْقِلُونَ ﴿٢﴾

نَحْنُ نَقُصُّ عَلَيْكَ أَحْسَنَ ٱلْقَصَصِ بِمَا أَوْحَيْنَا إِلَيْكَ
هَٰذَا ٱلْقُرْآنَ وَإِنْ كُنْتَ مِنْ قَبْلِهِ لَمِنَ ٱلْغَافِلِينَ ﴿٣﴾

In the name of Allah, the Merciful, the Mercifier.

❝ *Alif-Lām-Rā*. These are the verses of the Clear Book. Indeed, We have sent it down as an Arabic Qur'an so that you may understand. We narrate to you the best of stories in revealing to you this Qur'an; though before it you were among the heedless ❞[11]

From other than the Divine ﷻ, this would be a very bold introduction. In revealing the Qur'an with these discrete letters and mentioning

8 *al-Baqarah*, 1-2.

9 *Ṭā-Hā*, 1-2.

10 *Yā-Sīn*, 1-4.

11 *Yūsuf*, 1-3.

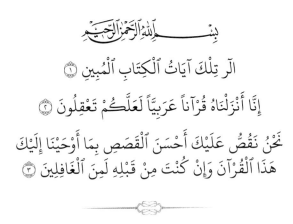

His revelation thereafter, it is as if Allah ﷻ is telling the Arabs: "These are the letters with which you write your poetry and deliver your sermons. Using these letters, here is something you will never come close to imitating."

Subḥān Allah! Truly, as Allah ﷻ Himself says about it, there is no uncertainty, mistake, or inconsistency in the Qur'an. Allah literally spells it out for us, as if telling us, "These are the basic units from which you produce language. With the very same units, I will bring about a literary miracle!"

All praise is due to Allah, Lord of the Worlds.

NON-ARABIC IN THE QUR'AN

On many occasions, Allah ﷻ describes the Qur'an as a clear Arabic exposition.[12] The nature of human language is that it evolves over time. There are many factors which influence this development, geography being one of the most important. Arabic is a Semitic language. Uniquely among this family of languages, it is native to a peninsula.[13] This, along with the disinterest neighbouring civilisations had in Arabia,[14] encouraged an isolated preservation which the Arabic language enjoyed for centuries.[15]

12 As in the third *āyah* of the *sūrah*. See also, for example, Q 13:37, 16:103, 39:28, 46:12.

13 Among the extant Semitic languages, Ethiopic varieties are native to East Africa and Hebrew to the Middle East, north of the Arabian Peninsula.

14 The Romans and the Persians warred for over six centuries, but did not view any excursions to Arabia as worth their time. As far as they were concerned, the Arabs were barbaric desert-dwellers with no value to offer.

15 Keep in mind that scientific classifications are post-fact. That is to say, there is first the

Nonetheless, there are what we can retrospectively refer to as 'non-Arabic' words that have been adopted by the native Arabs in their language. The phenomenon has always taken place among interacting demographics, but is especially evident in the modern age. Globalisation invites an interchange of cultural ideas unprecedented in antiquity. For example, English words like 'naïve', 'blasé', and 'savant' have been adopted from French over the last few centuries; whereas the word 'manga'—literally 'whimsical pictures' in Japanese—was only adopted in English some fifty years ago since the Japanese-style comics became popular in the West.

Therefore, it is of no surprise that there are words in the Qur'an which trace their origin from other than Arabic. For example, the names of non-Arab persons and places are Arabised. Nūḥ and Idrīs ﷺ lived before what we qualify as classical Arabic. Many of the prophets mentioned in the Qur'an are Hebrew by blood—*Banū Isrāʾīl* are the Children of Israel, Yaʿqūb ﷺ. There are many examples of this in the Qur'an.

Scholars have spoken about words like *Jahannam*, *dīnār*, *istabraq*, and others, exploring their origin and discussing their etymology. Regardless, these are words the ancient Arabs used in their language before revelation. Had it been perceived as an inconsistency by the idolaters post-revelation, they would have used this to attack the Qur'an.

Even if, for argument's sake, one qualifies such words as non-Ar-

---

organic phenomenon which takes place in the world, then our observing it and generalising 'rules' concerning it thereafter. Since Noam Chomsky's articulation of the theory, it is now a matter of consensus that human beings have a universal grammar. Thus, what we refer to as different languages and dialects is relative to our interest.

abic vis-à-vis their linguistic origin, this would not in any capacity take away from the essential Arabic nature of the Qur'an. Would a sound-minded, reasonable person seriously argue that a medical textbook written in English is in fact Greek by virtue of the etymology of certain technical terms within it? Today, the news broadcasted in the Arab world is in modern standard Arabic, where there are words directly transliterated from other languages.[16] No rational actor would argue that the language used is no longer Arabic due to the usage of such transliterations.

Consequently, to pontificate that the Qur'an 'has non-Arabic words' and attempt to use that as a tool to detract from its veracity is unfounded orientalist stickling.

TIMELESS PERFECTION

The will of Allah ﷻ dictated that the recipient of revelation be a human heart. It is the Heavy Word.[17] Mighty mountains would be left asunder in its wake, quaking in abject humility.[18] Yet, the heart of the Prophet ﷺ bore it. Allah ﷻ says: "Verily, it is what the Lord of the

16 The prevalence of certain words across cultures resulted in their being transliterated instead of translated, especially among the masses. For example, 'democracy' is rendered الديمقراطية (*dīmuqrāṭiyyah*) in Arabic, even though an effective translation may be حكم الأغلبية—'majority rule.' In fact, this is a perfect case in point. The word 'democracy' is itself not a native English word. It is adopted from the ancient Greek δημοκρατία, romanized: dēmokratía, from dēmos 'people' and kratos 'rule' [See: 'Democracy,' Oxford University Press]. If a contentious adversary were to see this argument through to its logical conclusion, English would not be English at all, rather some curious amalgam of Anglo-Saxon, Latin, Celtic, Norse, and Greek.

17 *al-Muzzammil*, 5.

18 *al-Ḥashr*, 21.

Worlds sent down—the Trustworthy Spirit came down with it—upon your heart so that you may be of the warners."[19]

There is nothing that affects the human heart like the Qur'an. Nothing has the potential to transform a person like it. To this very day, swathes of people accept Islam via a translation of its meanings. How would they have felt had they experienced it directly?! There is a unique incantatory quality to qur'anic recitation. Its cadence is entrancing and its rhythm captivating. Listeners, sometimes even non-Muslims, are moved to tears by it despite being unable to understand it. It is so beautiful that sciences have developed solely around its delivery.[20]

Wisdom is a primordial virtue. The stories of the Qur'an speak to an element of humanity that transcends space and time. A sound *fiṭrah* yearns for revelation. As such, the morals which the Qur'an inculcates within us are perfectly aligned with our God-given nature.

19 *al-Shu'arā'*, 192-194. A variant recitation renders the meaning: "Verily, it is what the Lord of the Worlds sent down—He sent the Trustworthy Spirit down with it—upon your heart so that you may be of the warners."

20 The science of *tajwīd* is primarily concerned with the veracity of one's recitation in terms of phonetics and tempo. However, what is often referred to as *tartīl* (also *taghannī* and *tarannum*) is an art that focuses on the splendour of the delivery and its melodic beauty.

DID YOU KNOW?

The Qur'an is revealed in 114 chapters, each referred to as a *sūrah*. Each *sūrah* is comprised of *āyāt* (pl.), translated as 'verses.' The word *āyah* (sg.) actually means 'sign,' 'marvel,' or 'miracle.' As such, there are *kawnī* (cosmological) and *shar'ī* (revelatory) signs of Allah and His divine oneness. The trees, clouds, mountains, planets, and stars are all cosmological signs, while the verses of the Qur'an are revelatory signs.

Allah ﷻ introduces *Sūrah Yūsuf* by saying that He relates to us the most excellent narratives. A good story has a strong theme, gripping plot, relatable characters, coherent structure, appropriate setting, and an appealing style. A good story resonates with its audiences at a deep level, touching their hearts and moving their souls as opposed to merely entertaining them. It is one that invokes vivid imagery and strikes powerful parables. It is one whose listeners love to be told and consequently love to tell. It is one that stands the test of time and echoes throughout the ages. The Qur'an not only excels in every one of these categories, but does so to a triumphantly incapacitating[21] degree.

Universal themes: There is no motif more moving, evocative, penetrating, and profound than transcending lowly impulses, repelling evil, and overcoming hardship through trusting God and being

21 The word *mu'jizah*, commonly translated as 'miracle,' literally means 'that which incapacitates.' The miraculous nature of the Qur'an is its *i'jāz*—its incapacitating quality: it cannot be replicated or imitated.

an agent of His will. It is the classic hero arc, and is the epitome of virtue. This is at the core of every passage in *Sūrah Yūsuf*. We all succumb to the vicissitudes of time, and we cannot but swim in the sea of divine destiny. Flowing with its preordained, powerful currents with faith, honour, and patience is what ultimately yields spiritual contentment as well as worldly prosperity. Resisting the irresistible is a fool's errand, and will only result in disappointment and humiliation.

Gripping plot: From humble beginnings to lofty heights, Yūsuf عليه السلام overcomes a myriad of challenges that are full of unexpected twists and turns. His brothers' treachery having him sold into slavery led him to the palace of a nobleman. His chastity and dignity led him to prison, favouring incarceration over promiscuity. If not for that, he would not have met the inmates who eventually led him to the king's chambers. Then, a dramatic reversal in the balance of power has the very brothers who betrayed him brought before him. His cleverness finds him reunited with his younger brother, and his clemency finally with his beloved father. There is not a single moment except that it is action-filled, capturing listeners and fascinating audiences of all ages and walks of life.

Relatable characters: If you cannot see yourself or people you know come before you in the story of Yūsuf عليه السلام, then what life are you living?! The *sūrah* gives us archetypes and character interactions that are so familiar, one would think some passages a parable for one's own personal circumstances! The loving, patient father figure, wise and forbearing. The dutiful son, walking in the footsteps of his ancestors. The sibling rivalry. The envious and the envied. The temptress and the tempted. The oppressor and the oppressed. The powerful and the weak. The king and the pauper. All these paradigmatic persons and more are presented in the story, each featuring their irreplaceable role in this profound prophetic saga.

Coherent structure: Dreams literally come true in this epic tale. The former half of the story is connected to its latter half in a synchronised ring structure. The *sūrah* begins with Yūsuf ﷺ sharing his dream with his father, and concludes with the vision manifesting itself before them. There is familial tension and separation in the beginning, and familial reconciliation and union at the end. Yūsuf ﷺ is enslaved as a young boy, and he's made treasurer as a mature man. The woman who tempts him and accuses him of indecency when he abstains from her advances, leading to his imprisonment, finally admits to his innocence and her own shortcomings. The inmate he meets in prison initially forgot to mention him to the king, but eventually remembers and returns back to him. At the centre of the story is the king's dream, the herald to change and the signifier of renewal—both the dream itself and its centrality in the narrative.

Appealing style and appropriate setting: We are told precisely enough to fuel the narrative and ignite our imagination such that we formulate the unspoken details in our minds. The camera constantly yet seamlessly shifts from one scene to another, immersing us in the narrative without boring us with irrelevant sidelines and insignificant trivia. In terms of scenery, we are transported to a world so ancient it is almost prehistoric, yet so familiar it could very well take place this very day. There are deserts, caravans, and wells. There are palaces, chambers, and halls. There are bustling markets and desolate dungeons, the fear of famine and the joy of harvest—opulence and privation. Pre-pharaonic Egypt and Palestinian Canaan serve as the geographical landmarks for the story, and the symbolism the two hold is significant throughout. The Arabic, as with the whole Qur'an, is incapacitatingly beautiful. It is *sahlun mumtani*ʿ—plain as to make one feel welcomed and drawn, yet impossible to imitate in its precision and specificity. Unlike thematic Makkan Qur'an, the *āyāt* are longer—as is the *sūrah* itself—to accommodate a storytelling style.

REFLECT...

It is a sufficient testament to its impact that the Qur'an is the only text that is fully recited off by heart—letter for letter and vowel for vowel—by millions of men, women, and children across the world, most of whom are not even Arab!

The epic of Yūsuf ☙ is a timeless story of faith and hope. It is narrated to us with such mastery that whole disciplines and modern fields of research draw benefit from it: theology, morality and ethics, psychology, parenting, sociology, spirituality, management and administration, economics, agriculture, and many more!

PART

V

PROPHETIC PARENTING

Allah ﷻ relates the best stories.

The narrative of Yūsuf ﷺ is one such story. The lessons and morals which Allah ﷻ teaches us in this incredible *sūrah* are profound. From the fourth to the fifth *āyah* of the *sūrah*, Allah ﷻ recounts a conversation between Yūsuf and Yaʿqūb ﷺ which showcases a strong bond of love and trust. Here, the relationship between father and son can truly be described as godly—prophetic parenting founded in a prophetic household. Allah ﷻ says:

إِذْ قَالَ يُوسُفُ لِأَبِيهِ يَا أَبَتِ إِنِّي رَأَيْتُ أَحَدَ عَشَرَ
كَوْكَبًا وَالشَّمْسَ وَالْقَمَرَ رَأَيْتُهُمْ لِي سَاجِدِينَ ﴿٤﴾

قَالَ يَا بُنَيَّ لَا تَقْصُصْ رُؤْيَاكَ عَلَىٰ إِخْوَتِكَ فَيَكِيدُوا لَكَ كَيْدًا
إِنَّ الشَّيْطَانَ لِلْإِنسَانِ عَدُوٌّ مُّبِينٌ ﴿٥﴾

وَكَذَٰلِكَ يَجْتَبِيكَ رَبُّكَ وَيُعَلِّمُكَ مِن تَأْوِيلِ الْأَحَادِيثِ وَيُتِمُّ نِعْمَتَهُ عَلَيْكَ
وَعَلَىٰ آلِ يَعْقُوبَ كَمَا أَتَمَّهَا عَلَىٰ أَبَوَيْكَ مِن قَبْلُ إِبْرَاهِيمَ
وَإِسْحَاقَ إِنَّ رَبَّكَ عَلِيمٌ حَكِيمٌ ﴿٦﴾

❝ Recall when Yūsuf said to his father, "O dear father, I saw eleven stars and the sun and the moon; I saw them prostrating to me." He said, "O my child, do not relate your vision to your brothers lest they plot a plot against you. Indeed, the devil is an evident enemy to man. And thus your Lord will choose you and teach you of the interpretation of dreams and perfect His blessing upon you and upon Yaʿqūb's folk, as He perfected it before upon both of your forefathers Ibrāhīm and Isḥāq. Indeed, your Lord is knowing, wise." ❩[1]

Before we dive into the shoreless ocean of qur'anic spiritual sustenance, the following are five principles which help the sincere reader in his ability to reflect upon the Book of Allah ﷻ:

I

Potent: The Qur'an is for the humble but wakeful heart. It forces you to be intellectually engaged. Its expressions are simultaneously concise and comprehensive. Just a few *āyāt* can have a deep impact on their reader, such that even a short passage is full of benefit.

II

Perfect: The creator of mankind is the one who sent down revelation. Allah ﷻ gave humans a unique desire for all things beautiful and true. In turn, He revealed a Wonderous Qur'an to satisfy this need. Thus, *fiṭrah* and *waḥy* perfectly match.

III

Persistent: A consequence of the previous two points is that no seeker is turned away from Allah's Banquet.[2] Furthermore, a single person will revisit the same passage dozens of times. Yet, each visit yields a different taste from the previous. One who reads the passage in question whilst first unmarried, then again when married with children, will not have the same experience on each occasion.

IV

Personal: The Qur'an gives you what you need and not what you want. It is uncompromising in its delivery and deliberate in its portrayal of truth. Consequently, *tadabbur* is subjective.

1 *Yūsuf*, 4-6.

2 It is narrated that Ibn Masʿūd ؓ said about the Book of Allah: "Indeed, this Qur'an is the Banquet of Allah, so let whoever sits at the Banquet of Allah take benefit from it." Reported by Ṭabarānī in *al-Muʿjam al-Kabīr* (8646), ʿAbd al-Razzāq in his *Muṣannaf* (376), and others.

On the other hand, *tafsīr* is a rigorous scholarly attempt at objectivity.[3]

 Plural: The Qur'an is guidance for all mankind until the end of time. Its morals are as relevant to a 21st century Western audience as they were to the Arabs listening to it when it was first revealed. Hence, the reflective reader is invited to read between the lines and extract gems when there are silences in the story.

With these principles at the front of our minds, let us return to the epic of Yūsuf and draw benefit from its opening passage.

BREVITY

There is no time wasted in getting to the crux of the narrative. Allah does not relay to us unnecessary information. Where did Yūsuf live with his family? What was the context in which he spoke to his father about the dream? How old was he when he saw the dream? These are details we may reflect over, but they are not significant variables in the story, especially given the universality of the Qur'an's message.

Instead, Allah begins the story from a critical moment—the dream brings news of dramatic change, and it is an omen of immense things to come. Yūsuf is to follow in the footsteps of his prophetic lineage. This is storytelling mastery at its absolute best.

---

3   In the scholarly tradition, exegesis (i.e. *tafsīr*) means to interpret what the text says, whereas eisegesis (i.e. *tadabbur*) is to bring your own interpretation and experience to the text. The former is a strict and complex science requiring expertise in various disciplines, while the latter is available for all Muslims in their approach to the Qur'an.

Precise speech is a feature of the Qur'an and the Sunnah. The Qur'an "is a decisive word, not a joke."[4] The Prophet ﷺ was uniquely blessed with brevity and eloquence (*jawāmiʿ al-kalim*).[5] We ought to adopt these qualities in our interactions, especially in formal situations.

TRANSFORMATIVE WISDOM

In this is an important lesson for our modern audience. We must learn to be clinical in disseminating information. Do not be too wordy or too dull in your discussions, conversations, and gatherings. Do not waste time by sharing what can be shared at a later time or does not need to be shared at all. Highlight your goals for a meeting and get to the bottom line with respectful intent.

FATHERHOOD

The closest person to Yūsuf ﵇, his role-model and idol, and the one he trusted above all others with his dream, was his father, Yaʿqūb ﵇. Though not an explicit part of the narrative, the upbringing and nurture which took place behind the scenes is showcased in this interaction. Undoubtedly, it was Yaʿqūb's superior level of upbringing

4 *al-Ṭāriq*, 13-14.

5 On the authority of Abū Hurayrah ؓ, the Prophet ﷺ said: "I have been favoured over other prophets by six: I am endowed with terse eloquence, I have been given victory by way of terror, war booty is lawful for me, the whole earth is made a pure prayer place for me, I have been sent to all mankind, and I am the seal to prophecy." Reported by Muslim (523).

that generated within the young Yūsuf knowledge of who his father was and his station with Allah. This led to the immense love Yūsuf 🕮 had for him.

There are ten ways in which a child can address his father in the Arabic language.[6] Allah 🕮 employs the most eloquent and endearing one when Yūsuf 🕮 addresses his father, highlighting the symbiotic veneration, benevolence, and moral excellence present in their relationship. Ya'qūb 🕮 is quoted as responding in kind. He says, *'Yā bunayy'*, the endearing form (*taṣghīr*) of *ibnī*—'My dear, young son.'

> ## TRANSFORMATIVE WISDOM
>
> The presence of a father figure in a young boy's life cannot be understated in its importance—a pillar, protector, provider, teacher, and pedagogical epicentre. There is no replacing a father in his son's life.

---

6   There are six syntactic forms for 'my father' and 'my mother' (when the *munādā* of *ab* or *umm* is *muḍāf* to the *yā'* of the *mutakallim*) in Arabic. The standard six forms for *nidā'* applied to the word *ab* (i.e. father) are: *abi, abī, abiya, abā, aba, abu*. Then there are a further four forms when the *tā* of endearment is added: *abati, abata, abatī,* and *abatā*. The form *abatī* is *abati* with an extended *kasrah* due to poetic license (*ḍarūrah shi'riyyah*; i.e. to maintain a sound meter via trivial morphological changes). The form *abatā* is an archaic form of the already less preponderant *abata* (the latter being a valid recitational variant in the quoted qur'anic passage). The most eloquent and endearing form to address one's father is *abati*.

TARBIYAH[7]

There is a tremendous lesson in nurturing children found in this passage. Yūsuf عليه السلام relaying his vision to his father and how his father responded to him hints at so much beauty that went on behind the scenes.

Firstly, Yūsuf عليه السلام was clear and precise in his description: "I saw eleven stars, the sun, and the moon—I saw them fall prostrate before me." Look at the maturity of young Yūsuf عليه السلام and his focus. This was an awesome dream and he was only a child. Other children may have not thought much of the incident. Youthful imagination can be very wild, after all. But Yūsuf عليه السلام was no ordinary child, nor was his household any old household. He was the son of Yaʿqūb, the son of Isḥāq, the son of Ibrāhīm عليهم السلام.

The response of Yaʿqūb عليه السلام indicates that he was a constant source of theological and spiritual nurture for his son. Yūsuf عليه السلام was already aware that Allah ﷻ is his Lord, the devil is his enemy, and his forefathers are prophets. This shows how much critical knowledge Yaʿqūb عليه السلام passed over to him over the years. Yet, it is even deeper than that. Perhaps surprisingly for an unsuspecting audience, Yaʿqūb عليه السلام did not directly comment on the dream itself. He did not tell Yūsuf عليه السلام its interpretation. Instead, he indirectly affirmed its apparent meaning, then prepared his son for what was to follow. Yūsuf عليه السلام was to attain a high station with Allah, but he was to be severely tested in the process.

---

7 In Islamic pedagogy, the term *tarbiyah* refers to the proper physical, intellectual, and spiritual nurture of Muslims, especially children.

Yaʿqūb 🕮 read so far ahead of the dream. He had so much foresight and wisdom. He helped his son understand concepts necessary to pass the trials he will go through. Notice how he gave advice to Yūsuf 🕮: "O my child, do not relate your vision to your brothers lest they plot a plot against you. Indeed, the devil is an evident enemy to man." In modern speech pattern analysis, a command should be followed with a justification, then any extra, useful information should be given after that. Command: "Do not relate your vision to your brothers." Justification: "Lest they plot a plot against you." Useful information: "The devil is an evident enemy to man."

TRANSFORMATIVE WISDOM

We must not shy away from explaining things to our children. The young are naturally curious and imaginative. Asking, 'why?' is not disobedience! It is a duty upon parents to nurture understanding in their sons and daughters. They should not teach them to be submissive and blindly accept things as this risks rebellion in their later years.

It is as if Yaʿqūb 🝉 was telling Yūsuf 🝉:

> *"My dear, beloved child,*
>
> *Among my sons, you are to be chosen by Allah to fulfil the favour bestowed upon us from Him. You are to attain a lofty station with your Lord, similar to mine, your grandfather's, and your great grandfather's. You come from a noble lineage of prophecy, and you are to inherit this divine grace.[8]*
>
> *However, my son, Allah initiates His most beloved and tests them. My son, the devil is ever a clear enemy to man. He is to sprout a seed of envy between you and your brothers.[9]*
>
> *My son, always remember your Lord. Remember that Allah knows all and is wise to all. Wherever you find yourself, He is your guardian and protector. He will not forsake you, and He is the best disposer of affairs.*
>
> *My son, rely on your Lord, place your trust in Him, and never despair of His mercy!"*

This is the message that Yūsuf 🝉 carried throughout his trials. He was abducted from the prophetic household, kidnapped by passers-by, sold into Egypt's slave market, then seduced by his mistress. It is as if every time affliction struck him, and at every instance in

---

8 Later on, when he was imprisoned, Yūsuf 🝉 quoted this to his fellow inmates, invoking what his father told him about himself and his ancestors of monotheism and prophecy: "I followed the way of my forefathers Ibrāhīm, Isḥāq and Yaʿqūb. Never was it for us to associate partners with Allah. This is from Allah's favour upon us and upon mankind, but most people do not show thanks." Q 12:38.

9 The hesitancy showed by Yaʿqūb 🝉 when his sons asked his permission to go out with Yūsuf 🝉 shows he was aware of their ill feelings towards him.

which he felt abandoned by all of creation, his father's reminder rang in his ears and echoed in his heart:

إِنَّ رَبَّكَ عَلِيمٌ حَكِيمٌ

❝ Indeed your Lord is knowing, wise… ❞

Imagine such a gentle boy in such harsh environments. Distressed, homeless, in bondage, and with no shoulder to cry on nor loving parent to wipe his tears away, Yūsuf repeats his father's timeless advice:

"Allah is my Rabb! He is my protector and guardian. He knows full well my state, and is wise as to why I am there."

Allāhu Akbar! Such patience, faith, and hope is truly befitting of a prophet of Allah! And it is all borne of prophetic parenting.

Parents are the most appropriate source of the most important lessons in a child's life. Notice how Yaʿqūb ﷺ did not hesitate before speaking about *shayṭān*. This taught Yūsuf ﷺ to excuse others' faults and instead remember the devil's hand in misguiding creation.

When his brothers finally returned, destitute and dishevelled, he said to them, "Do you remember what you did with Yūsuf when you were an ignorant people?"[10] He cites ignorance as the source of their crime. Furthermore, when they recognised him and were contrite for their wrongdoing, he said to them, "There is no blame upon you today. May Allah forgive you, He is the most merciful of those

10 *Yūsuf*, 89.

who show mercy."[11] The immediacy with which he accepted their repentance was not only incredibly moving and a sign of his moral excellence, but it was borne of his father's reminder in his former years—'Indeed, the devil is an evident enemy to man!'

From that momentous lesson delivered by his father all the way until he reached his prime[12], we did not hear Yūsuf's voice. When his mistress tried to seduce him, however, the first words he is quoted as saying are: "Allah is my refuge!"[13] He seeks refuge in Allah from the lowly and demonic whispers of *shayṭān*.

When the family is joyously reunited in Egypt, and they all fall prostrate before him, Yūsuf ﷺ recognises that this is the manifestation of his vision as a boy. He proclaims: "Father, this is the fulfilment of my dream from before. My Lord has made it come true and has been gracious to me: He released me from prison and He brought you here from the desert after the devil sowed discord between me and my brothers."[14] Neither does he cite the incident of the well, nor does he attribute the evil deed to his brothers. Instead, he blames the devil.

11 *Yūsuf*, 92.

12 Allah ﷻ says about Yūsuf ﷺ: "When he reached his prime (*ashuddah*), We gave him wisdom and knowledge." Many exegetes understand the qur'anic term *ashuddah* to be a reference to forty years in age. This was the age of the Prophet ﷺ when he received the first revelation. This may also be understood from Q 46:15. The point is that it had been some thirty years since he heard his father's reminder, yet he still honoured his advice.

13 *Yūsuf*, 23.

14 *Yūsuf*, 100.

Such is the impact of a father's lesson on his young son: it persists with him through the toughest of tribulations, and allows him to not only endure them, but to pass every test with flying colours. If this does not highlight the value of prophetic parenting, nothing else will.

TRANSFORMATIVE WISDOM

There is an endless list of services that may be outsourced. Raising righteous children is not one of them. In Islam we raise leaders, not children. To do so, we cannot afford to be absent from our children's lives. At best, the *madrasah* and school effort is there to compliment the parents' effort, but never can it be a replacement for it.

GUIDANCE

Allah ﷻ says to the Prophet ﷺ: "Indeed, you do not guide whom you like. Rather, Allah guides whom He wills. He is best knowing of those who are guided."[15] This passage was revealed in reference to Abū Ṭālib,[16] the uncle of the Prophet ﷺ and his carer and supporter. The Prophet ﷺ really wanted Abū Ṭālib to accept Islam and was deeply saddened when he passed away upon the religion of his forefathers. It is important to note here, especially in the context of parenting, that guidance is in the hands of Allah alone. The Prophet ﷺ is the

15 *al-Qaṣaṣ*, 56.

16 The erudite exegete al-Ṭāhir Ibn ʿĀshūr ؒ mentions in his *al-Taḥrīr wa al-Tanwīr* that al-Zajjāj cites scholarly consensus that this *āyah* is primarily revealed about Abū Ṭālib.

best caller to Islam, but necessarily there are those who have denied—and will deny—his call to truth. It is an inevitable consequence of *taklīf.* Allah endowed mankind with the ability to identify right from wrong and to pursue either path. He ﷻ says: "Indeed, We created man from a mingled sperm drop to try him, and We made him hearing and seeing. Indeed, We have guided him to the way, be he thankful or a staunch denier."[17] He ﷻ also says: "By the soul and Him who perfected it, and inspired it with its own wickedness and piety. He is indeed successful the one who purifies it, and he is indeed a failure the one who pollutes it."[18]

Just as Yūsuf was the son of Yaʿqūb and was raised in his household, so were his older brothers.[19] Yet, they plotted against him and held a gathering to discuss how they will get rid of him.[20] Yūsuf and Binyāmīn were younger and inevitably required more attention. The older brothers interpreted that as favouritism. Out of jealousy and

17 *al-Insān*, 2-3.

18 *al-Shams*, 7-10.

19 Yaʿqūb ﷺ had four wives and twelve sons: Raʾūbīn, Shamʿūn, Lāwā, Yahūdhā, Yasākir, and Zabūlūn were his sons from his wife Līʾah; Yūsuf and Binyāmīn were his sons from his wife Rāḥīl; Dān and Naftālā were his sons from his wife Bilihah; and finally Jād and Ashīr were his sons from his wife Zulfah. See Ibn ʿĀshūr's commentary on Q 2:133. Mentioned also by Zamakhsharī in his *Kashshāf*. The precise *ḍabṭ* (pronunciation) of these names is differed over. The common Latinised renditions of these names are, in the same order as before: Reuben, Simeon, Levi, Judah, Issachar, and Zebulun (Leah); Joseph and Benjamin (Rachel); Dan and Naphtali (Bilhah); Gad and Asher (Zilpah).

20 As has been mentioned and as Allah explicitly recounts in the story, they repent from their wrongdoing. In fact, some scholars believe them to have become messengers of Allah, understanding the label *al-Asbāṭ* to be referring to them. Commenting on Q 2:136, Ṭabarī ﷺ says: "*al-Asbāṭ*—they are the prophets from the progeny of Yaʿqūb." Commenting on Q 2:133, Ibn ʿĀshūr ﷺ says: "The children of Yaʿqūb are *al-Asbāṭ*; i.e. the grandsons of Isḥāq."

envy, they sought to remove Yūsuf away from their father.[21]

Yaʿqūb ﷺ is not the only prophet who was tried in his children. Prophet Nūḥ ﷺ called his son to come onto the ark, but he stubbornly denied and ultimately drowned as a disbeliever. Allah ﷻ says: "It sailed with them on waves like mountains, and Nūḥ called out to his son, who stayed behind, 'Come aboard with us, my son, do not stay with the disbelievers.' But he replied, 'I will seek refuge on a mountain to save me from the water.' Nūḥ said, 'Today there is no refuge from Allah's command, except for those on whom He has mercy.' The waves cut them off from each other and he was among the drowned."[22]

The inversion of this took place with the Intimate Friend of Allah, Ibrāhīm ﷺ. His father, Āzar, denied the truth and threatened to harm him if he persisted upon pure monotheism.[23] There is also a parable struck in the ending of *Sūrat al-Taḥrīm* for all womenfolk to heed.[24] The wife of Pharaoh lived under the paragon of tyranny. Yet, she endured his torture and was firm upon the truth. We honour her as one of the greatest women to ever live.[25] Conversely, the wife of Lūṭ and the wife of Nūḥ disobeyed their husbands and perished with the disbelieving people.

We are to do our best in whatever context we find ourselves in, but

21 *Yūsuf*, 8-10.

22 *Hūd*, 42-43.

23 See, for example, Q 19:41-50.

24 See Q 66:10-12.

25 On the authority of Abū Mūsā al-Ashʿarī ؓ, the Prophet ﷺ said: "Many among men have attained moral perfection. None have done so among women except Maryam the daughter of ʿImrān and Āsiyah the wife of Pharaoh. The virtue of ʿĀʾishah over other women is like that of stew over other food." Reported by Bukhārī (3411) and Muslim (2431).

results are in the hands of Allah ﷻ. He ﷻ says: "If they submit, they will be guided, but if they turn away, your only duty is to convey the message. Allah is watchful over the slaves."[26] We must ourselves embody prophetic character and qur'anic values. This is our first priority. It is also the best way to portray the message and consequently become guided guides (*hudāh muhtadūn*). Thereafter, whether it be our children, spouses, or parents: "We do not guide whom we like; Allah guides whom He wills. He knows best those who will follow guidance."

TRANSFORMATIVE WISDOM

It is very easy to blame our circumstances for our shortcomings. This is not the way of the greats of this ummah. Take on responsibility and try your best. Allah does not burden a soul more than it can bear. Know that deep down you have the capacity to overcome your struggles and attain a lofty station with Allah!

26 *Āl 'Imrān*, 20.

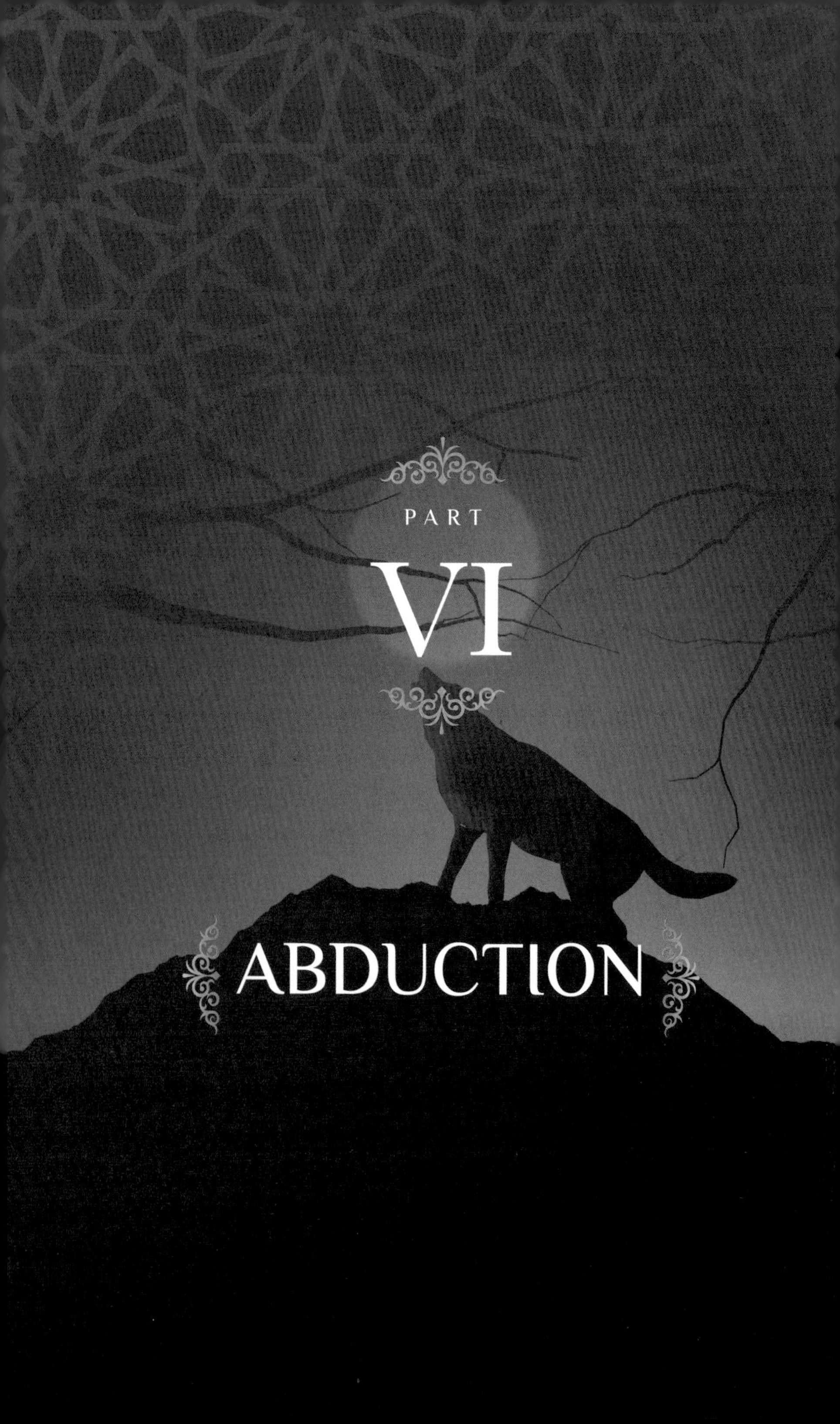

PART VI

ABDUCTION

Jealousy is a blinding disease.

In gripping fashion, Allah ﷻ shifts the focus from the conversation between Yaʿqūb and Yūsuf ﵉ to a much more sinister setting. Driven by envy, Yūsuf's half-brothers have gathered to decide how they will remove him from their father and hence have the latter all to themselves.[1] The manifestation of what Yaʿqūb ﵇ feared is already afoot. Allah ﷻ says:

لَقَدْ كَانَ فِي يُوسُفَ وَإِخْوَتِهِ آيَاتٌ لِلسَّايِلِينَ ٧

إِذْ قَالُوا لَيُوسُفُ وَأَخُوهُ أَحَبُّ إِلَىٰ أَبِينَا مِنَّا وَنَحْنُ
عُصْبَةٌ إِنَّ أَبَانَا لَفِي ضَلَالٍ مُبِينٍ ٨

اقْتُلُوا يُوسُفَ أَوِ اطْرَحُوهُ أَرْضًا يَخْلُ لَكُمْ وَجْهُ أَبِيكُمْ
وَتَكُونُوا مِنْ بَعْدِهِ قَوْماً صَالِحِينَ ٩

قَالَ قَايِلٌ مِنْهُمْ لَا تَقْتُلُوا يُوسُفَ وَأَلْقُوهُ فِي غَيَابَةِ الْجُبِّ
يَلْتَقِطْهُ بَعْضُ السَّيَّارَةِ إِنْ كُنْتُمْ فَاعِلِينَ ١٠

❝ Surely, in Yūsuf and his brothers are signs for those who ask. Recall when they said, "Yūsuf and his brother are dearer to our father than we are and we are many. Indeed, our father is in clear error." "Kill Yūsuf or cast him to some land and your father's attention will be yours alone;

1 It is worth mentioning that the following qur'anic passage is used by exegetes as evidence that the brothers of Yūsuf ﵇ never became prophets. For them, *al-Asbāṭ* are the progeny of Yaʿqūb ﵇ generally, but not his own immediate sons. In other words, they are the various tribes among the Children of Israel and their leaders. See Ibn Kathīr's commentary on Q 12:10 for a detailed exposition of this view.

then afterwards you become a righteous people." One of them said, "Do not kill Yūsuf. Rather, throw him in the depth of the well so that some wayfarers may pick him up, if you must do something." [2]

COGNITIVE DISSONANCE

Cognitive dissonance is the palpable tension felt when one's beliefs are in contrast to one's actions. The disassociation creates internal conflict that is only resolved via changing the belief, the action, or how either is perceived. Here, it was via hyperbole that Yūsuf's brothers justified their plotting against him. "Our father is in grave error, for he is wholly smitten by Yūsuf!"—a falsity they fed themselves and wholly consumed to dignify their crime with a cloak of duty. At most, Yaʿqūb ﷺ had an organic soft spot for Yūsuf and Binyāmīn which he never externalised as unjust favouritism. After all, they were the youngest of his sons and naturally needed more attention. That was all the fuel they needed to stoke up their envy.

Another demonic delusion they fell into is *tamannī*—wishful thinking. The brothers of Yūsuf ﷺ convinced themselves that they could commit an unspeakable act—harming or even killing their own sibling—and yet still claim righteousness afterward. It was as if they saw their imminent crime as a singular event, divorced from a context of intent, preparation, execution, and repercussion. This conception,

2 *Yūsuf*, 7-10.

however, is a deceit: an illusion spun by the architect of lies himself, *shayṭān* the accursed.

TRANSFORMATIVE WISDOM

There is a lesson we must learn and internalise from how Allah ﷻ describes the devil's ploys. Throughout the Qur'an, Allah commands us to not follow *khuṭuwāt al-shayṭān*—the devil's **footsteps.** There is a chain of events that eventually results in destructive sin. A fleeting notion becomes an idea, the idea turns to consolidated thought, consolidated thought becomes a plan, the plan yields action, which if repeated becomes a habit, and a habit is a mode of being. We must nip this chain in the bud and foil *shayṭān's* guile.

The words of Allah ﷻ do not corroborate this falsehood. Instead, they reveal that a crime does not exist in isolation. One crime begets another, forming a chain of sins that binds the wrongdoer. One act of deliberate and wilful transgression sends ripples across the fabric of one's moral integrity, instigating a chain reaction that may lead to damnation. Allah ﷻ tells us about the devil: "He makes them promises and raises false hopes, but the devil's promises are nothing but delusion."[3] Allah ﷻ also describes how a person may be engulfed by a certain sin they indulged in such that it drags them to the Fire! He ﷻ says: "Yes indeed, whoever has earned an evil deed and whose offense has surrounded him—then those are the fellows of the Fire; therein they abide."[4]

3 *al-Nisā'*, 120.

4 *al-Baqarah*, 81.

The brothers' assumption that they would have the remainder of their lives to seek Allah's forgiveness was a fallacy birthed from *shayṭān*'s deception. Who can guarantee life's duration, promising that one will have the chance to atone for their wrongs? While Allah, the most forgiving and the most merciful, never denies His creation the opportunity for redemption, no one can guarantee that they will have the time or the inspiration to seek it.

TRANSFORMATIVE WISDOM

It's imperative to take *shayṭān* as an enemy in practice and not just in theory. Allowing our children unrestricted use of smartphones and tablets is not taking *shayṭān* as an enemy. Giving them 24/7 access to TV is not taking *shayṭān* as an enemy. Letting ideologically driven and harmful curricula inculcate their doctrines within our youth is not taking *shayṭān* as an enemy. Seek refuge in Allah from the devil and act accordingly!

The devil whispers to us, peddling deceit, and pushing us towards actions that tarnish our morality and weaken our relationship with Allah ﷻ. He tries to make us forget about the inevitability of death and entices us to act on whims and fancies. He is our sworn enemy, so we ought to treat him as such: in our households and communities, as well as our private moments of seclusion. Allah ﷻ says: "Indeed, the devil is an enemy to you, so take him as an enemy. Indeed, he calls his faction to be inmates of the Blaze."[5]

5 *Fāṭir*, 6.

UNSEEN PROTECTION

There is a subtle benefit from this conversation that lies behind the apparent narrative. At one point, the brothers' resolve could have settled on killing Yūsuf ﷺ. Yet, *qā'ilun minhum*—'a sayer among them'—intervened. He rejected the idea of murdering Yūsuf in cold blood. Evidently, the alternative offered was not exactly compassionate, but it nonetheless averted the certain death of Yūsuf ﷺ. Here lies an important lesson that is constantly stressed at every single stage in the story: trust *qadr*. The divine destiny which dictated that this 'sayer' intervene is that which led to Yūsuf being thrown in the well. It is the same one which took him out of it, had him sold as a slave, raised in a house of nobility, seduced by his mistress, unjustly incarcerated, bequeathed as the minister of Egypt, dragged his brothers from the desert before him, and ultimately reunited him with his family in a scene of unmatched forbearance and joy.

REFLECT...

There are times in which we can feel overwhelmed with worry or grief. There are times in which the future looks dark and gloomy. Looking at the current state of the ummah, it is easy to feel despondent. But we forget how Allah takes care of us at every moment while we are unaware. The unfolding of history is in good hands, for Allah ﷻ is its author.

We are also invited to reflect over a curious omission. The identity of the speaker in question is not given. Some scholars of qur'anic commentary are of the view that this is the eldest of Yaʿqūb's sons.[6] Of course, he is deliberately made anonymous, and this is the source of our reflection. Later on and in a different context, Allah ﷻ directly quotes him as 'the eldest among them'.[7] The difference between the two scenarios is that the first is one of evil plotting while the second is fulfilling a covenant. In other words, his identity was omitted when involved in an evil deed, but highlighted when involved in a good deed. Such is the favour of Allah ﷻ upon His slaves: He wishes that He only sees them upon obedience.

TRANSFORMATIVE WISDOM

The characteristic trait of our religion is *ḥayāʾ*. It is a holistic and grand moral which encompasses a plethora of virtues, including modesty, humility, bashfulness, dignity, and having a sense of shame. It includes that one dislikes seeing another in a compromised state. The Qur'an is nurturing us to cover the wrongdoings of others. When mentioning their error, there is no need to peddle their names. However, when they do something good, advertise their identity. Conceal others' faults, focus on your own, and set your sight on all things noble and beautiful!

6 Exegetes differ whether it was Raʾūbīn, Shamʿūn, or Yahūdhā. The first of the three, Raʾūbīn, is the eldest. See Ibn Kathīr's commentary on Q 12:10.

7 See Q 12:80.

EMOTIONAL MANIPULATION

The cameras once again make a dramatic shift onto the next critical development. Having agreed on what they will do to their young sibling, the band of brothers direct their focus to luring him away from his father's protective hold. They altogether came before Yaʿqūb عليه السلام and addressed him in a singular, stern voice. Allah سبحانه وتعالى says:

قَالُوا يَا أَبَانَا مَا لَكَ لَا تَأْمَنَّا[8] عَلَىٰ يُوسُفَ وَإِنَّا لَهُ لَنَاصِحُونَ ﴿١١﴾

أَرْسِلْهُ مَعَنَا غَدًا يَرْتَعْ وَيَلْعَبْ وَإِنَّا لَهُ لَحَافِظُونَ ﴿١٢﴾

قَالَ إِنِّي لَيَحْزُنُنِي أَن تَذْهَبُوا بِهِ وَأَخَافُ أَن يَأْكُلَهُ
الذِّئْبُ وَأَنتُمْ عَنْهُ غَافِلُونَ ﴿١٣﴾

قَالُوا لَئِنْ أَكَلَهُ الذِّئْبُ وَنَحْنُ عُصْبَةٌ إِنَّا إِذًا لَّخَاسِرُونَ ﴿١٤﴾

فَلَمَّا ذَهَبُوا بِهِ وَأَجْمَعُوا أَن يَجْعَلُوهُ فِي غَيَابَتِ الْجُبِّ وَأَوْحَيْنَا إِلَيْهِ
لَتُنَبِّئَنَّهُم بِأَمْرِهِمْ هَٰذَا وَهُمْ لَا يَشْعُرُونَ ﴿١٥﴾

8 This word has a specific way in which it is recited. Its linguistic origin is (تَأْمَنُنَا): *ta'manunā*. The *nūn* with a *ḍammah* is merged into the *nūn* with a *fatḥah*, rendering the word (تَأْمَنَّا): *ta'mannā*. However, for all the ten *qurrā'* other than Abū Jaʿfar al-Madanī, an element of the first *nūn* and its *ḍammah* should remain in the recitation. This is achieved via one of two deliveries: *rawm* or *ishmām*. In this word specifically, *rawm* is that the first *nūn ḍammah* is recited lazily—the vowel is not given its full tempo nor is it as clear as a normal *nūn ḍammah* would be. *Ishmām* is that the *idghām* (merging) takes place with a pouting of the lips (to imply the *ḍammah*) which initiates immediately after the *nūn shaddah* is held and ceases right before the *ghunnah* (nasality) ends and the *fatḥah* of the second *nūn* is pronounced. The qur'anic traditions of *talaqqī* and *mushāfahah* (direct oral transmission from teacher to student) are required to fully appreciate the intricacies of recitation.

•• They said, "O our father! Why do you not trust us with Yūsuf although we truly wish him well? Send him with us tomorrow that he may enjoy himself and play and we shall surely take good care of him." He said, "It makes me sad that you should take him with you, and I fear that some wolf may eat him up when you are heedless of him." They said, "If a wolf eats him up while we are a united many, we are then losers indeed." Then, when they led him off and were of one mind that they should place him in the depth of the well, We inspired in him, "You will tell them of this deed of theirs while they are unaware." ••[9]

The brothers chose to use manipulation as their weapon, casting doubts upon their father's trust in them. "Why don't you let Yūsuf join us? We are all brothers, aren't we?" This was their cleverly disguised emotional blackmail—exploiting the very values of fidelity and brotherhood their father had instilled within them. This manoeuvre is akin to a student questioning the teacher using the principles they taught them: an audacious reversal of roles.

REFLECT...

At the very least, it is improper for a person to remind another of what they previously said about them to further their personal agenda. This is especially reprehensible with parents. "You're the one who said you want me to be more responsible! Why won't you let me travel?" Such statements reek of disrespect.

Thus, Yaʿqub 🕮 found himself cornered. In his anxiety, he expressed

---

9   *Yūsuf*, 11-15.

his fear of a wolf devouring Yūsuf while his brothers were engrossed in their games. Scholars who have reflected on this incident pointed out that, in his moment of fear, Ya'qub unintentionally handed his sons the very excuse they would later use against him. After dealing with Yūsuf —thankfully opting to abandon him in a well rather than murder him—they found themselves at a loss for words. How were they to explain their brother's absence? In their original plot, they had not accounted for this part. But here, they found their excuse gifted to them by their father's benign concern.

TRANSFORMATIVE WISDOM

Never give your opponent a weakness they can exploit and use against you. It is like handing them a weapon on a silver platter. Be wary of the personal information you hand those of questionable intentions.

HOPE AND INSPIRATION

After the heartbreak of betrayal, and from none other than his own brothers, one can only imagine how young Yūsuf felt in the secluded, dark depths of the well. Abandoned by those who should be responsible for his wellbeing, only Allah knew of his hurt. It was at that moment that Allah inspired within him hope and certitude— the good end is for the God-conscious and the patient. "You shall tell them of this deed of theirs when they know you not."[10] That was his source of solace and perseverance. "One day, the power dynamics shall be inverted, and you, Yūsuf, will remind them of their misdeed."

DID YOU KNOW?

According to the Old Testament, it was Ra'ūbīn (Reuben) who saved Yūsuf ﷺ from his brothers wishing to kill him, and it was Yahūdhā (Judah) who guided the caravan to his location. [See Genesis: 37]

It is appropriate to make the distinction between revelation (*waḥy*) and inspiration (*ilhām*) at this point. In its technical sense, revelation is solely for prophets, whereas inspiration is a divine grace which extends to all creation. Yūsuf ﷺ was not yet a prophet in the well. A contention may be that the word used in the 15th *āyah* is *awḥaynā* which comes from *waḥy*; literally: 'We revealed.' However, this verb is also used to refer to inspiration. This is made unequivocally clear when Allah ﷻ says: "Your Lord inspired (*awḥā*) the bee, 'Take for yourself homes of the mountains, trees, and in what people trellis.'"[11] The inspiration which Allah ﷻ bestowed upon Yūsuf ﷺ was not revelation. Non-prophets may also experience this blessing.[12] It is

10 *Yūsuf*, 15. This divine promise manifested decades later when the brothers returned to Egypt and Yūsuf ﷺ was its minister. Following the unfolding of various events, Yūsuf ﷺ says to them: "Do you know what you did with Yūsuf and his brother when you were ignorant?" Q 12:89.

11 *al-Naḥl*, 68.

12 Regarding the mother of Mūsā ﷺ and her decision to place him in the river, Allah ﷻ says: "We inspired to Mūsā's mother, 'Nurse him, then when you fear for him, cast him into the waters and do not fear nor grieve; We shall return him to you and make him one of the messengers'" Q 28:7. She was not a messenger herself according to scholarly consen-

an overwhelming feeling or emotion that is begotten within one by Allah's favour, and may manifest as a dream[13] or a mental inclination or clarity. It entails subjective though certain knowledge within the person it is bestowed upon, especially if they are a devoted, worshipful, acquainted slave of Allah.

THE WOLF, THE SHIRT, AND BEAUTIFUL PATIENCE

The deed was done. The brothers' mission had been accomplished. Now, the only puzzle left to solve is how they were going to confront their father. In a twisted turn of events, they decided to project his insecurities upon him. Under the cover of darkness, they returned to him with crocodile tears in their eyes and Yūsuf's blood-stained shirt in their hands—the artefact that has become a symbol of innocence, injustice, and eventual triumph.[14] Allah ﷻ says:

وَجَاءُوا أَبَاهُمْ عِشَاءً يَبْكُونَ ﴿١٦﴾

قَالُوا يَا أَبَانَا إِنَّا ذَهَبْنَا نَسْتَبِقُ وَتَرَكْنَا يُوسُفَ عِنْدَ مَتَاعِنَا فَأَكَلَهُ الذِّئْبُ
وَمَا أَنْتَ بِمُؤْمِنٍ لَنَا وَلَوْ كُنَّا صَادِقِينَ ﴿١٧﴾

وَجَاءُوا عَلَىٰ قَمِيصِهِ بِدَمٍ كَذِبٍ قَالَ بَلْ سَوَّلَتْ لَكُمْ أَنْفُسُكُمْ أَمْرًا
فَصَبْرٌ جَمِيلٌ وَاللَّهُ الْمُسْتَعَانُ عَلَىٰ مَا تَصِفُونَ ﴿١٨﴾

---

sus.

13 This is discussed in detail in Part XII.

14 In expressing someone's innocence, the following words are effectively a proverb among Arabs: *barī'un barā'ata al-dhi'bi min dami ibni Ya'qūb*— "As innocent as the wolf was from the blood of Ya'qūb's son." Additionally, 'the Coat of Many Colours' is a well-known reference in Western popular culture.

✦✦ They came to their father at nightfall, weeping. They said, "O our father, we went off racing one another and left Yūsuf by our belongings so the wolf ate him. You would never believe us even if we were truthful." And they came with false blood on his shirt. He said, "Rather, your souls have tempted you to do something. So, a comely patience! It is Allah whose help is sought against what you describe." ✦✦[15]

The irony was cruel. The very fear their father had voiced, the fear of a wolf attacking Yūsuf, was the lie they returned with. It's as if they were saying, "Your worst fear, father, it came true!" A valuable lesson to consider here is that we should monitor our negative thoughts and unseemly words. There are moments in our lives when we encounter unintended self-fulfilling prophecies. Retrospectively, we bemoan how overemphasising a certain worry was the inadvertent cause of its realisation.

> ### REFLECT...
>
> Cognisance is certainly a virtue. Being perceptive and aware is important. However, we must be careful not to project our personal insecurities onto others. Who knows what effect that may have on their subconscious?

One of the most devastating experiences a parent can endure is the loss of a child, especially a young and innocent one. In the case of Yaʿqūb 🕊, the pain is exponentially magnified since the loss is instigated by his own sons, Yūsuf's siblings. The grief of this noble

---

15 *Yūsuf*, 16-18.

prophet of Allah encapsulates this profound agony. When faced with a trial like no other, the words uttered by Yaʿqūb ﷺ ring across time and space as a slogan for the trialled: "A beautiful patience!" Despite unimaginable loss and immeasurable anguish, he portrayed sobriety and steadfastness becoming of a prophet: "I can only endure with patience. That is most fitting for me. Allah's help alone is what I seek in my state!"

Allah ﷻ has taught us the precise words to say when calamities befall us. He tells us of the nature of this world—that it is a test—and that it is the patient who are successful. He ﷻ says: "We will certainly test you with something of fear and hunger, and loss of wealth, life, and crops. Give glad tidings to the patient—those who, when disaster strikes them, say, 'Indeed we belong to Allah, and indeed to Him we shall return.' Those are the ones upon whom are blessings from their Lord and mercy. It is those who are rightly guided."[16] Allah is the King, and in His hand is the dominion of the heavens and the earth: we belong to Him. He is the Just, the Owner of Judgement: we will return to Him. This life is but a fleeting fancy and a temporary test.

This powerful invocation isn't merely a mantra of resilience, but an affirmation of identity and belief in the Divine ﷻ. During these testing times, the expression, "Indeed we belong to Allah, and indeed to Him we shall return," takes on an extraordinary significance. Patience then becomes a means of holding oneself together; binding soul, mind, body, and heart in a protective and comforting mantle of faith. Faith that Allah ﷻ is the Merciful, the Knowing, the Wise, and that He is guiding us to His pleasure despite our inability to fully

16 *al-Baqarah*, 155-157.

grasp it. Faith that He will never forsake His true slaves nor do away with the reward of the patient. Faith that we will all stand before Him, and that He will recompense us for our trust in Him. This is the quintessence of *ṣabr* (patience), and is why this fundamental Islamic virtue encompasses all of religion. This is what Yaʿqūb ﷺ exemplified when he said: *fa-ṣabrun jamīl*—"I will exercise a beautiful patience."

REFLECT...

Islam can be summarised in terms of patience: patiently persevering upon what Allah commanded us, and patiently keeping away from what He prohibited us.

At a macro level, the abduction of Yūsuf ﷺ delivers stark lessons about community ethics and dynamics. It prompts us to take a step back, seek refuge in Allah, and assess our actions objectively. If the sons of Yaʿqūb ﷺ were able to engage in such a heinous crime, how dare we feel safe from the whispers of *shayṭān*? It is easy to judge others and detach ourselves from a narrative as sanctimonious observers. Yet, many of the vices Allah ﷻ indirectly warns against in this passage we readily fall into among ourselves. How often have families broken up over inheritance? How often do we hold grudges and nurture malice against our brothers and sisters in Islam? How often does envy play a role in dividing our communities?

Are we a people who fear Allah, aware of His ever-watchful gaze, or are we simply pandering to *shayṭān*'s demonic desires? How would the Prophet ﷺ react if he were to witness our behaviour? In our quest for victory, we sometimes resort to misrepresentation, exaggeration, and pretence, building a distorted narrative to win at all costs. The story of the abduction serves as a stark reminder of the dangers of such conduct.

PART

VII

SOLD INTO SLAVERY

Freedom is a blessing we take for granted.

One of the trials Yūsuf ﷺ went through was being sold into bondage. From the loving and nurturing home of a prophet to the harsh slave markets of ancient Egypt, young Yūsuf had to experience this intense inversion of circumstance. But Allah's mercy is always close to the good-doers. Allah ﷻ says:

وَجَاءَتْ سَيَّارَةٌ فَأَرْسَلُوا وَارِدَهُمْ فَأَدْلَىٰ دَلْوَهُ قَالَ يَا بُشْرَىٰ هَٰذَا غُلَامٌ
وَأَسَرُّوهُ بِضَاعَةً وَاللَّهُ عَلِيمٌ بِمَا يَعْمَلُونَ ١٩

وَشَرَوْهُ بِثَمَنٍ بَخْسٍ دَرَاهِمَ مَعْدُودَةٍ وَكَانُوا فِيهِ مِنَ الزَّاهِدِينَ ٢٠

وَقَالَ الَّذِي اشْتَرَاهُ مِن مِّصْرَ لِامْرَأَتِهِ أَكْرِمِي مَثْوَاهُ عَسَىٰ أَن يَنفَعَنَا أَوْ نَتَّخِذَهُ
وَلَدًا وَكَذَٰلِكَ مَكَّنَّا لِيُوسُفَ فِي الْأَرْضِ وَلِنُعَلِّمَهُ مِن تَأْوِيلِ الْأَحَادِيثِ
وَاللَّهُ غَالِبٌ عَلَىٰ أَمْرِهِ وَلَٰكِنَّ أَكْثَرَ النَّاسِ لَا يَعْلَمُونَ ٢١

❝ There came a caravan, and they sent their water-drawer and he let down his pail. He said, "What good tidings! Here is a youth." They hid him as merchandise, and Allah is knowing of what they did. They sold him for a paltry sum, a few dirhams, so little did they value him. The man from Egypt who purchased him said to his wife, "Tend graciously to his dwelling. Hopefully he may be useful to us or we may take him as a son." Thus We established Yūsuf in the land, and so that we might teach him of the interpretation of dreams. Allah always prevails in His affairs, yet the majority of people do not know. ❞[1]

1 *Yūsuf*, 19-21.

LOST AND FOUND

The world was not always as we perceive it today. Being psychologically isolated in an incredibly niche few annals of the human story, we all too readily forget how the luxuries we take for granted have impacted even the most basic of our interactions. Going back a mere few centuries, we immediately appreciate how much has changed in such little time. Now imagine how unrecognisable the ancient world would be for us were we to witness it with our modern expectations. Without advanced communication, transportation, and navigation systems, travel is a completely different endeavour to what we know—a life-altering decision rather than a jovial excursion. The amenities we regularly enjoy are non-existent. Instead, bandits and brigands[2] are a norm, whereby one's very life is at risk upon such an unfortunate encounter, let alone one's wealth and property. Furthermore, if a person is lost, they well and truly become lost. There is no route—literally or figuratively—that a wayward person can follow to find their way home.

With all this in mind, think what some ignoble commoners with ill intentions would do if they were to stumble upon a healthy, beautiful young man. Yūsuf ﷺ was found and immediately perceived as a source of income. Allah ﷻ uses the words *biḍāʿah*—'merchandise'—and *thaman bakhs*—'lowly price', highlighting this reality.

2 The Arabic for these terms is *quṭṭāʿ ṭuruq*—literally 'path cutters.'

DID YOU KNOW?

There is a discussion among exegetes as to who did the concealment and the selling mentioned in the *āyah*. Either it is referring to the water-drawer and his mates who concealed him from the rest of the caravan so that they may sell him quietly and benefit from him themselves, or Yūsuf's brothers concealed the fact he's their brother and consequently sold him to the water-drawer when he found him, as they waited by the well for three days to see what would happen to him [See Ibn Kathīr's commentary on Q 12:20]. Though the *āyah* is describing either scenario, it is perfectly possible and even likely that Yūsuf ؊ was sold into bondage multiple times: by his brothers to the water-drawer, the water-drawer to Egypt's slave market, and the market to the minister of Egypt.

Consider the day Yūsuf ؊ was taken to the marketplace in Egypt—a scene that sends shivers down the spine. A bustling hub of human transaction, rampant with squalor, pollution, and a blatant lack of decorum. Slaves were treated less like humans and more like cattle, their dignity stripped away as they were inspected for any hint of disease or frailty. Despite the horrifying spectacle, Yūsuf ؊ held onto his faith, for he knew divine mercy was within arm's reach. Indeed, Allah is as His faithful slave expects Him to be.

> ## REFLECT...
>
> Bukhārī reports in his *Ṣaḥīḥ* (7505) on the authority of Abū Hurayrah ☀ that Allah's Messenger ☀ said: "Allah said, 'I am to My slave as he thinks of Me.'" Allah ☀ says: "What then is your opinion of the Lord of the Worlds?" Q 37:87

ENABLEMENT

Allah's command is irresistible, and He always prevails in His affairs. Of all the potential owners and buyers, Allah ☀ guided young Yūsuf to the household of what must have been one of the most powerful men on earth at the time. In this arena of dehumanisation, emerged the ʿAzīz,[3] the finance minister of Egypt;[4] a man of wealth, respect, and authority. He was drawn to Yūsuf, and so the divine mercy poured in the form of an unexpected benefactor. There was no account of the transaction in the marketplace, for Allah ☀ took us directly to the heart of the matter. Yūsuf ☀ was swiftly bought and housed within the comforts of the ʿAzīz's palace, signalling Allah's benevolent hand directing the course of events.

---

3   The word *ʿazīz* comes from *ʿizzah*—honour, might, and nobility. One of the names of Allah ☀ is *al-ʿAzīz*. In the *sūrah*, the word is used as a title for this regal person—his name is not mentioned in the Qurʾan. It may be effectively translated as 'nobleman', and it refers to a governor, minister, or ruler of some sort. Notably, Yūsuf ☀ is himself referred to by this title when he becomes the finance or agricultural minister of Egypt.

4   His exact role is left unknown in the *sūrah* and is hence disputed by commentators. Muḥammad ibn Isḥāq ☀ relays: "His name was Iṭfīr and he resided over the storehouses (*khazāʾin*; i.e. treasury) of Egypt." See Ibn Kathīr's commentary on Q 12:21.

REFLECT...

On the authority of Abū al-Aḥwaṣ ﵀, Ibn Masʿūd ﵁ said: "Those of greatest clairvoyance (*firāsah*) were three: the ʿAzīz when he said to his wife [about Yūsuf ﵇], 'Tend graciously to his dwelling that he may be useful to us or we may take him as a son' [Q 12:21]; the woman who said to her father [about Mūsā ﵇], 'Father, hire him; the best you can hire is the strong and trustworthy' [Q 28:26]; and Abū Bakr al-Ṣiddīq when he appointed ʿUmar as his successor." Reported by Ṭabarī in his *Tafsīr* (see his commentary on Q 12:21) and Ḥākim in his *Mustadrak* (1301).

In the palace, Yūsuf ﵇ found care from the ʿAzīz who instructed his wife to treat him with kindness and dignity. This command carried an important lesson, especially for those in positions of influence—the power of clear communication. The ʿAzīz did not merely demand obedience; he explained his expectations, thus making his intent transparent. It is a crucial lesson for those in leadership roles today. When issuing commands, providing clear context and reason can foster understanding and strengthen bonds between leaders and their subordinates. This understanding keeps hearts united and wards off dispute and discord, creating a healthy environment of mutual respect and cooperation.

TRANSFORMATIVE WISDOM

When we are in positions of authority or power, we often make decisions and implement actions based solely on our convictions without giving much thought to the implications they might have on those around us. We shun discussions and debates in fear of opposition and conflict. Yet, an essential aspect of leadership is communication. A simple gesture of explaining the reasons behind our decisions can close the gates of discord, the inroads for *shayṭān*.

It is essential in our fast-paced world to remember that relationships are built on a foundation of reciprocity. The ʿAzīz of Egypt understood this. He knew that by ensuring Yūsuf's comfort, he could unlock his potential, ultimately benefiting both parties. We are familiar with this dynamic, whether it's leaving a good tip for a waiter in the anticipation of better service next time, or simply treating people with kindness and respect to foster a healthy, mutually beneficial relationship. Allah ﷻ says: "Is the reward for goodness anything but goodness?"[5]

CHILDREN

Allah ﷻ says: "Wealth and children are an adornment of the worldly life."[6] The gift of offspring is undoubtedly one of the greatest Allah

5 *al-Raḥmān*, 60.

6 *al-Kahf*, 46.

can bestow upon His slaves. A righteous progeny carries the ancestors' legacy and honours their grand generational goals. Many prophets of Allah made direct supplications for children. Ibrāhīm and Zakariyyā ﷺ were granted sons in old age. Ibrāhīm was gifted Ismāʿīl and Isḥāq, and Zakariyya was gifted Yaḥyā ﷺ. At the end of *Sūrat al-Furqān*, Allah describes a very virtuous category of people: *ʿibād al-Raḥmān*—'the slaves of the Merciful.' One of their characteristics is that they supplicate Allah, saying: "Our Lord, give us from our spouses and our children comfort of eyes, and make us heads of the God-conscious."[7]

TRANSFORMATIVE WISDOM

We should see our own selves in our children. They are literally a part of us. We should direct them to avoid our mistakes, set them on lofty paths, and help them to accomplish goals even greater than ours. They are the most beautiful burden, and the greatest of investments.

Witnessing the physical as well as spiritual beauty of Yūsuf ﷺ, the ʿAzīz could not help but be drawn. Thus, he not only anticipated goodness from him, but hoped that he and his wife may take him as their own son.[8] Allah ﷻ says: "To Allah belongs the kingdom of the heavens and the earth. He creates what He wills. He grants females to whom He wills, and grants males to whom He wills. Or He combines for them couples, both males and females, and makes whom

7 *al-Furqān*, 74.

8 It is mentioned in many works of exegesis that they were likely unable to bear their own children.

He wills barren. Surely, He is knowing, powerful."[9] One of the three avenues which continue to benefit the deceased after their death is a righteous offspring who supplicates for them. On the authority of Abū Hurayrah ﷺ, the Prophet ﷺ said: "When the son of Adam dies, his deeds cease except via three: a continuous charity, knowledge that is benefited from, and a righteous child who supplicates for him."[10]

9 *al-Shūrā*, 49-50.

10 Reported by Muslim (1631).

PART

VIII

SEDUCTION

Temptation is ugliness cloaked in a beautiful mantle.

Yūsuf ﷺ has come of age. Not only has he become a man at the height of his maturity and sound-mindedness, but he is now a prophet of Allah. He has grown in the palace of the ʿAzīz and is grateful to him for his magnanimity. But, as his father taught him all those years ago, *shayṭān* is ever an enemy to man. The accursed has been busy casting whispers of lust in the household, and his handiwork is evidently at play. Allah ﷻ says:

وَلَمَّا بَلَغَ أَشُدَّهُ آتَيْنَاهُ حُكْمًا وَعِلْمًا وَكَذَٰلِكَ نَجْزِي الْمُحْسِنِينَ ﴿٢٢﴾

وَرَاوَدَتْهُ الَّتِي هُوَ فِي بَيْتِهَا عَن نَّفْسِهِ وَغَلَّقَتِ الْأَبْوَابَ وَقَالَتْ هَيْتَ لَكَ قَالَ
مَعَاذَ اللَّهِ إِنَّهُ رَبِّي أَحْسَنَ مَثْوَايَ إِنَّهُ لَا يُفْلِحُ الظَّالِمُونَ ﴿٢٣﴾

وَلَقَدْ هَمَّتْ بِهِ وَهَمَّ بِهَا لَوْلَا أَن رَّأَىٰ بُرْهَانَ رَبِّهِ كَذَٰلِكَ لِنَصْرِفَ
عَنْهُ السُّوءَ وَالْفَحْشَاءَ إِنَّهُ مِنْ عِبَادِنَا الْمُخْلَصِينَ ﴿٢٤﴾

❝ When he reached his prime We gave him wisdom and knowledge; thus do We reward the good. Then she in whose house he was living sought to seduce him, and she shut the doors and said, "Come to me!" He said, "Allah is my refuge! He is my lord, who has given me a good dwelling. Indeed, the unjust never succeed." So she advanced towards him, and he would have advanced towards her had he not seen the proof of his Lord. Thus it was, so that We would divert evil and obscenity away from him. Indeed, he is one of Our chosen slaves. ❞[1]

1 *Yūsuf*, 22-24.

KNOWLEDGE AND ACTION

The prophets are the paragons of virtue. When he reached his peak physical and spiritual prowess,[2] Allah ﷻ endowed Yūsuf ﷺ with wisdom and knowledge; that is to say: prophecy.[3] The words in Arabic are *ḥukm* and *ʿilm*. The former, *ḥukm*, has connotations of both wisdom and judgement. A *ḥakīm* is a sage, a *ḥākim* a ruler, and a *ḥakam* a judge. Among the Divine Names are *al-Ḥakīm* and *al-Ḥakam*: the Wise, the Judge. Thus, there is a practical element that lies within the Arabic virtue of *ḥikmah*—it is the ability to rule justly and decide on the best course of action. The virtue of *ʿilm* on the other hand is more abstract. It is to have acute, detailed, and holistic awareness of realities (*ḥaqāʾiq*). An *ʿālim* is a scholar,[4] and an *ʿallāmah* an erudite

2 When exactly this was and at what precise age is subject to scholarly discussion. Ibn Kathīr ﷺ mentions various positions in his commentary on Q 12:22. He says: "There have been differences with regards to the age at which he (Yūsuf ﷺ) reached his prime (*ashuddah*). Ibn ʿAbbās, Mujāhid, and Qatādah said: thirty-three. The view of thirty-something is also attributed to Ibn ʿAbbās. Ḍaḥḥāk said: twenty. Ḥasan said: forty years. ʿIkrimah said: twenty-five years. Suddī said: thirty years. Saʿīd ibn Jubayr said: eighteen years. Imam Mālik, Rabīʿah, Zayd ibn Aslam, and Shaʿbī said: *ashudd* is puberty (*ḥulum*). There have also been other views espoused on the matter. Allah knows best." After similarly citing a number of opinions in this regard, Ṭabarī ﷺ says that it is difficult to ascertain an age without an unambiguous proof, which is lacking. If Allah ﷻ did not explicitly specify an age, then it is an area of positive scholarly engagement, but one that is neither apodictic (*qaṭʿī*—beyond disute) nor critical to the narrative.

3 Ibn Kathīr ﷺ said: "*Ātaynāhu ḥukman wa ʿilmā*—'We gave him wisdom and knowledge'; meaning: prophecy." Ṭabarī quotes Mujāhid ﷺ as saying: "*Ḥukman wa ʿilmā*—'wisdom and knowledge'; meaning: intellect and knowledge prior to prophecy." Ibn ʿĀshūr ﷺ explained *ḥukm* as prophecy, and *ʿilm* as surplus knowledge atop the status of prophethood, as Allah ﷻ says about Dāwūd and Sulaymān ﷺ: "And each did We endow with *ḥukm* and *ʿilm*" Q 21:79.

4 These are all examples of the linguistic connotations of the values in question. However,

expert with encyclopaedic knowledge. Allah ﷻ is *al-ʿAlīm*: the Knowing. He is *ʿĀlim al-Ghayb wa al-Shahādah*: the Knower of the Unseen and the Witnessed. As such, *ḥukm* and *ʿilm* together are signifiers of both applied and theoretical knowledge.[5]

These are the morals which Allah ﷻ bestowed upon Yūsuf ﷺ when He chose him as a prophet. It is these very gifts which we constantly pray for every single day as Muslims. When we recite *Sūrat al-Fātiḥah*, we plead Allah ﷻ: "Guide us to the straight path! The path of those You have blessed; not those who have anger upon them, nor those who have gone astray."[6] Those who have incurred the anger of Allah are the ones who overindulge in theory and fail to act upon the wisdom they learn. Those who have gone astray are the ones who are emphasising action but at the expense of sound reason and knowledge.

---

from an Islamic perspective, a *ʿālim* is someone who couples between knowledge and action. Allah ﷻ says: "Indeed, from among His servants, only the knowledgeable fear Allah" Q 35:28. Here, Allah describes those who are knowledgeable as those who are God-fearing, necessarily manifesting this in everything they do.

5 Commenting on Q 12:22, Ibn ʿĀshūr quotes Fakhr al-Dīn al-Rāzī making this exact point, ؓ. He says: "*Ḥukm* is practical wisdom because it is judgement that is conducive to one's guidance. *ʿIlm* is theoretical wisdom."

6 *al-Fātiḥah*, 6-7.

DID YOU KNOW?

There is an abundance of benefits the scholars have extrapolated from the two categories *al-maghḍūb ʿalayhim* and *al-ḍāllīn*. They are often juxtaposed as a dichotomy. Here are a few of these binaries:

Maghḍūb ʿAlayhim	**Ḍāllīn**
Only knowledge	Only action
Overly physical	Overly spiritual
Reason	Emotion
Emphasis on law	Emphasis on mysticism
Focus on divine *jalāl*	Focus on divine *jamāl*

The former are paradigmatically understood to be the Jews, while the latter the Christians.

Allah ﷻ says: "Thus We have appointed you a middle nation."[7] We are a people of action guided by sound knowledge. We do not reside wholly in either extreme. Rather, we perfectly balance this nexus. Our faith itself is necessarily all of: belief in the heart, affirmation by the tongue, and manifestation on the limbs.[8] Acquiring knowledge without following it up with action is hollow and stale, while activ-

7 *al-Baqarah*, 143.

8 There are scholars who opine that the essence of faith is heartfelt acceptance (*taṣdīq*), and action (*ʿamal*) follows suit as a consequence, but is not itself *īmān*. The difference is ultimately semantic and has no legal implications, as Ibn Taymiyyah ؒ articulated in many of his works. After thoroughly discussing the topic in *Sharḥ al-ʿAqīdah al-Aṣfahāniyyah*, he says: "After all this, arguing whether *īmān*—'faith'—linguistically refers to only belief (*taṣdīq*) without its entailments or both comes down to a semantic dispute (*nizāʿ lafẓī*)."

ism without a foundation of knowledge is often more harmful than beneficial.

There is another significance to the two timeless virtues of *ḥukm* and *ʿilm* in the *sūrah*: the names of Allah related to these virtues are mentioned together multiple times throughout. Thrice to be exact. Allah ﷻ is referred to as *ʿAlīmun Ḥakīm* in Yaʿqūb's early-years' advice to Yūsuf ﷺ.[9] After Binyāmīn goes with his older brothers to Egypt but does not return to his father, Yaʿqūb ﷺ says: "Perhaps Allah will bring them all back to me. Indeed, He is the Knowing, the Wise."[10] At the culmination of the story, Yūsuf is reunited with Yaʿqūb ﷺ, and the whole family enters Egypt unified and prosperous. Yūsuf ﷺ then says to his father: "Indeed, my Lord is kind to whom He wills. Indeed, He is the Knowing, the Wise."[11]

When Yaʿqūb ﷺ was teaching his young son about the great responsibilities he was to bear in assuming the prophetic office, he taught him: Your Lord is always knowing of your affairs, wise as to your journey and its challenges, guiding you every step of the way. Every time Yūsuf ﷺ felt alone, abandoned, and alienated, he reminded himself: Allah is knowing of my circumstances, wise to why I am here, actively taking care of me at every moment. After the unimaginable pain of losing three of his children,[12] Yaʿqūb ﷺ consoled himself: Allah has full knowledge of all three of them, and His wisdom dictates that they be away from me, He is just in His decree, aware

9 *Yūsuf*, 6.

10 *Yūsuf*, 83.

11 *Yūsuf*, 100.

12 The narrative implies that, upon failing to uphold his father's covenant, the eldest son could not bear returning to his father having failed him in protecting Binyāmīn. He therefore stayed behind. See Q 12:80.

of His slave's strife. In a scene of unparalleled triumphant joy, son and father finally find themselves together again in a prestigious and honourable setting. With serene contentment, Yūsuf said to Yaʿqūb ﷺ: Truly, dear father, Allah knew how every event we went through was leading us to this one, and His wisdom was such that our being here together would have been impossible otherwise! Such is the criticality of these beautiful names of Allah ﷻ in the infinitely intricate woven tapestry of *Sūrah Yūsuf*. And such is the importance of us properly acquainting ourselves with the Divine ﷻ through them.

LUST

The worldly life is a test. Allah ﷻ says: "He is the one who created death and life to test you who is best in deed."[13] Our tests come in different shapes and forms, and the greater the slave's value in the sight of Allah, the greater the test He makes him go through. On the authority of Muṣʿab ibn Saʿd ﷺ, he asked the Prophet ﷺ: "Messenger of Allah, who among the people are most severely tested?" He ﷺ replied: "The prophets, then the exemplars, one after the other [in rank]. One is tested in accordance with his religion—if he is strong, his test is severe; and if he is frail, he is tested accordingly. The slave continues to be tested until he is left walking sinless upon the earth."[14] Furthermore, the Messenger ﷺ said: "Verily, great reward comes with great tribulation.

13 *al-Mulk*, 2.

14 Reported by Tirmidhī (2398) and Ibn Mājah (4023).

Verily, if Allah loves a people, He tests them. Whoever is content, upon him is pleasure; and whoever is rebellious, upon him is wrath."[15]

REFLECT...

Every believing soul is necessarily tested. Thus, every believing soul necessarily has a share in Allah's love! The greater the test, the greater the perseverance, and the greater the love from Allah ﷻ!

One of the most destructive diseases of the heart is lust. Its temptation may overcome one to a degree of blind infatuation, whereby one sees nothing but one's object of desire. It is important to highlight that desiring the opposite gender is in itself natural and even praiseworthy. Ours is a way that does not circumvent natural desires, rather one which invites to their righteous fulfilment and mitigates their harm. The Prophet ﷺ himself—the most masculine and chivalrous of all men—has said: "It has been made beloved to me from your worldly life: women and perfume. The comfort of my eye has been placed in the prayer."[16] Thus, what is reprehensible is entertaining evil thoughts and immoral fancies, not the attraction itself, which is part and parcel of manly virtue.

15 Reported by Tirmidhī (2396) and Ibn Mājah (4031).

16 Reported by Nasāʾī (3939), Bayhaqī (13836), and Aḥmad (14068) with a minor difference in wording.

TRANSFORMATIVE WISDOM

Allah's Messenger ﷺ gives young men direct advice with regards to safeguarding their chastity. He ﷺ said: "Young men! Whoever among you can support a wife should marry, for it helps restrain one's gaze and preserve one's chastity. Whoever is unable to do so should fast, for it will blunt his urges."
Reported by Muslim (1400)

Yūsuf ﷺ found his master's wife compromising herself before him. She was a woman of status, power, and beauty, and she offered herself to him. Though possible, it is unlikely that this was an isolated incident. Her glances, approaches, and mannerisms led up to this moment. It was probably a pre-planned ordeal on her behalf, especially given the female sexual psyche.[17] She had cunningly created a secluded environment, locking doors and windows, leaving no witnesses to their actions.

It is of paramount importance to recognise that the final act of fornication[18] does not take place in an isolated context. There are glances exchanged, illicit intentions verbalised, meetings and places planned, and so on. The Prophet ﷺ said: "Every son of Adam has his share of fornication. The eyes fornicate and their fornication is looking. The ears fornicate and their fornication is hearing. The hand fornicates and its fornication is touching. The foot fornicates

17 Unlike men, women are less able to exercise immediate arousal. Generally, men are triggered via visual stimuli, while women more via emotionally relevant stimuli.

18 From a legal (*shar'ī*) perspective, fornication (*zinā*) is realised via penile insertion. Any lewd interactions before that are undoubtedly unlawful and incur grave sin. They serve to incite and instigate towards the final act, but are strictly speaking not *zinā* in and of themselves.

and its fornication is walking. The heart wishes and desires. The sexual organ then substantiates this or belies it."[19] This is why there are means and legislations given by Allah ﷻ to curtail obscenity.

Allah ﷻ says: "Tell the believing men to lower their gazes and guard their private parts. That is more decent for them. Indeed, Allah is aware of what they do. And tell the believing women to lower their gazes and guard their private parts, and to not expose their adornment except that which appears thereof, and to cover their necklines with their headscarves."[20] Additionally, Ibn ʿAbbās ؓ narrated that he heard the Prophet ﷺ say: "Let no man be secluded with a woman except she has a *maḥram*[21], and let no woman travel except she does so with a *maḥram*."[22] The Prophet ﷺ advised ʿAlī ibn Abī Ṭālib ؓ by telling him: "ʿAlī, do not follow up one [involuntary] glance with another [illicit one]. The first is for you, but the second is against you."[23] Allah ﷻ is most aware of His slaves and their vulnerabilities and dispositions. He ﷻ wishes dignity and honour for them, not decadence and immorality.

---

19 Reported by Bukhārī (6243) and Muslim (2657) on the authority of Abū Hurayrah ؓ, with some minor differences of certain bodily parts being included or excluded.

20 *al-Nūr*, 30-31.

21 The word *maḥram* comes from the trilateral root *ḥ-r-m* and is of the morphological form *mafʿal*. It refers to a man whom a woman cannot legally marry, usually her family members; e.g. her father, uncle, brother, son, etc.

22 Reported by Muslim (1341) and Bukhārī (3006) with minor differences in the wording.

23 Reported by Tirmidhī (2701).

TRANSFORMATIVE WISDOM

There is that which one has no conscious control over, and that which is borne of deliberate and wilful contemplation. Any introspective person can recognise the difference. What is important is that we never entertain immorality and keep a tight rein on our imagination. Instead, we must treat each other with dignity and respect, as we would like our own family members to be treated by the opposite gender.

Yūsuf ﷺ was a stunningly handsome man.[24] He was in a situation where, from a materialistic perspective, everything was set up perfectly. The wife of the ʿAzīz was both beautiful and his superior, and there she was giving him the vantage point. Where many men would have thought they had everything to gain, Yūsuf ﷺ realised he had everything to lose—his connection with Allah ﷻ and his moral integrity. He exclaimed: "Allah forbid! He is my refuge!" Despite having the natural inclination to an attractive woman,[25] he remembered His creator, sustainer, and protector. He remembered his Lord, and consequently remembered his lord[26]—the ʿAzīz. He was a man who

24 In the lengthy and beautiful account of the Ascension (*Miʿrāj*), the Messenger ﷺ encounters and converses with many other prophets. Upon meeting Yūsuf ﷺ in the third heaven, he ﷺ said: "I saw Yūsuf, and surely he was given half of beauty (*shaṭr al-ḥusn*)." Narrated on the authority of Anas ibn Mālik ﷺ and reported by Muslim (162). Other narrations of this account reported by Bayhaqī and Ṭabarānī are even more explicit in how the Prophet ﷺ described the beauty of Yūsuf ﷺ.

25 We will speak shortly about the statement of Allah ﷻ: *Wa hamma bihā*—'He proceeded towards her.'

26 The wording in the *āyah* is: *Innahū rabbī aḥsana mathwāy*—'It is my lord who honoured my dwelling.' This is referring to the ʿAzīz. The word *rabb* means 'lord' or 'master,' and may possibly be referring to Allah ﷻ. However, given the context and the repeated mention of

generously opened his house to Yūsuf ﷺ and ennobled him despite Yūsuf ﷺ being his servant. He even wished to take him as his son. Yūsuf ﷺ was not going to betray his trust.

REFLECT...

Committing adultery with a married woman is oppression towards her husband, as well as the man and woman sinning against themselves and each other. It is compound injustice, "an abomination, and an evil path to follow." Q 17:32

Allah ﷻ protected His prophet and slave from major sin.[27] When she advanced towards him, Yūsuf ﷺ would have[28] responded in kind[29]

---

mathwā (dwelling), her husband and their relationship is likely what is being invoked as a deterrent. Qurṭubī ﷺ says in his commentary on Q 12:23: "*Innahū rabbī*—'It is my lord'; meaning: her husband. That is: he is my master who honoured me, so I shan't betray him. This is the view of Mujāhid, Ibn Isḥāq, and Suddī. Zajjāj said: 'This means: it is Allah, my Lord, who safeguarded me with his kindness, so I will not commit what He ordained unlawful.'" There is no contradiction either way, and both interpretations hold a complementary, positive meaning.

27 This is referred to as *'iṣmah*. In their messengerhood, the prophets are infallible and secured from committing sin.

28 Some exegetes interpret *hamma bihā*—'he inclined towards her'—as Yūsuf ﷺ almost yielding to her advances. However, this should be properly read in context and is an incomplete statement by itself. Yūsuf ﷺ would have responded to her, but Allah protected him by showing him a sign. See the following two footnotes.

29 There is a useful note regarding *tilāwah* here. Ibn 'Āshūr ﷺ cites a felicitous anecdote from Abū Ḥātim al-Sijistānī, the well-known Qur'an scholar, Hadith scholar, and grammarian. The latter is reported to have said: "I was going through the *gharīb* (peculiar or ambiguous passages) of the Qur'an with Abū 'Ubaydah [Mu'ammar ibn al-Muthannā]. I reached the statement of Allah, 'She advanced towards him, and he advanced...' Q 12:24 Abū 'Ubaydah then said: 'This is articulated via a sentence-order reversal (*taqdīm* and *ta'khīr*)—mentioning the answer to the condition before the condition. That is, it is as if the statement is: She advanced towards him, and, but for the proof of his Lord, he

had Allah ﷻ not shown him a sign[30] to remind him of who he was and wake him to the evil setting he inadvertently found himself in. We ought to take Prophet Yūsuf ﷺ as a role model in chastity and integrity. Despite all worldly enticement to the contrary, he chose Allah ﷻ over his base urges.

The completeness of one's character lies in the ability to control one's desires and not be enslaved to one's whims and fancies. Imagine a person who prioritises his primitive impulses above all else. Such a person is no better than animals, or even worse. At least beasts cannot transcend their biology. Human beings can go against theirs in pursuit of virtue. Allah ﷻ strikes this very example. He ﷻ says: "Have you seen the one who takes his whim as his god: would you be a trustee for him? Or do you assume that most of them hear or reason? They are but like livestock; rather, they are even further astray."[31]

---

would have advanced towards her.'" Thus, the appropriate delivery here is to recite: *Wa laqad hammat bih* [**stop**]. [**start**] *Wa hamma bihā lawlā an ra'ā burhāna Rabbih.* This would deliver the correct meaning as: "She advanced towards him. And he would have advanced towards her but for the proof of his Lord." A *waqf* (stopping point) that would be considered *qabīḥ* (ugly) would be: *Wa laqad hammat bihī wa hamma bihā*—implying they respectively advanced towards one another.

30 There is an abundance of scholarly positions on what the *burhān* in question was and its exact nature. Ibn 'Āshūr ﷺ summarises these eloquently in his commentary on Q 12:24. He said: "Exegetes differed over what the *burhān* was. Some implied it was a theoretical proof which laid bare the ugliness of the deed before him. It was said that it was a form of revelation, and it was said it was divine preservation. It was also said that it was images which appeared before him."

31 *al-Furqān*, 43-44.

TRANSFORMATIVE WISDOM

They say that opportunity knocks, while temptation leans on the doorbell. Nonetheless, every temptation has an escape. Despite what your carnal desires may suggest, you have everything to lose and almost nothing to gain. Every moment temptation is resisted is a victory. No one is known to be truly good until they have a choice to be bad. While it should never be sought out, temptation should be viewed as a chance to prove one's mettle to Allah ﷻ. May Allah ﷻ safeguard us from falling for our primitive inclinations.

IKHLĀṢ

Allah ﷻ chooses for Himself those who choose nothing else but Him. There is a beautiful benefit to be drawn here from the science of the *qirāʾāt*[32]. Concluding this passage, Allah ﷻ says regarding Yūsuf ﷺ: "He is one of Our chosen (*mukhlaṣīn*) slaves."[33] In a variant recitation, we read: "He is one of Our sincere (*mukhliṣīn*) slaves."[34] The two words *mukhlaṣ* and *mukhliṣ* are respectively a done-to noun (*ism mafʿūl*) and a doing noun (*ism fāʿil*)[35] of the trilateral root *kh-l-ṣ*

32 The variant, overabundantly prevalent (*mutawātir*) recitations of the Qur'an.

33 This is the interpretation as per the *qirāʾah* of Nāfiʿ, ʿĀṣim, Ḥamzah, Kisāʾī, Abū Jaʿfar, and Khalaf al-ʿĀshir ﷺ.

34 This is the interpretation as per the *qirāʾah* of Ibn Kathīr, Abū ʿAmr, Ibn ʿĀmir, and Yaʿqūb ﷺ.

35 The words 'subject' and 'object' were deliberately avoided since they are commonly used as a grammatical categorisation. The categorisation in question is of a morphological nature (the form of the word and how that impacts its meaning, not its position in the sentence). To clarify this, consider the following sentence: "The ball hit the batter." From

(خلص). In other words, a *mukhliṣ* is someone who does *ikhlāṣ*, and a *mukhlaṣ* is someone who has *ikhlāṣ* done to them.

Ikhlāṣ is to cleanse a thing from all excess matter, getting rid of the undesirable and leaving only the desirable. This is why it is used to refer to 'sincerity.' If someone is *mukhliṣ* in their endeavours, they are wholly focused on them without distraction. In the religious context, a *mukhliṣ* is someone who has singled out Allah ﷻ alone for worship, devotion, and adoration. *Sūrat al-Ikhlāṣ* is referred to as such because it so eloquently and emphatically describes Allah's oneness, uniqueness, and sublime unlikeness—there is no mistaking to whom it is referring other than Allah ﷻ.

In this short sentence, Allah ﷻ describes Yūsuf ﷺ as both a *mukhliṣ* and a *mukhlaṣ*. In doing so, He ﷻ is teaching us that there is no seeking Him out without a pre-ordained portion of His grace (*tawfīq*).[36] Without that, we would all be lost. All goodness initiates from Him, belongs to Him, and goes back to Him.

---

a grammatical perspective, the word 'batter' is the object of the sentence. From a morphological perspective—i.e. analysing the form of the word in isolation—the word 'batter' is a doing noun, since a batter is a person who bats (does the action of 'batting'). In Arabic, grammar is *naḥw*, and it is the science concerned with the syntactic relationship of words in a sentence. Morphology is *ṣarf*, and it is the science concerned with how changing the form of the word impacts its meaning in abstraction.

36 This concept is found in passages pertaining to *mashī'ah* (divine will). For example, Allah ﷻ says: "You do not will except that Allah wills" Q 81:29, 76:30. It is also implied in the passage: "He turned to them [in mercy] so that they may turn to Him [in repentance]" Q 9:118. Meaning: He relented towards them that they may repent to Him.

TRANSFORMATIVE WISDOM

The crux of our struggles today, it seems, lies in our ignorance of who Allah ﷻ truly is. The antidote? Deepening our understanding of Allah and acquainting ourselves with Him. This knowledge inversely correlates with our susceptibility to sin. The less we know of Allah, the more likely we are to stumble; the more we learn about Him, the stronger we become in resisting temptation.

PART

IX

ALLEGATION DENIED

Speak the truth, even if your voice shakes.

Realising what will ensue if he lies idle, Yūsuf ﷺ made a dash for the exit, trying by any means to escape his predicament and get out of the room. The wife of the ʿAzīz was not going to make things easy for him, though. She chased after him, grabbing his clothes from behind. The struggle led both of them to the chamber's door, and it was at that very moment that the ʿAzīz pulled it open. Allah ﷻ says:

وَاسْتَبَقَا الْبَابَ وَقَدَّتْ قَمِيصَهُ مِنْ دُبُرٍ وَأَلْفَيَا سَيِّدَهَا لَدَى الْبَابِ قَالَتْ مَا جَزَاءُ مَنْ أَرَادَ بِأَهْلِكَ سُوءًا إِلَّا أَنْ يُسْجَنَ أَوْ عَذَابٌ أَلِيمٌ ﴿٢٥﴾

قَالَ هِيَ رَاوَدَتْنِي عَنْ نَفْسِي وَشَهِدَ شَاهِدٌ مِنْ أَهْلِهَا إِنْ كَانَ قَمِيصُهُ قُدَّ مِنْ قُبُلٍ فَصَدَقَتْ وَهُوَ مِنَ الْكَاذِبِينَ ﴿٢٦﴾

وَإِنْ كَانَ قَمِيصُهُ قُدَّ مِنْ دُبُرٍ فَكَذَبَتْ وَهُوَ مِنَ الصَّادِقِينَ ﴿٢٧﴾

فَلَمَّا رَأَى قَمِيصَهُ قُدَّ مِنْ دُبُرٍ قَالَ إِنَّهُ مِنْ كَيْدِكُنَّ إِنَّ كَيْدَكُنَّ عَظِيمٌ ﴿٢٨﴾

يُوسُفُ أَعْرِضْ عَنْ هَذَا وَاسْتَغْفِرِي لِذَنْبِكِ إِنَّكِ كُنْتِ مِنَ الْخَاطِئِينَ ﴿٢٩﴾

❝ They raced towards the door, and she tore his shirt from behind, and they found her master at the door. She said, "What is the penalty for him who intended evil towards your family except that he be given prison or a painful punishment?" He said, "It was she who sought to seduce me." A witness from her own family testified: "If his shirt has been torn from the front, then she has told the truth and he is of the liars. But if his shirt has been torn from the back, then she has lied and he is of the truthful." So, when he saw his shirt ripped from behind, he said, "This is certainly of your trickery, O women. Great is your trickery indeed. Yūsuf, disregard this. And you, ask forgiveness for your misdeed; for surely you have been of the wrongdoers." [1]

A GOOD WORD

The Messenger of Allah ﷺ said: "Let whosoever believes in Allah and the Last Day say a good word or stay quiet."[2] The words we speak have a grave impact on ourselves as well as those around us. It is the utterance of the *shahādah*—the testimony of faith—which confirms one as Muslim to the community, verbalising by the tongue that which is in the heart. Likewise, evil words incur grave sin—as in slander and backbiting—and can even take one out of the fold of the religion—as in blasphemy and mockery. The Qur'an and the Sunnah are full of statements emphasising the value of the spoken word.

TRANSFORMATIVE WISDOM

How many of our internal conflicts and disputes would be avoided if we adhered to this beautiful prophetic command? How many people do we unwittingly repel and how many loved ones do we hurt by our words? How far would a kind word of encouragement or gentle accountability go in creating leaders and role models? Speak a good word, or do not speak at all!

1 *Yūsuf*, 25-29.

2 Reported as part of a longer report in Muslim (47) on the authority of Abū Hurayrah ﷺ.

The Prophet ﷺ said: "Surely, the slave speaks a word from [what earns] Allah's pleasure, not thinking much of it, and Allah raises him in stations through it. And surely, the slave speaks a word from [what incurs] Allah's wrath, not thinking much of it, and he is cast into Hellfire due to it."[3] A lot of what transpires in this passage is borne of quick, unprepared utterances—the wife of the ʿAzīz and her calumny against Yūsuf ﷺ, Yūsuf ﷺ denying her false claims, the fair judge who was a voice of reason amidst the chaos, and the ʿAzīz with his final exhortations. Some of these statements were borne of justice and goodness, while others were borne of deceit and evil.

REFLECT...

It is said that between what is meant but not said and what is said but not meant, most of love is lost. Before you speak, let your words pass through three gates: Is it true? Is it necessary? Is it kind?

Allah ﷻ says: "Allah does not like that evil words be said openly except from anyone wronged. Allah is hearing, knowing."[4] To his dismay, Yūsuf ﷺ found himself accused of dishonouring the man he refused to betray. He was standing before him, and the circumstances were certainly sufficient to arouse anyone's suspicion. Then, the woman who had just been trying to seduce him against his will changed roles in the blink of an eye.[5] She cried to her husband, feigning victimhood, and accused Yūsuf ﷺ of indecency.

3 Reported in Bukhārī (6478) on the authority of Abū Hurayrah ؓ.

4 *al-Nisāʾ*, 148.

5 More on this later.

He stood up for himself. He did not allow his reputation to be maligned and his good name be tarnished. He spoke the truth, firmly and clearly, without addition, omission, or alteration: "She tried to seduce me." A simple and direct statement of fact. Compare that to the wife's Greek-tragedy of an accusation, playing on the heartstrings of her husband with emotive language, as well as suggesting ready-made penalties.[6]

TRANSFORMATIVE WISDOM

Clearing one's name from false allegations is a noble deed. It is not self-aggrandising, but a necessary vocalisation of truth. Allah ﷻ says: "You who believe, stand for the sake of Allah as witnesses for justice" [Q 5:8]. We did not hear Yūsuf's voice since his conversation with his father until now, not even when he was abducted and sold as a slave. Yet, when his chastity was brought into question, he spoke up!

TRUTH TRUMPS ALL

Allah ﷻ says: "Say, 'The truth has come and falsehood has withered away—falsehood is ever perishing.'"[7] He ﷻ also says: "Rather, we hurl the truth against falsehood so that it obliterates it; and thus it

6 This is the second time in the story where there is a direct contrast between a liar's alibi when compared to an honest person's account of an event. The first was pertaining to Yūsuf's brothers and their excuse for how they lost him. Later on, they actually do lose their younger brother—Binyāmīn—through no fault of their own (See Q 12:81-82). The wording and psychological implications are starkly different in each case.

7 *al-Isrā'*, 81.

vanishes."[8] All things remaining equal, whenever there is a standoff between truth and falsehood, the truth always triumphs. Our problem as human beings is that we are often distracted by the means through which we receive the truth, obfuscating matters and pulling us in different directions. If we do not like the person speaking it, we are disinclined to accept it. Likewise with books and their presentation: if certain standards of ours are not met, we neglect the truth-value within the content.

There are two extremes: not honouring the truth by failing to adorn it with what it deserves of proper delivery; and only focusing on embellishments, letting the vessel distract us from the core message. We ought to strike the correct balance. The Prophet ﷺ said: "Indeed, Allah is beautiful and He loves beauty."[9] 'Uthmān ibn 'Affān and his wife Ruqayyah ؓ (the daughter of the Prophet ﷺ) were the first to migrate to Abyssinya and deliver the message of Islam to the Negus (al-Najāshī)—both of them were strikingly beautiful. With regards to writing and presentation, an *athar* (relayed report) states: "Beautiful writing increases the truth in clarity."[10] On the other hand, we must aim for objectivity in formulating our verdicts. The truth is the truth, even if spoken by *shayṭān* himself![11] Furthermore, despite delivering

---

8   *al-Anbiyā'*, 18.

9   Reported by Muslim (91) on the authority of Ibn Mas'ūd ؓ.

10   Reported by Daylamī in *Musnad al-Firdaws* on the authority of Umm Salamah ؓ. The statement cannot be authentically attributed to the Prophet ﷺ, and is often ascribed to 'Alī ibn Abī Ṭālib ؓ. Regardless, it is an adage with sound meaning given our context.

11   This literally took place with one of the Companions ؓ. On one occasion, Abū Hurayrah ؓ was given authority by the Prophet ﷺ to supervise the obligatory Ramdan charity given towards the end of the month (*zakāt al-fiṭr*). A man came one night to unlawfully take from it. Abū Hurayrah ؓ caught him, but the man complained that he was in severe poverty and that he needed to feed his wife and many starving children.

incredibly powerful and profound truths to him, Pharaoh belittled Mūsā due to the way he spoke: "Am I not better than this nobody who can barely express himself?"[12]

REFLECT...

How blessed is the ummah of Islam that we are not merely given truth and instructed to follow it, but we have the most stunning husk carrying the most precious kernel! Our Messenger is the best of all creation, and our revealed manifesto is the best of all speech!

Allah says: "You who believe, always stand for justice as witnesses for the sake of Allah, even if it be against yourselves, parents, or relatives."[13] Allah allowed objective and just judgement to flow from the tongue of none other than a relative of Yūsuf's accuser. Since it was her word against his, the criterion to establish either testimony as true would be to analyse the way in which Yūsuf's garments were severed. If his shirt was torn from the front, she was fending him off while he was forcing himself onto her. If it was torn from the back, he was fleeing her grasp while she tried to draw him

Abū Hurayrah pitied him and let him go. The same thing happened again the next night. On the third night, Abū Hurayrah caught him and was adamant he would deliver him to the Prophet. The man offered to teach him words which will protect him from *shayṭān* on the condition he let him go. Abū Hurayrah agreed, and the man taught him to recite *Āyat al-Kursī* (the Verse of the Stool, Q 2:155) before going to sleep. Having narrated this to the Prophet, he told him: "He told you the truth even though he is a liar. Do you know whom it was you met three nights in a row, Abū Hurayrah? It was a devil." The full, lengthy account is reported by Bukhārī (2311).

12 *al-Zukhruf*, 52.

13 *al-Nisā'*, 135.

to her. Lo and behold, the shirt of Yūsuf 🕊—a recurring symbol in the story—came to bear witness to his innocence. He was vindicated.

TRANSFORMATIVE WISDOM

It is very difficult to judge against one's own interests or against one's family, especially in a context where emotions are running high and close relations are being invoked. To calm our trepidations and calibrate our intentions, we must remind ourselves of the One before whom all are ultimately to be judged. Forget other people's opinions—the judge of the earth should fear lest the Judge of the heavens and the earth and all that is within them disapproves of his verdict! When all is said and done, there is only one court: His court 🕊.

FEMININE GUILE

The Prophet ﷺ said about women: "I have not seen ones lacking *'aql*[14] and *dīn*[15] more able to steal a stern man's heart than you."[16] This is neither praise nor dispraise, but an innate feature of the feminine woman which she may then utilise for goodness or for evil. Generally speaking, women have higher emotional intelligence than men.

When the wife of the ʿAzīz found herself compromised before her husband, she was instantaneously able to assume the character of the damsel in distress. She realised that her best course of action was to place herself in the victim's shoes, and call upon her husband as her saviour. She was playing on his *ghīrah*—masculine protective jealousy. "Look, dear husband, what this scoundrel wished to do to your wife. How should you punish such ignoble insolence? Jail? Lashing? Please, come to my rescue and be by my side!" Notice how Allah ﷻ described her plea: *man arāda* ***bi-ahlika*** *sū'an*—'one

14 The deficiency of *'aql*—intellect—is explained in the full narration by the Prophet ﷺ to be in reference to a woman's legal testimony being half that of a man, as Allah revealed in the Qur'an. It is not that a woman is lacking intelligence as is often misquoted and misunderstood. Allah ﷻ says: "If two men are not available, then [appoint] a man and two women from those you approve as witnesses so that if one [lady] wavers, the other reminds her [to remain steadfast]" Q 2:282. Accordingly, and as per this verse, this legislation is related to the paradigmatic feminine personality which is unique and distinct from that of a male. It is not referring to mental prowess. It is worth noting that even Western psychological literature showcases this feature: women are on average more agreeable than men. Thus, there should be no doubt that the Law of Allah protects and honours women.

15 The deficiency of *dīn*—religion—is explained in the full narration by the Prophet ﷺ via the woman's menses barring her from fasting and performing the ritual prayer.

16 Reported by Ibn al-ʿArabī in his *Aḥkām al-Qur'ān* (1/1531). A similar wording is reported by Muslim (79) on the authority of ʿAbdullāh ibn ʿUmar ﷺ.

who wished evil upon **your family**[17]'. She did not say that Yūsuf ﷺ did this or that. Instead, she spun the narrative into an emotionally charged plot: a hapless maiden who needs her knight to protect her from an uncouth low-life.

TRANSFORMATIVE WISDOM

In the modern world, we are all too familiar with this picture-perfect feminine virtue signalling. Just as the family member was able to remain objective in the face of a tumultuous scenario, it is absolutely critical for a judge to not be swayed by the helpless tears and sobs of a lady. Regardless of whether they are justified or not, it is the facts that should dictate a verdict, not who feels sorry for whom.

17 A wholesome element within the Arabic language (approved by revelation) is the use of the word *ahl* to refer to one's wife. *Ahl* literally means 'family', implying that one's wife is one's kin, and the source of familial comfort and recourse.

PART X

TALK OF THE TOWN

Do not look down on others because they sin differently than you.

Wishing that the scandal not spread, the ʿAzīz commanded his wife to repent[1] and Yūsuf ﷺ to forget about the ordeal. Despite this, the walls have ears, and word managed to get out. Such tantalising gossip spread like wildfire. The lady and her servant boy became the talk of the town. But the wife of the ʿAzīz was not going to let this go. Allah ﷻ says:

وَقَالَ نِسْوَةٌ فِى الْمَدِينَةِ امْرَأَةُ الْعَزِيزِ تُرَاوِدُ فَتَاهَا عَن نَّفْسِهِ
قَدْ شَغَفَهَا حُبًّا إِنَّا لَنَرَاهَا فِى ضَلَالٍ مُّبِينٍ ﴿٣٠﴾

فَلَمَّا سَمِعَتْ بِمَكْرِهِنَّ أَرْسَلَتْ إِلَيْهِنَّ وَأَعْتَدَتْ لَهُنَّ مُتَّكَأً وَآتَتْ كُلَّ وَاحِدَةٍ
مِّنْهُنَّ سِكِّينًا وَقَالَتِ اخْرُجْ عَلَيْهِنَّ فَلَمَّا رَأَيْنَهُ أَكْبَرْنَهُ وَقَطَّعْنَ أَيْدِيَهُنَّ
وَقُلْنَ حَاشَ لِلَّهِ مَا هَٰذَا بَشَرًا إِنْ هَٰذَا إِلَّا مَلَكٌ كَرِيمٌ ﴿٣١﴾

قَالَتْ فَذَٰلِكُنَّ الَّذِى لُمْتُنَّنِى فِيهِ وَلَقَدْ رَاوَدتُّهُ عَن نَّفْسِهِ فَاسْتَعْصَمَ
وَلَئِن لَّمْ يَفْعَلْ مَا آمُرُهُ لَيُسْجَنَنَّ وَلَيَكُونًا مِّنَ الصَّاغِرِينَ ﴿٣٢﴾

“ Some women in the city said, “The governor’s wife is trying to seduce her slave! Love for him consumes her heart! Indeed, we see her in clear misguidance.” So when she heard of their taunts, she sent for them and prepared for them a banquet and brought each one of them a knife, and

1 This refers to her seeking her husband’s forgiveness, and is the interpretation of the majority of exegetes. It is also possible that they were believers in a supreme being to whom sins must be atoned for, though as polytheists, such that they associated partners with God and engaged in idol worship.

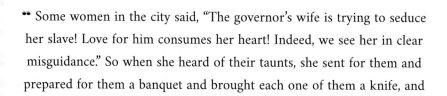

she said, "Come out before them." So when they saw him, they marvelled at him and cut their hands and said, "Good God! In no way is this a human; this is but a noble angel!" She said, "Here he is—the one you blamed me for. And yes, I did seek to seduce him, but he abstained. Though if he does not do what I command him, he will most surely be imprisoned, and he will become among the disgraced." ﴾[2]

SANCTIMONY

Thinking oneself too great to fall into others' sins is a perfect recipe for disaster. In fact, it often leads one to eventually commit them![3] Furthermore, this holier-than-thou attitude is usually a greater sin than whatever wrong is being committed, for it is borne of *kibr*—arrogance and pride: one of the deadliest diseases of the heart. It is the first sin ever committed. Allah ﷻ created Ādam ﷺ and commanded the angels to prostrate to him. All obliged but one: Satan the Accursed. Allah ﷻ says: "He (Allah ﷻ) said, 'What prevented you from prostrating when I commanded you?' He (Iblīs) said, 'I am better than him; You created me from fire and created him from clay.'"[4] It was thinking himself special that was the source of his damnation.

2 *Yūsuf*, 30-32.

3 There are traditions to this effect, but none of them are authentically attributed to the Prophet ﷺ. For example: "Do not gloat at your brother['s misfortune], lest Allah grants him wellness and trials you." Also: "Whosoever mocks his brother's sin will not die until he falls into it." Nonetheless, the wisdom can be derived from collective experience, and is a concept that is discussed by scholars concerned with spiritual purification [See Ibn al-Qayyim's *Madārij al-Sālikīn* (1/177-1778) for example].

4 *al-Aʿrāf*, 12.

TRANSFORMATIVE WISDOM

The Prophet ﷺ said: "He will not enter the Garden who has an atom's worth of *kibr* in his heart" [Reported by Muslim (91)]. The reason why *kibr* is such a severe sin is that it attributes to the self that which may only be attributed to Allah ﷻ. Whatever goodness one likes in themselves is purely a gift from Allah, and not the product of one's own doing. Our physical, intellectual, and spiritual qualities are bestowed upon us by Him. Thus, we submit to His will and say as Sulaymān ﷺ said, "This is from the favour of my Lord" Q 27:40. Not as Qārūn—Pharaoh's ally—said: "I was surely given this of my own, personal knowledge" Q 28:78.

In this light, it is important to keep in mind the primacy of the heart's actions. A regretful sinner is categorically closer to Allah ﷻ than a boastful worshipper. Regarding a man who would continuously receive the penal punishment for drinking, the Prophet ﷺ forbade others from cursing him and said: "By Allah, I know he loves Allah and His Messenger."[5] On the other hand, there are plenty of warnings in the Qur'an and the Sunnah for those who marvel at their deeds, believing themselves too good to not enter the Garden.

Allah ﷻ says: "Say, 'Shall We inform you of the biggest losers regarding deeds? Those whose efforts in the worldly life have gone astray, while they assumed that they were doing well.' Those are the ones who denied the signs of their Lord and the meeting with Him,

5 Reported by Bukhārī (6780) on the authority of 'Umar ibn al-Khaṭṭāb ﷺ. In a similar report, the Prophet ﷺ continued: "Do not be aids to *shayṭān* against your brother. Rather say, 'May Allah forgive him.'"

so their deeds were nullified, and on the Day of Resurrection We will consider them of no weight."[6] The first three people who will be judged and consequently flung into the Fire are: the fighter who was martyred in battle, the knowledgeable reciter of the Qur'an, and the wealthy person who spent in charity—all of them did what they did for other than Allah's sake, and rather wished for notoriety and fame so got the reward they desired in the worldly life.[7] Additionally, the Prophet ﷺ warned his ummah of a punishment that will overtake both the wicked and the few good-doers left among them.[8] The reason is the lack of enjoining good and forbidding evil (*al-amr bil-ma'rūf wa al-nahy 'an al-munkar*).[9]

REFLECT...

Intention is the key in directing the actions of the limbs. Two people may be performing the exact same manifest deed, yet one is drawn to Allah and the Garden through his action, while the other is incurring His wrath and the Fire. Arrogance, ostentation, self-amazement, and narcissistic egoism are major and destructive sins of the heart.

6 *al-Kahf*, 103-105.

7 Reported by Muslim (1905).

8 There are many reports to this effect, especially with regards to the end of times. See, for example, Bukhārī (3346), Muslim (2880), and Tirmidhī (2185).

9 Commenting on one such narration, Qurṭubī says in his *Tadhkirah*: "If the wicked become abundant and the righteous become but a few, the latter are destroyed along with the former if they do not enjoin them towards common good (*amr bil-ma'rūf*) and detest the actions of the wicked. It is the meaning of Allah's statement: 'Beware of a chastisement that shall not only befall the wrongdoers among you.' Q 8:25"

When the town womenfolk heard of what happened, they ran the wife's name through the gutters. They spoke about her with such malice[10] that it bespoke their internal sense of smug self-righteousness. "We see her in plain error!"; "She's wholly smitten by him!"; "She can't keep her hands to herself!"; "How unbecoming of a lady, let alone the governor's wife!" What ensued, of course, was them falling into the very trial that plagued her. They cut their hands in awe of Yūsuf 🕊 and his stunning appearance. On top of that, they ended up doing the same deed which they were mocking her for not so long before this—calling Yūsuf 🕊 to indecency.[11]

Their hearts were troubled with haughtiness, and perhaps even a subtle envy. They were allured by what had taken place and potentially wished to explore further, using their jibes as a means to get a reaction from the wife of the ʿAzīz.[12] Here lies another important lesson: we should thank Allah 🕮 for safeguarding us from trials and tribulations, and never hope that we find ourselves in their midst. If we do, then we are patient and resilient, holding fast onto His commands and believing His promise of reward.

---

10 See next subheading, where Ibn al-Qayyim 🕮 speaks about ten rhetorical tools used in their describing her deed.

11 This is deduced from the statement: *Wa illā taṣrif ʿannī kaydahunna aṣbu ilayhinn*—'If You do not avail me from **their** (fem. pl.) scheming, I may soften towards **them** (fem. pl.)' Q 12:33.

12 This is hinted towards from the statement: *Fa-lammā samiʿat bi-makrihinn*—'When she heard of their **plotting'** Q 12:31. Their gossip was referred to as *makr*—deceitful scheming and trickery.

TRANSFORMATIVE WISDOM

The Prophet ﷺ said: "All within my ummah are well except the public sinners." [Reported by Bukhārī (6069)]. We are invited to cover up the sinner's mistake so long as it was privately committed and those involved wish to repent, not to publicise it and help *shayṭān* against them. In their remorse for their error and their adamance not to return to it, they may be better than many who did not fall into it. Judging is all too easy. This is one of the meanings of the prophetic statement: "Indeed, a man may do the deeds of the Garden dwellers according to what appears to the people while he is among the inhabitants of the Fire. And indeed, a man may do the deeds of the Fire dwellers according to what appears to the people while he is among the inhabitants of the Garden." [Reported by Bukhārī (2898)]

SMEAR CAMPAIGN

DID YOU KNOW?

The 30th *āyah* of the *sūrah* is the only time the word *ḥubb*—'love'—is used in the Qur'an with connotations of lust. The wording is: *Qad shagh-afahā ḥubbā*—'her heart is impassioned with love for him.'

Reflecting over the way in which Allah ﷻ described the women gossiping, Ibn al-Qayyim ﷺ derived ten points which serve to emphasise their ill-intention and the Qur'an's linguistic prowess in portraying it. In his commentary[13] on Q 12:30, he ﷺ says:

> " "Some women in the city said, 'The governor's wife is trying to seduce her slave! Love for him consumes her heart! Indeed, we see her in clear misguidance.'"
>
> This statement includes many elements of malicious intent (*makr*).
>
> **The first** is their saying, "The governor's wife is trying to seduce her slave." They did not refer to her by her name. Rather, they referred to her by the description which highlights the ugliness of her deed: the fact that she has a man—her husband. Fornication from a married woman is uglier than from an unmarried one.
>
> **The second** is that her husband is Egypt's grand governor and minister, making her deed even worse.
>
> **The third** is that the one she is seducing is a slave[14] not a free man, making her crime more heinous.

13 Known mostly for carrying Ibn Taymiyyah's banner in theology (his shaykh and teacher), Ibn al-Qayyim ﷺ has nonetheless made noteworthy contributions in *tazkiyah* (spiritual sciences) and even *tafsīr* (qur'anic commentary). His *tafsīr* work is widely referred to as *al-Tafsīr al-Qayyim*.

14 The word used is *fatāhā*—'her servant boy.'

The fourth is that it is her slave who lives in her home and under the same roof as her. Her dealing with him ought to be in that light—as part of the household (*ahl al-bayt*); not the way in which one would deal with an unknown foreigner [where promiscuity is more conceivable].

The fifth is that she is the seductress (*al-murāwidah*).

The sixth is that love for him has completely infatuated her, such that it penetrates the innermost depths of her heart.[15]

The seventh is what this (the three previous points) implies: he is more chaste, loyal, and noble than she is. She is tempting him and he is abstaining out of decency, dignity, and a sense of shame. This further compounds the lampooning against her.

The eighth is that the word *turāwid* (seduces/is seducing) was used, implying continuity and futurity—that is to say: it is her nature [to act this way]. They did not say: *rāwadat*—'she seduced him' [implying a deed done singularly in the past]. There is a difference between saying: "So-and-so hosted his guests'; and saying: "So-and-so hosts his guests and is hospitable to his visitors." The latter implies that this is how he is [as opposed to an isolated incident in the past].

15 Referring to the passage: *Qad shaghafahā ḥubbā*—'love for him consumes her heart.'

> **The ninth** is their saying, "Indeed, we see her in clear misguidance." That is: "We are utterly appalled at her behaviour." They ascribed to themselves disgust and rebuke; whereas these whimsical matters are usually ones where women unite upon and help one another in regards, just as men do.[16] Yet, they were seemingly outraged, thus implying this to be an abominable matter, such that they could not support her in it despite the tendency to do so.
>
> **The tenth** is that they coupled between blaming her for excessive lust (*al-ʿishq al-mufriṭ*) as well as excessive enticement (*al-ṭalab al-mufriṭ*)—neither was she moderate in her lusting over him nor was she moderate in her seeking him out. As for lust, it is their saying: *qad shaqhafahā ḥubbā*—'love for him consumes her heart.' And as for enticement, it is their saying: *turāwidu fatāhā*—'is trying to seduce her slave.' *Murāwadah* is the repeated seeking out of some desired thing. Thus, they ascribed to her intense lust as well as intense lewdness. ”

Such was the potency and incessance of their taunting gossip that it merited a direct retaliation from the wife of the ʿAzīz. She invited all of them to her palace for casual dining, only she was setting them up to witness first-hand what they oh-so-piously blamed her for. As they reclined, she gave them citrus fruit[17] and knives with which

16 Referring to the stereotypical chitter-chatter each gender engages in with regards to the opposite.

17 Commentators are almost unanimous in their mention of *utruj*—citron.

to peel and cut them. She then commanded Yūsuf ﷺ to make his grand entrance. Astounded at his unearthly physical beauty, they did not pay heed to what their hands were doing, and ended up cutting themselves. They exclaimed thereafter, "This cannot be a man; rather it is a blessed angel!"

The wife of the ʿAzīz had gotten her own over them: "So this is Yūsuf, the one you looked down on me for desiring. I very much did try to seduce him, though to no avail. But I shall have him, or he will surely be imprisoned, and he will be humbled!" Not only did they excuse her for her misdeed, but they were now resolved in joining her in its pursuit!

TRANSFORMATIVE WISDOM

The Prophet ﷺ visited a severely unwell man and asked him if he had been making any specific supplication. He replied in the positive, and said that he would supplicate: "Allah! Whatever You wish to punish me with in the Hereafter, hasten it for me in the worldly life!" He ﷺ reprimanded him and said: "*Subḥān Allāh*! You cannot bear it! Rather, you should say, 'Allah, grant us goodness in this life, goodness in the next, and save us from the torment of the Fire.'" The Prophet ﷺ prayed for him, and he regained his health [Reported by Muslim (2688)]. Do not wish for what you cannot bear, for "Allah does not overburden a soul with more than it can carry." Q 2:286

There is another beautiful note with regards to the language used by the wife of the ʿAzīz in this passage. There are many rhetorical tools for emphasis in the Arabic language. One is the use of the *nūn* at the end of imperative and present tense verbs.[18] One *nūn* is *muthaqqalah* (a 'heavy' *nūn* with a *shaddah*) and another is *mukhaffafah* (a 'light' *nūn* with a *sukūn* only). The generic maxim states: *al-ziyādatu fī al-mabnā ziyādatun fī al-maʿnā*—increase in the foundation [of words] is an increase of meaning. That is to say, the heavy *nūn* implies a greater emphasis than the light *nūn* (the former is literally a double *nūn*, while the latter is a singular one).

Here, Allah ﷻ says quoting the wife's threat to Yūsuf ﷺ: *La-yusjanann* (heavy *nūn*) *wa la-yakūnan* (light *nūn*) *min al-ṣāghirīn*—'He will most surely be imprisoned and surely be made from the abased.' In other words: the wife of the ʿAzīz may indeed have the power to imprison him, and even physically harm him, but unconditional disgrace is not in the hands of any human being, but in the hands of Allah ﷻ alone.

TRANSFORMATIVE WISDOM

Even if one is afflicted with the most severe forms of outward humiliation, they may still retain honour by virtue of their internal faith in Allah ﷻ and their reliance upon Him. So long as a person endures their afflictions with dignity and is patient over Allah's decree, they maintain their uprightness and moral integrity.

18 For example, Allah ﷻ says: "They shall certainly bear (*la-yaḥmilunn*) their own loads, and some other loads along with their own loads, and they will certainly be questioned (*la-yusʾalunn*) about what they used to forge." Q 29:13

DIVINE DEVOTION

The trials of Yūsuf ﷺ with women had just gotten much more complicated. Though he was saved from the wife of the ʿAzīz the first time, it seems like that was the first of many instigations. Not only has she vowed that she will not give up pursuing him, but now the ladies of the city have joined her in her vice, attempting to go after him as well. Having no other means, Yūsuf ﷺ calls out to his creator. Allah ﷻ says:

قَالَ رَبِّ السِّجْنُ أَحَبُّ إِلَيَّ مِمَّا يَدْعُونَنِي إِلَيْهِ وَإِلَّا تَصْرِفْ عَنِّي كَيْدَهُنَّ أَصْبُ إِلَيْهِنَّ وَأَكُن مِّنَ الْجَاهِلِينَ ﴿٣٣﴾

فَاسْتَجَابَ لَهُ رَبُّهُ فَصَرَفَ عَنْهُ كَيْدَهُنَّ إِنَّهُ هُوَ السَّمِيعُ الْعَلِيمُ ﴿٣٤﴾

ثُمَّ بَدَا لَهُم مِّن بَعْدِ مَا رَأَوُا الْآيَاتِ لَيَسْجُنُنَّهُ حَتَّىٰ حِينٍ ﴿٣٥﴾

❝ He said, "My Lord, prison is dearer to me than what they call me to, and unless You turn their plotting away from me, I might yield to them and become one of the ignorant." Thereupon his Lord answered him and diverted their plotting away from him; indeed, He is the Hearing, the Knowing. In the end, they[19] thought it best—despite seeing all the signs—that they should imprison him for a while. ❞[20]

How important is our relationship with Allah to us? How much do

19 The authorities or the ʿAzīz himself along with his guards.

20 *Yūsuf*, 33-35.

we actually sacrifice for His sake? Lip service is easy. If push came to shove, what are you truly willing to give up in His path? For Yūsuf 🕊, the answer was clear as day. He exclaimed: "My Lord! It is more beloved to me that I be thrown in prison than engage in what these women call me for!" Imagine… it was not a choice between Allah and a physically repugnant or painful outcome, but a choice between Allah and what many materialistic young men would consider a dream come true. Yet, Yūsuf 🕊 called upon Allah 🕊 and his plea was emphatic: "Anything over Your displeasure, my Lord!"

There are concessions in revealed law which allow one to do and utter what would otherwise be unlawful or even tantamount to unbelief. Allah 🕊 says: "Whoever disbelieves in Allah after attaining faith—except for one who was compelled while his heart rests securely in faith, but rather whoever openheartedly chooses denial—upon them is wrath from Allah and for them is a great punishment."[21] He 🕊 also says: "The believers must not take the disbelievers as friends instead of the believers. And whoever does that has no relation with Allah whatsoever—unless you do so as a protective measure to save yourselves from them."[22] However, if not for the steadfastness of the few, all religion would be lost!

Consider the sacrifices made by the likes of Malcolm X and Muhammad Ali. Consider the sacrifices made by great imams like Shaykh

---

21 *al-Naḥl*, 106.

22 *Āl ʿImrān*, 28.

al-Islām Ibn Taymiyyah[23] and Imam Aḥmad ibn Ḥanbal.[24] Consider what the Prophet ﷺ and his closest companions went through and sacrificed for the sake of Allah ﷻ. Prophet Yūsuf ﷺ was another exemplar of uprightness and devotion to the Divine ﷻ. He feared losing his relationship with his creator and sustainer—his guardian and helper throughout his life. He called out to Him: "If You do not help me against them, I may incline towards them and become among the ignorant!" Above all, he feared becoming ignorant of Allah ﷻ.

TRANSFORMATIVE WISDOM

There is no greater reward than proximity to, and acquaintance with, Allah ﷻ, and no greater punishment than furtherance from, and ignorance of, Him ﷻ. There are seven types of people who will be shaded in His shade when there will be no shade but His. Among them is a man called for illicit intimacy by a woman of beauty and status, yet he replies: "I fear Allah!" [Reported by Bukhārī (6806)] Let all men in such a trial take solace in this immense reward and the role model set by Prophet Yūsuf ﷺ!

23 He ﷺ famously stated: "What can my enemies do to me? My paradise is in my heart: it goes with me wherever I am. If they kill me, it is martyrdom. If they exile me from my land, it is a retreat in the path of Allah. If they imprison me, it is to allow me private seclusion with Allah."

24 All of these noble personalities took principled stances against tyranny and stood uncompromisingly for the sake of truth. Their faith and courage led to imprisonment, torture, or martyrdom. May Allah accept their sacrifice and have mercy on them all.

PART

XI

DUNGEONS, DREAMS, AND DA‘WAH

A believer sees the opportunity in every difficulty.

Allah ﷻ answered the call of His prophet. Yūsuf ﷺ was cast into prison. Yet, even within the walls of his confinement, his spirit remained unbroken, and his faith in Allah unwavering. His ministry would persist despite the harsh environment, and he was at the service of those around him. Recognising him as a beneficent and insightful man, two of his inmates approached Yūsuf ﷺ with a request. Allah ﷻ says:

وَدَخَلَ مَعَهُ السِّجْنَ فَتَيَانِ قَالَ أَحَدُهُمَا إِنِّي أَرَانِي أَعْصِرُ خَمْرًا وَقَالَ الْآخَرُ
إِنِّي أَرَانِي أَحْمِلُ فَوْقَ رَأْسِي خُبْزًا تَأْكُلُ الطَّيْرُ مِنْهُ نَبِّئْنَا بِتَأْوِيلِهِ
إِنَّا نَرَاكَ مِنَ الْمُحْسِنِينَ ﴿٣٦﴾

قَالَ لَا يَأْتِيكُمَا طَعَامٌ تُرْزَقَانِهِ إِلَّا نَبَّأْتُكُمَا بِتَأْوِيلِهِ قَبْلَ أَن يَأْتِيَكُمَا ذَٰلِكُمَا مِمَّا
عَلَّمَنِي رَبِّي إِنِّي تَرَكْتُ مِلَّةَ قَوْمٍ لَّا يُؤْمِنُونَ بِاللَّهِ وَهُم بِالْآخِرَةِ هُمْ كَافِرُونَ ﴿٣٧﴾

وَاتَّبَعْتُ مِلَّةَ آبَائِي إِبْرَاهِيمَ وَإِسْحَاقَ وَيَعْقُوبَ مَا كَانَ لَنَا
أَن نُّشْرِكَ بِاللَّهِ مِن شَيْءٍ ذَٰلِكَ مِن فَضْلِ اللَّهِ عَلَيْنَا وَعَلَى
النَّاسِ وَلَٰكِنَّ أَكْثَرَ النَّاسِ لَا يَشْكُرُونَ ﴿٣٨﴾

❝ There entered the prison with him two young men. One of them said, "Indeed, I see myself pressing wine." The other said, "Indeed, I see myself carrying upon my head bread from which the birds were eating. Inform us of its interpretation; indeed, we see you to be among the good-doers." He said, "You will not receive food provision except that I shall inform you of its interpretation before it arrives. That is from what my Lord has taught me. Indeed, I have left the way of a people who do not believe in

Allah, and they, in the Hereafter, are disbelievers. And I have followed the religion of my fathers, Ibrāhīm, Isḥāq, and Yaʿqūb. It is not for us to associate anything with Allah. That is from the favour of Allah upon us and upon the people, but most of the people do not show thanks." ●●¹

A DIAMOND IN THE ROUGH

The Arabic proverb goes: "Man is a product of his environment."² While this certainly holds true on many occasions, the truly virtuous leader is he who moulds his environment according to what is right and noble. For such revolutionary reformers, it is most apt to say: "The environment is a product of its man."

Yūsuf 🙿 did not allow his unfavourable circumstances to hamper his good works. Whether unjustly incarcerated or the grand minister of Egypt,³ his duty was always to Allah 🙿 and realising His will on earth. Yūsuf 🙿 must have been carrying out acts of kindness in the prison.⁴ How else could he have been recognised as a benevolent person by

---

1 *Yūsuf*, 36-38.

2 The original Arabic states: *al-insānu walīdu al-bīʾah* (الإنسان وليد البيئة).

3 The statement: *innā narāka min al-muḥsinīn*—'we see you to be among the good-doers' is said to him here by his inmates as well as when he is in a position of power as the treasurer of Egypt (Q 12:78).

4 In his commentary on Q 12:36, Qurṭubī 🙿 quotes Ibn ʿAbbās 🙿 as saying: "The woman said to her husband, 'This Hebrew slave has disgraced me, and I wish that you imprison him'; and so he did. In prison, he (Yūsuf 🙿) would give solace to the aggrieved, take care of the sick, treat the wounded, and pray all night—he would weep till the walls, ceiling, and doors wept with him! Prison was cleansed through him. The people enjoyed his company, such that when an inmate would be freed, he would return to visit Yūsuf."

his inmates? Firstly, he was warm enough that they felt it reasonable to share their dreams with him. Secondly, they must have seen in him signs of wisdom, insight, and heavenly orientation—they are asking him to interpret their dreams after all. Thirdly, having narrated their visions to him, they explicitly justified their approach and their request by saying, "We see you to be among the good-doers."

TRANSFORMATIVE WISDOM

Do not take your surroundings as an excuse to not aim for the loftiest moral heights. We do not choose to whom we are born and where we grow up, but we choose what we aim for and how we conduct ourselves. There is always goodness to be done.

The word for 'good-doer' in Arabic is *muḥsin*, from *iḥsān*, having connotations of excellence, beauty, and benefaction. That is to say, Yūsuf ﷺ did not just seem like a good person, but someone who was constantly at the service of others. When he first received revelation, the Prophet ﷺ feared for his sanity given the awesome interaction he had experienced. His wife Khadījah ؓ cited his good works as proof that it could not have been of a demonic source. She ؓ told him ﷺ: "By Allah, Allah will never let you down. You uphold ties of kinship, speak truthfully, carry the burdens of the weak, honour the guest, give to the destitute, and are always there for those in need."[5] He ﷺ was of unassailable character, even prior to the advent of prophecy. Likewise Prophet Yūsuf ﷺ, as well as all the prophets and messengers ﷺ.[6]

5 Reported by Bukhārī (6982) on the authority of ʿĀʾishah ؓ.

6 Allah ﷻ says about the prophets: "They used to hasten towards all types of good and call

REFLECT...

The prophets ﷺ were the most severely tested, yet they all excelled in their tests in the most magnanimous ways. Even though they had the most right to take their trials as an excuse for apathy, they never did, and always persevered with dignity and honour.

DA'WAH 101

Yūsuf ﷺ has been endowed with the knowledge of dream interpretation. Dreams are a significant theme throughout the *sūrah*.[7] On this occasion, his fellow inmates were seeking out the meaning of their respective visions and saw that Yūsuf ﷺ was an upright man of deep understanding. When they asked, it would have been perfectly normal and even expected to give them what they want and be done with it. But this is not the way of prophets.

There is what you want, and there is what you need. The truth is sometimes the former, but always the latter; and the messengers are the masters of its delivery. Appreciating the other's context, empathising with their struggles, and supporting them accordingly is the way of those who assume the prophetic office. Some seamen approached the Prophet ﷺ and enquired as to the purificatory quality of seawater—is it acceptable to perform the ritual ablution (*wuḍū'*) using it? He ﷺ replied by saying: "It (the sea) is that whose water is

---

upon Us in hope and awe, and were reverent before Us." Q 21:90.

7 More on this in Part XII.

purifying and its dead [meat] lawful."[8] They only asked about seawater and *wuḍūʾ*, yet the Prophet ﷺ gave them further information that will benefit them in their fishing excursions.

TRANSFORMATIVE WISDOM

When interacting with others and calling them to Islam, do not just put yourself in their shoes, but walk a mile in them. Their personal experiences and lifestyles will inform how best to approach the *daʿwah* setting. You will likely be able to capture their hearts with a kind, appropriate gesture that is relevant to what they know.

Allah ﷻ says: "Call to the way of your Lord with wisdom and good counsel."[9] Yūsuf ؑ saw an opportunity to save others from misguidance and false practices. Instead of responding directly, he told them, "You shall receive the interpretation of your dreams before your next meal.[10] Allah has blessed me with the knowledge to under-

8 Reported by Aḥmad (8720), Tirmidhī (69), Nasāʾī (59), and others.

9 *al-Naḥl*, 125.

10 There are three main ways in which exegetes understood the statement of Yūsuf ؑ: *Lā yaʾtīkumā ṭaʿāmun turzaqānihī illā nabbaʾtukumā bi-taʾwīlihī qabla an yaʾtiyakumā*—'You do not receive any food provided for you except that I inform you of its interpretation before it comes to you.' They are summarised as follows:
That it means: "You do not receive any food in your dreams except that I inform you of its interpretation (i.e. in wakefulness) before said interpretation becomes manifest (in real life)." This is the understanding offered by Ṭabarī, attributing it to Suddī and Ibn Isḥāq. It is also what is mentioned by Ibn Kathīr in his commentary on this passage.
That it means: "You do not receive any food (in wakefulness) except that I am able to interpret for you its significance before it manifests." This is a secondary understanding offered by Ṭabarī, attributing it to Ibn Jurayj. The idea is that the king would give certain meals to inmates before their sentence transpires—either via freedom or capital pun-

stand such signs."[11] He achieved two important goals through these very subtle and sagacious words:

I. He simultaneously gave them the comfort of knowing that their matter will be dealt with, as well as ensured their attention for the next few moments. He did not simply start rambling about a certain topic. They are seeking a very specific thing, so he assured them it will be seen to. He recognised they have a want which he is happy to help with. But, more importantly, there

---

ishment. Here, there is no dream interpreted (it is possible that they lied about seeing a dream; see below re: Qurṭubī).

That it means: "You will not receive the next meal you are provided with in prison except that I will let you know of your dreams' interpretation before it arrives." This is the understanding offered by Ibn ʿĀshūr and al-Saʿdī, and is the most accurate and consistent with the context. Allah ﷻ knows best.

Qurṭubī offers even more possible and speculative interpretations, going into extra-scriptural details and providing background information. For example, he mentions that it was possible each man was a servant of the king—a winemaker and baker respectively, and that there was a plot to poison the king where they were implicated. The winemaker did not take part in it, while the baker did. They were both incarcerated under suspicion of treason (he offers scenarios as to how this may have happened). When the case became clear, the baker was given capital punishment for sedition and the winemaker exonerated. It is also therefore possible that they lied about the dream. According to this understanding, they would have approached Yūsuf ﷺ to test him or tease him. One understanding Qurṭubī offers in this regard is that, when Yūsuf ﷺ interpreted their purported dreams, they said it was only pretence, to which he replied, "The matter about which you enquired has been settled (i.e. it shall be realised as interpreted)" Q 12:41. This is somewhat commensurate with what Ṭabarī cites from Ibn Jurayj.

11 In their commentary on this section of Q 12:37, Ibn ʿĀshūr ﷺ said: "Through this reply, he wished to oblige them to engage and converse with him further. They are awaiting their dreams' interpretation, so he inserted within that an invitation to proper faith, while promising that he won't delay answering their request too long." Saʿdī ﷺ said: "Perhaps Yūsuf ﷺ wished to call them to belief [in Allah alone] whereupon they clearly needed it. This way, his calling them is more effective and more appealing to them."

is something they need which he will endeavour to give them first. To deliver the latter, he hooked them onto the conversation with this engaging introduction.

II. He indirectly began speaking about his Lord and Master—Allah ﷻ. And not at an abstract, philosophical level; rather a very real and practical level. It is as if he was saying, "You think I am good? You see me to possess some insight that I can benefit you with? This is not of my own doing. It is a gift from Allah. He alone taught me this knowledge, and He is the source of all goodness. Let me tell you about the path to His pleasure."

This is *da'wah* mastery. The conversation is organic yet captivating. Yūsuf ﷺ was unassumingly able to direct it from the topic of their personal dreams to inviting them to his Lord.

REFLECT...

The godly cannot help but relate everything back to God. They cannot help but have Him in their minds and hearts, and constantly remember Him and make mention of His name.

KNOW THYSELF

Aristotle is quoted as having said: "Knowing yourself is the beginning of all wisdom." Yūsuf ﷺ was acutely aware of his status and what made him stand out from the crowd. "I have left the way of the indigenous Canaanites—they did not believe in Allah and the Afterlife." He was confident in setting himself apart on account of his faith. He told them of his rejection of the false beliefs of his people and how he had embraced the path of monotheism, the worship of one true God. "I follow the faith of my forefathers—Ibrāhīm, Isḥāq, and Yaʿqūb", he declared. That was his lineage, and these were his role models: "I am the son of a prophet, the grandson of a prophet, the great-grandson of a prophet, and I follow in their footsteps." He continued to his fellow inmates, "We worship none but Allah alone, and we associate no partners with Him. This is a grace from Allah upon us and upon all of humanity, yet most people do not give thanks."

On many occasions in the Qur'an, Allah commands the Prophet to distinguish himself from idolatry and false rituals.[12] To stand out by virtue of following the truth is no shame at all. To appreciate that a person's identity lies first and foremost in their relationship with their Lord is indeed the beginning of wisdom.

TRANSFORMATIVE WISDOM

Never be shy to proclaim who you are to others. In a world where people have lost their purpose and question their identity, proudly proclaim, "I am Muslim. I submit my will to the one true God—Allah. I worship none other but Him, direct my devotion towards Him, and place my faith solely in Him!" That in itself is one of the greatest forms of *daʿwah*.

12 See for example: Q 6:14-15, 6:56-57, 6: 161-164, 39:11-13.

Yūsuf ﷺ was telling his prison companions what a great favour guidance is. He embodied the virtues of pure, Abrahamic monotheism—*ḥanīfiyyah*. Had he not, he would not be the good-doer they approached for the interpretation of their dreams in the first place. In other words, he is telling them as well as showing them what an immeasurable blessing it is to have people oriented towards Allah ﷻ around you. They simply make everything better through their faith and optimism. There he was, in a dark, desolate dungeon, seeing to the needs of the needy, consoling the distraught with a tender smile and a warm embrace, and standing during the night in devotional prayer. Who would not want such an inspirational, upright moral figure in their life?!

TRANSFORMATIVE WISDOM

Do not tell people why Islam is the truth, but show them! Be the change you wish to see around you. Countless people accepted Islam simply through the generosity and magnanimous character of the Prophet ﷺ. Have vision, and create the world you wish to see before you die.

THE ONLY WAY IS GOD

Yūsuf ﷺ continued conversing with his now-captivated companions. He had their full and undivided attention. He must now speak plainly and drive the point of monotheism home before he interprets their dreams. Allah ﷻ says:

يَا صَاحِبَيِ السِّجْنِ أَأَرْبَابٌ مُتَفَرِّقُونَ خَيْرٌ أَمِ اللَّهُ الْوَاحِدُ الْقَهَّارُ ﴿٣٩﴾

مَا تَعْبُدُونَ مِنْ دُونِهِ إِلَّا أَسْمَاءً سَمَّيْتُمُوهَا أَنْتُمْ وَآبَاؤُكُمْ مَا أَنْزَلَ اللَّهُ
بِهَا مِنْ سُلْطَانٍ إِنِ الْحُكْمُ إِلَّا لِلَّهِ أَمَرَ أَلَّا تَعْبُدُوا إِلَّا إِيَّاهُ ذَلِكَ
الدِّينُ الْقَيِّمُ وَلَكِنَّ أَكْثَرَ النَّاسِ لَا يَعْلَمُونَ ﴿٤٠﴾

يَا صَاحِبَيِ السِّجْنِ أَمَّا أَحَدُكُمَا فَيَسْقِي رَبَّهُ خَمْرًا وَأَمَّا الْآخَرُ فَيُصْلَبُ
فَتَأْكُلُ الطَّيْرُ مِنْ رَأْسِهِ قُضِيَ الْأَمْرُ الَّذِي فِيهِ تَسْتَفْتِيَانِ ﴿٤١﴾

وَقَالَ لِلَّذِي ظَنَّ أَنَّهُ نَاجٍ مِنْهُمَا اذْكُرْنِي عِنْدَ رَبِّكَ فَأَنْسَاهُ الشَّيْطَانُ
ذِكْرَ رَبِّهِ فَلَبِثَ فِي السِّجْنِ بِضْعَ سِنِينَ ﴿٤٢﴾

❝ “O my fellow inmates, are diverse lords better or Allah, the One, the Subduer? You worship not besides Him except mere names you have named, you and your fathers, for which Allah has sent down no authority. Judgement belongs to none but Allah. He has commanded that you worship none besides Him. That is the right religion, but most people do not know. O my fellow inmates, as for one of you, he will serve wine to his master. As for the other, he will be crucified, and the birds will eat from his head. The matter about which you inquire has been decreed. And he said to the one whom he knew would go free, “Mention me before your master.” But the devil made him forget the mention to his master, and Yūsuf remained in prison several years.❞[13]

Yūsuf ﵇ has gained his companions’ trust. He was able to critique polytheism without insulting or degrading their personal beliefs.

13 *Yūsuf*, 39-42.

Allah ﷻ says: "Do not insult those who call upon other than Allah lest they insult Allah out of hostility without knowledge."[14] Yūsuf ﷺ has established rapport with his fellow inmates such that shaking them up internally would be conducive to their spiritual awakening as opposed to pushing them away.

He posed a rhetorical question, one which they already know the answer to: "Which do you think is better: many different and conflicting gods who are divided among themselves or the one, single, true God, whose volition is irresistible and His will inescapable?" There is no doubting which is greater. This is the prompt through which Yūsuf ﷺ incited them to rethink their ways, provoking their *fiṭrah*.

"These deities are but names you and your forefathers named—they have no sovereignty", Yūsuf ﷺ continued. "Kingship, dominion, and legislation belong to Allah alone! He ordains for us what to do, how to do it, and when to do it. He has decreed that we devote ourselves in worship to none other than Him. This is the right way, but most people are unaware." A simple and direct message that, once the groundwork has been laid out, cannot but penetrate the sincere listeners' hearts.

14 *al-Anʿām*, 108.

DID YOU KNOW?

There is an emphasis that has been placed on 'names' in our pure religion: they are the vessels of meaning and value. Ādam ﷺ sat atop the hierarchy of creation once Allah ﷻ breathed into him from His spirit and taught him all the names. Polytheists are rebuked for worshipping false idols—they are names without heavenly authority. The Prophet ﷺ would change names of people and places with negative connotations: ʿĀṣiyah (disobedient one) to Jamīlah (beautiful one), and Ḥarb (war) to Salm (peace).

A DONE DEAL

Finally, it was time to tell the inmates the significance of their dream: one of them will be freed and will serve wine to his master, while the other will be crucified to death and birds will peck at his head. This combination of glad tidings and horrific news must have been quite the shock to their system, especially for the one who was to receive capital punishment. The interpretation would have undoubtedly been met with denial and horror.[15] This is one of a few rare occasions where the sternness of Yūsuf ﷺ was apparent. He exclaimed, "It is a done deal—a matter ordained!"[16] There is a legislated Islamic

15 As alluded to previously, some exegetes say that once the dreams were interpreted, the inmates said they were only jesting and they did not really see anything in their sleep, attempting to avoid the inevitable outcome.

16 This statement has become a qur'anic adage and used by many when a ruling is given between two parties: *Quḍiya al-amru alladhī fīhi tastaftiyān*—'Ordained is the matter about which you have both enquired.'

value to the first interpretation given for a dream: once a vision is interpreted by a qualified interpreter, that interpretation is taken and no further interpretations may be sought thereafter.[17]

Many a time, we seek out others' counsel and advice, or even official religious verdict, but when the result does not manifest in our favour, we turn back on our heels and either downplay the person or the advice. This is borne of emotional immaturity and mental frailty. We should not expect echo chambers where all our experiences are validated and we are constantly praised. Pushback, and even admonishment, are necessary at times. Without them, we may persist on bad ideas that will only conclude in failure in this life, or worse, the next life.

TRANSFORMATIVE WISDOM

Especially in the age of social media, bans and blocks are easy to come by when we offer a word of firm advice to others. Do not be so unwise as to think yourself beyond criticism, and when you receive it, do not be so haughty as to think yourself above it! It is narrated that ʿUmar ibn al-Khaṭṭāb ﵁ said: "Allah have mercy on a person who gifts me [with knowledge of] my faults."

17 This is discussed further in Part XII.

TIE YOUR CAMEL

A man enquired to the Prophet ﷺ about the nature of *tawakkul*—reliance upon Allah ﷻ and having trust in His plan. He asked him ﷺ: "Messenger of Allah, should I keep my camel loose and rely on Allah?" The Prophet ﷺ replied: "Tie it then rely on Him."[18] Taking the appropriate means is part of having faith in Allah. Doing nothing and expecting miraculous results is not the way of the believer. Allah ﷻ could have split the sea for Mūsā ﷺ without his involvement, yet He ﷻ commanded him to strike it with his staff.[19] During her contractions, a caller called out to Maryam ﷺ to shake the palm tree so that dates may come down to her for sustenance.[20] She was a young, frail woman in labour, yet Allah ﷻ commanded her to take the means.

TRANSFORMATIVE WISDOM

We are held to account for what we pursue and exert effort to achieve, not the worldly outcomes themselves. Allah ﷻ says: "Man will only have what he sought after" Q 53:39. Do your part, and leave the results in the hands of Allah ﷻ.

Yūsuf ﷺ knew[21] that one inmate was going to be exonerated and have proximity to a regal figure,[22] so wished that his innocence

18 Reported by Tirmidhī (2517) and Ibn Ḥibbān (731).

19 See Q 26:63.

20 See Q 19:25.

21 The word *ẓann* in Arabic may refer to both speculative thinking and certain knowledge. The latter is what is intended here. Allah ﷻ knows best.

22 The word in Arabic is, once again, *rabbik*—'your lord.' See the next footnote regarding

be mentioned before him.[23] But, alas, as the days turned to weeks and months, the devil played his role, and the inmate who had been promised freedom forgot to convey Yūsuf's message. And so, Yūsuf ﷺ remained imprisoned for a number of years,[24] his patience unshakeable and faith unwavering, awaiting the divine plan that would one day lead him out of the darkness and into the light.

---

exegetes' commentary on this passage.

23 The statement: *Fa-ansāhu al-shayṭānu dhikra rabbih*—'The devil made him forget the mention to/of his lord', may have one of two meanings:

- It means: "The devil made Yūsuf ﷺ forget the remembrance of his Lord (Allah ﷻ)." That is to say, in his urgency to be released from imprisonment, Yūsuf ﷺ asked for this man's help instead of directly pleading Allah ﷻ and as a result he remained in prison for a number of years as a form of divine discipline. This is the main interpretation offered by Ṭabarī.
- It means: "The devil made the freed man forget the mention of Yūsuf to his master." That is to say, Yūsuf ﷺ took the means by asking this man to mention his case before his superior, but Allah ﷻ willed otherwise, and the devil made the exonerated inmate forget Yūsuf ﷺ. This is the main interpretation offered by Ibn Kathīr and Saʿdī, and is the most accurate understanding. Allah ﷻ knows best.

Qurṭubī offers both possibilities without choosing one over the other, while Ibn ʿĀshūr couples between them, saying, "Perhaps both possibilities are linguistically intended, and this is a form of rhetorical brilliance: Yūsuf ﷺ not asking Allah directly was the devil casting inspiration into his call, which was a divine cause in the winemaker not remembering to bring the issue up with his master, which in turn resulted in Yūsuf ﷺ being disciplined by Allah ﷻ [by staying longer in prison] for not seeking His aid alone."

24 The word *biḍʿ* refers to a number between three and nine. Some scholars said that Yūsuf ﷺ stayed in prison for seven more years.

PART

XII

THE REALM OF DREAMS

When you sleep in this world, you are awake in another.

Dreams are a fundamental and enigmatic part of the human experience. Sleep itself is a spiritual journey into the Unseen. It is the 'minor death.'[1] Allah ﷻ says: "Allah takes back souls at their death, and those who have not died during their sleep—He keeps that upon which He has decreed death and sends back the other until an appointed time. Indeed, there are signs in this for a people who reflect."[2] He ﷻ also says: "He is the one who calls back your souls by night and knows what you commit in the day."[3]

DID YOU KNOW?

A noteworthy occasion where Allah ﷻ exercised *wafāh* over one of His slaves' complete being—body and soul—is ʿĪsā the son of Maryam ﷺ. Allah ﷻ says: "Allah said, 'O ʿĪsā, I am taking you back (*mutawaffīk*) and raising you to Me." Q 3:55

What we see in our sleep is often a reflection of our concerns when awake. A person's conscious engagement in evil and filth will usually be reflected in their subconscious. Likewise, a person with deep-seated fears and spiritual insecurities is a sitting duck for demonic whispers. On the other hand, an honest, upright, righteous person will see dreams that support their noble vision. Naturally, there are also dreams that belong to neither category and are sim-

1 The word *wafāh* is used for when the soul returns to its maker. The *wafāh ṣughrā*—minor death—is sleep, and the *wafāh kubrā*—major death—is the ceasing of our worldly life.

2 *al-Zumar*, 42.

3 *al-Anʿām*, 60.

ply borne of jumbled thought along with incomplete memories. On the authority of Abū Hurayrah ﷺ, the Prophet ﷺ said: "Dreams are of three types: a righteous dream is glad tidings from Allah, a dream that causes sadness is from the devil, then there is the dream that is a reflection of one's subconscious."[4]

The story of Yūsuf ﷺ is one where dreams and visions play a significant role throughout. The major arc is outlined by Yūsuf's dream as a young boy which is later recalled and made manifest at the conclusion of the story. There are also two more occasions where dreams are cited and interpreted: the inmates' dreams and the king's vision. The following is an exposition into dreams from a general Islamic perspective, with a return to the narrative of Yūsuf ﷺ at the end.

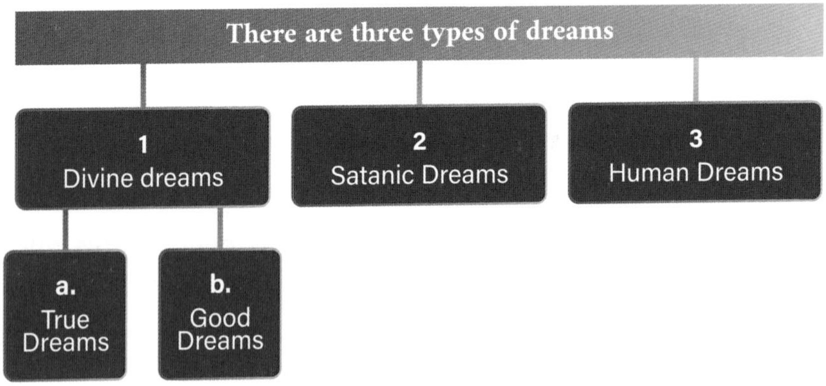

4 Reported by Bukhārī (7017) and Muslim (2263).

DIVINE DREAMS

Dreams were one of the ways through which Allah ﷻ communicated with His chosen prophets. Revelation was conveyed to the prophets in three distinct modes: direct revelation, communication from behind a veil, or transmission through angelic emissaries. Allah ﷻ says: "It is not granted to any mortal that Allah should speak to him except through revelation or from behind a veil, or by sending a messenger to reveal by His command what He will. Indeed, He is exalted, wise."[5] Revelation includes, but is not exclusive to, dreams.[6] An example of speaking behind a veil is Allah ﷻ directly conversing with Mūsā ﷺ.[7] Sending angelic messengers is Allah ﷻ sending Jibrīl ﷺ or any other angel to reveal unto His prophets whatever He wills.[8]

The story of Prophet Ibrāhīm ﷺ serves as a vivid illustration of the connection between prophetic dreams and divine revelation. In his dream, he received clear and unambiguous instructions, prompting him to take immediate action. He shared this dream with his son, Ismāʿīl, wherein he saw himself sacrificing him. The remarkable obedience and submission displayed by both father and son underscore the fact that both viewed the vision as direct revelation from Allah ﷻ, and not just a passing dream. Of course, this was a test from Allah ﷻ

5 *al-Shūrā*, 51.

6 Commenting on this, Qurṭubī ؒ said: "It was also said: *illā waḥyan*—'except through revelation' refers to a vision he (the prophet) sees in his sleep. This is the position of Muḥammad ibn Zuhayr."

7 Allah ﷻ says: "Allah spoke to Mūsā directly." Q 4:164

8 Also in his commentary on Q 42:51, Qurṭubī ؒ quotes Ibn ʿAbbās ؓ as having said: "Jibrīl ﷺ descended upon every prophet, but only Muḥammad, ʿĪsā, Mūsā, and Zakariyyā ﷺ saw him. For all other than them, their revelation was inspiration in their sleep."

which both Ibrāhīm and Ismāʿīl ☙ passed with flying colours. Allah ☙ gifted Ibrāhīm ☙ with a mighty ram to sacrifice instead.[9]

For the Seal of Prophecy ☙ himself, dreams were his initiation to prophethood. ʿĀʾishah ☙ said: "The first form of revelation that Allah's Messenger experienced was true visions which he would see in his sleep. He would not see a vision but that it would later manifest as clear as day."[10]

True dreams are considered a divine gift from Allah ☙. On the authority of Abū Qatādah ☙, the Prophet ☙ said: "True dreams originate from Allah, while bad dreams are from *shayṭān*."[11] Furthermore, as the Day of Resurrection approaches, the dreams of a believer are prophesised to have a remarkably high likelihood of coming true. On the authority of Abū Hurayrah ☙, the Prophet ☙ said: "When the end times are near, the dream of the believer will hardly fail to come true. True dreams are one of forty-six parts of prophecy, and whatever is borne of prophecy is never untrue."[12]

---

9   For the full qur'anic account, see Q 37:101–111.

10   Reported by Bukhārī (6982).

11   Reported by Bukhārī (3292).

12   Reported by Bukhārī (7017).

DID YOU KNOW?

There is a quaint numerical reflection that can be extrapolated from true dreams being 1/46th of prophecy [as per Bukhārī (7017) as well as many other reports]. If prophecy is 46 parts, 1 part is true dreams.

The Prophet ﷺ was 40 years old when he began to receive true dreams, and he continued to do so for six months [as per Ibn Ḥajar's commentary on the narration of ʿĀʾishah ﵂ in *Fatḥ al-Bārī*]. He ﷺ formally assumed the prophetic office for about 23 years; and **6** months are **1/46th** of **23** years. [This is one understanding cited by Khaṭṭābī in his *Maʿālim al-Sunan*, commenting on the "1/46th" narrations]

It is important to note that the authenticity and truthfulness of dreams are intricately linked to an individual's character. The Prophet ﷺ emphasised that those who are most truthful in speech are likely to experience the truest dreams, highlighting the connection between one's moral character and the clarity of divine communication through dreams. In another version of the aforementioned report, the Prophet ﷺ said: "When the end times are near, the dream of the believer will hardly fail to come true: the truest among them in their visions will be the truest in speech."[13]

The question may arise: Are true dreams specific to believers alone? The answer lies in the divine nature of dreams. They can manifest as a form of glad-tidings or warning for anyone chosen by Allah ﷻ,

13 Reported by Muslim (2263).

irrespective of their faith. However, the extent to which dreams are understood and acted upon may differ among individuals. For the prophets ﷺ, dreams are revelation from Allah ﷻ. For the believers, a good dream is a form of solace and a catalyst towards good deeds. For non-Muslims, it may be a from of guidance or a clarification of some truth. An example of the latter is the vision of the king in the story of Yūsuf ﷺ. As far as we can deduce from the narrative, he was not a monotheist, yet saw a true dream which Yūsuf ﷺ interpreted.

Good dreams may be shared with others in the same way as good news is shared. However, the Prophet ﷺ explained that we should not share good dreams with everyone. Abū Qatādah ؓ heard the Prophet ﷺ say: "Good dreams are from Allah, so if any one of you sees that which he likes, he should not disclose it to other than whom he loves."[14]

SATANIC DREAMS

Iblīs the Accursed wishes for nothing more than to drag as many of us to damnation along with him as he can. He wishes to deceive the progeny of Ādam ﷺ and tempt them into sin and despair. Allah ﷻ says: "He (Iblīs) said, 'Now, because You have sent me astray, I shall certainly lurk in ambush for them on Your right path. Then I shall come upon them from before them and from behind them and from their right and from their left, and You will not find most of them grateful.'"[15] He ﷻ also warns us against him, and tells us that he is of a realm unlike ours: "O Children of Adam, let not the devil lure

14 Reported by Bukhārī (6995).

15 *al-A'rāf*, 16-17.

you like he brought your parents out of the Garden, stripping them of their garments to show them their private parts. He surely sees you, He and his clan, whence you cannot see them. Indeed, We have made the devils allies to those who do not believe."[16] Just as devils can introduce evil thoughts into the human mind while it is awake, they are able to do so while it is asleep.

There are etiquettes one should follow if they see an evil dream. Abū Salamah ﵁ said: "I would see dreams that ail me, until I heard Abū Qatādah saying, 'I also would see dreams that ail me until I heard the Prophet ﷺ say: "The good dream is from Allah. If one of you sees that which he likes, let him narrate it to only those whom he likes. If he sees that which he dislikes, let him seek refuge in Allah from its evil and the evil of the devil, dry-spit thrice to his left, and inform no one of it, for it will not harm him."'"[17] Furthermore, one should change the side they were sleeping on, or even get up and perform supererogatory prayers, for that is more severe against the devil as well as a source of spiritual solace and steadfastness.[18]

Allah ﷻ taught the Prophet ﷺ to seek refuge from the devils. He ﷻ says: "Say, 'My Lord, I seek refuge in You from the goadings of the devils; and I seek refuge in You, my Lord, lest they be present with me.'"[19] There are a few supplications in the Sunnah that revolve around this qur'anic one, specifically made to protect against bad

16 *al-Aʿrāf*, 27.

17 Reported by Bukhārī (7044).

18 The vast majority of these narrations are reported by Bukhārī and Muslim on the authority of Abū Qatādah al-Ḥārith ibn Ribʿī al-Anṣārī al-Salamī ﵁, the Knight of Allah's Messenger ﷺ.

19 *al-Muʾminūn*, 97-98.

dreams.[20]

As a preventative measure, we are also advised to recite certain words of divine remembrance before going to sleep. Most prominent of those is reciting *Āyat al-Kursī*,[21] *Sūrat al-Ikhlāṣ*,[22] *al-Muʿawwidhatān*[23] (*al-Falaq* and *al-Nās*),[24] and the last two verses from *Sūrat al-Baqarah*.[25] These passages, by Allah's grace and His might alone, protect one from evil during sleep.

HUMAN DREAMS

Whatever one is constantly busy with, or engaged in, will usually leave its mark on one's subconscious. Additionally, one may see in their dream that which reflects a physical state they are experiencing: hunger, thirst, cold, arousal, or a desire to relieve oneself. These are neither divine nor demonic dreams, and are simply ramblings of the mind.

Scientists have categorised sleep as "quiet sleep" (Non-Rapid Eye Movement or NREM) and "active" or "paradoxical sleep" (Rapid Eye Movement or REM). During REM sleep, the brain is active and the

20 See, for example: Imam Mālik in his *Muwaṭṭa'* (51/1741) and Imam Aḥmad in his *Musnad* (6696).

21 Verse number 255 from *Sūrat al-Baqarah*.

22 *Sūrah* number 112.

23 Literally, 'the Two Protectors.' Each *sūrah* is a plea of refuge from Allah ﷻ. *Sūrat al-Falaq* begins: *Qul aʿūdhu bi-Rabb al-falaq*—'Say, "I seek refuge in the Lord of daybreak."' *Sūrat al-Nās* begins: *Qul aʿūdhu bi-Rabb al-nās*—'Say, "I seek refuge in the Lord of mankind."'

24 *Sūrahs* number 113 and 114 respectively.

25 Along with *Sūrat al-Fātiḥah*, these passages form the core of any set of Islamic invocations, especially when seeking physical and spiritual well-being.

eyes are constantly moving: the sleeper is dreaming. The term "paradoxical sleep" refers to the fact that while the brain is as active as it is during wakefulness, the body is in a state of complete muscular relaxation that is quite unlike the wakeful state. Numerous studies have confirmed that REM sleep is important for brain development and consolidation of memory, and that it improves learning. Interestingly, 50% of a newborn baby's sleep consists of REM sleep, and this proportion decreases with age. It has also been discovered that a certain growth hormone is released nocturnally, particularly during REM sleep.

INTERPRETATION

Only divinely inspired and positive dreams may be interpreted. Demonic inspiration and mental drivel should be disregarded and dealt with as explained above. Dream interpretation is not quite a science in the formal, conventional sense. It is not something where fundamental principles (*uṣūl*) are used to generate secondary derivatives (*furūʿ*). It is a combination of a God-given gift coupled with a keen awareness of the Qur'an, the Sunnah, and their subtle imagery and symbolism.[26] Ideally, though not necessarily, it may be useful if the interpreter of the dream is acquainted with the one who saw it.

26 The Prophet ﷺ would interpret certain objects as having grander implications. For example, upon approaching the fort of Khaybar, he ﷺ saw many workers with axes, mattocks, and the like, before they scurried inside the garrison. These are all tools of destruction. Thereupon, he ﷺ said: "Khaybar has been destroyed!" See Bukhārī (4197).

DID YOU KNOW?

The Eminent Successor (*Tābiʿī*) and Erudite Imam, Muḥammad Ibn Sīrīn al-Baṣrī (d. 110 AH), is the earliest and most prominent figure to give dream interpretation scholarly attention. His *Tafsīr al-Aḥlām* is an abecedarian exposition into the significance of certain common dreams and their symbolism.

The dream interpreter must not seek financial compensation for interpreting a dream. Interpretation of dreams, unlike certain trades or services, carries an inherent uncertainty regarding its utility and benefit. Dreams are subjective experiences, and their significance may vary greatly from one individual to another. Additionally, the outcome of dream interpretation is not always tangible or measurable. In Islamic ethics, payment is generally accepted for services that have a clear and well-defined benefit. Since dream interpretation lacks this clarity, accepting compensation for it is discouraged.

One way to contextualise the prohibition of accepting payment for interpreting dreams is by drawing an analogy to the issuance of fatwas—religious rulings or verdicts. It is widely accepted among Islamic scholars that a mufti—a religious scholar qualified to issue fatwas—should not seek or accept payment for providing religious guidance or rulings. Just as fatwas are considered an act of religious service, dream interpretation falls within the realm of spiritual guidance, making it undesirable to seek financial gain for such a service.[27]

27 This is unlike the practice of *ruqyah*—spiritual and physical healing by way of prayers

DID YOU KNOW?

Some take dreams to be the categorical answer to *istikhārah*—a prayer Muslims should make before making critical decisions. They assume that they have to see a dream guiding them either way. The answer to the *istikhārah* prayer is facilitation towards the favourable choice. This may manifest in many different forms, one of which is potentially a dream. However, to specifically wait for a good dream following *istikhārah* is a mistake.

THREE VIVID VISIONS

In *Sūrah Yūsuf*, there are three occasions where dreams and their interpretations are critical to the narrative: Yūsuf's dream as a child and his eventual prominence, the inmates' dreams in prison and their implication on their sentences, and the king's dream and the future of Egypt's agriculture.

and qur'anic recitation. A *rāqī*—one who performs *ruqyah*—may earn a living through their services. *Ruqyah* is an act of treating illness, and Islamic jurisprudence allows for compensation for services related to healthcare. Nonetheless, one should avoid asking others for *ruqyah* (unless absolutely necessary) and should instead recite the morning and daily invocations—among other prayers—for the sake of protection and wellbeing.

These are summarised in the table below:

SUBJECT	DREAM	INTERPRETATION
Yūsuf ﷺ	Sun, moon, and 11 celestial bodies prostrating to him	Father, mother, and 11 brothers prostrating before him
Inmate 1	Pressing wine	Serving wine to his master
Inmate 2	Carrying bread atop his head from which birds were eating	Crucified and birds pecking at his head
The king	7 fat cows eaten by 7 lean ones, and 7 green grain ears and 7 withered ones	7 years of good harvest followed by 7 years of severe drought

PART

XIII

A TURN OF FATE

Be never hopeless, rather hopelessly hopeful.

Though Yūsuf ﷺ remained in prison for many more years, the mercy of Allah is always close to the good-doers. He was being prepared for unimaginable ennoblement. Far away from the dark depths of desolate dungeons and up in the palatial heights of the monarch's chambers, the king of Egypt himself was irked by a recurring dream. This was to be the turning point for our prophetic protagonist. Allah ﷻ says:

وَقَالَ الْمَلِكُ إِنِّي أَرَىٰ سَبْعَ بَقَرَاتٍ سِمَانٍ يَأْكُلُهُنَّ سَبْعٌ عِجَافٌ وَسَبْعَ سُنْبُلَاتٍ
خُضْرٍ وَأُخَرَ يَابِسَاتٍ يَا أَيُّهَا الْمَلَأُ أَفْتُونِي فِي رُؤْيَايَ إِنْ كُنْتُمْ لِلرُّؤْيَا تَعْبُرُونَ ﴿٤٣﴾

قَالُوا أَضْغَاثُ أَحْلَامٍ وَمَا نَحْنُ بِتَأْوِيلِ الْأَحْلَامِ بِعَالِمِينَ ﴿٤٤﴾

وَقَالَ الَّذِي نَجَا مِنْهُمَا وَادَّكَرَ بَعْدَ أُمَّةٍ أَنَا أُنَبِّئُكُمْ بِتَأْوِيلِهِ فَأَرْسِلُونِ ﴿٤٥﴾

يُوسُفُ أَيُّهَا الصِّدِّيقُ أَفْتِنَا فِي سَبْعِ بَقَرَاتٍ سِمَانٍ يَأْكُلُهُنَّ سَبْعٌ عِجَافٌ وَسَبْعِ
سُنْبُلَاتٍ خُضْرٍ وَأُخَرَ يَابِسَاتٍ لَعَلِّي أَرْجِعُ إِلَى النَّاسِ لَعَلَّهُمْ يَعْلَمُونَ ﴿٤٦﴾

❝ The king said, "I see seven fat cows which seven lean ones eat, and seven green ears of corn and others dry. O chiefs, elucidate for me my vision, if visions you do explicate." They said, "Jumbles of dreams, and of the interpretation of dreams we know nothing." And he of the two who had been released and had recollected after a long time said, "I will inform you of its interpretation, so send me out." "Yūsuf! O you truthful one! Expound for us the seven fat cows which seven lean ones were eating and the seven green ears of corn and the others dry that I may return unto the people so that they may know. ❞[1]

DESTINY

Allah ﷻ says: "He has created everything and determined its measure."[2] He ﷻ also says: "Surely Allah is to accomplish His purpose. Allah has appointed for everything its destined measure."[3] He ﷻ also says: "Indeed, We have created everything with due measure."[4]

'What are the odds?!' People often exclaim upon witnessing a seemingly impossible or highly improbable event. We do not see the full picture, nor can we account for all the variables. Our perception of randomness is merely an admission of ignorance. Ours is a fleeting existence that is bound by countless limitations. But the One, the Unique—He is not fettered by our shackles.

The reality is that everything that is, has been, or will be, is perfectly and masterfully orchestrated by the master planner, the one true God, Allah ﷻ. He is the Dominant (*al-Muhaymin*), the Irresistible (*al-Qahhār*), and the Compeller (*al-Jabbār*). He is the First (*al-Awwal*) without beginning and the Last (*al-Ākhir*) without end. The Externally Manifest (*al-Ẓāhir*) and the Inwardly Hidden (*al-Bāṭin*). The Know-

1 *Yūsuf*, 43-46.

2 *al-Furqān*, 2.

3 *al-Ṭalāq*, 3.

4 *al-Qamar*, 49.

ing, the Wise. The Merciful, the Mercifier. The Lord of the Worlds—all praise, extolment, and thanks are eternally due to Him ﷻ.

REFLECT...

Unlike how some people take it, belief in *qadr* (divine destiny) is immensely liberating. It is not that you are forced to do what you do. Rather, via personal volition, you are actively realising what Allah ﷻ preordained for you. "Work, for each person is eased towards what he was created for." [Bukhārī (4949)]

What were the odds, indeed? Everything was impeccably set up, both at a macro and a micro level. At a macro level, Allah ﷻ sends prophets who are ideally equipped for the specific needs of their people. Yūsuf ﷺ could interpret dreams. This served him well in prison and, as we are to find out, will be the cause of his eventual release and empowerment. Every prophet was sent with blessings and guidance, but each prophet sent to a people answered to their particular temporal and spatial requirements.

REFLECT...

Each prophet and his miracles catered for the customs of his nation and what they knew best. The miracle came to outdo what they thought cannot be outdone. The following table presents some prominent examples.

PROPHET	CUSTOM	MIRACLE
ʿĪsā ﷺ	Medicine: the mystery of life and death	"I create for you out of clay the shape of a bird, then I breathe into it so it becomes a bird by Allah's leave; and I heal the born-blind and the leper; and I revive the dead by Allah's leave." Q 3:49
Mūsā ﷺ	Magic, sorcery, and the supernatural	"We revealed to Mūsā: 'Throw your staff,' and, lo and behold, it swallowed what they were faking! So the truth prevailed and their illusions failed. There and then, they were defeated and brought low." Q 7:117-119
Muḥammad ﷺ	Linguistic prowess and enchanting eloquence	"If you are in doubt about what We have revealed to Our slave, then bring a *sūrah* similar to this and call your supporters other than Allah, if you are true. If you do not—and you cannot—then beware the Fire!" Q 2:23-24

As for the micro, then the king saw a dream. Not only did he see a dream, but his close and eminent advisors failed to interpret it and told him to dismiss it. Not only that, but who else was present to hear about the dream than the wine-pourer which Yūsuf ﷺ foresaw would be freed? Not only that, but he was able to remember Yūsuf ﷺ at that moment after so many years of having forgotten him. At every instance, it could have been otherwise, and matters could have transpired other than how they did. The king may have been of those who do not see true dreams or may have seen it and not thought much of it. He could have listened to his advisors and just brushed it under the carpet as unimportant. The freed inmate may have been elsewhere and never have come across the news of the dream, or he may have heard about it but continued in his heedlessness of Yūsuf ﷺ regardless. But, as Allah ﷻ reminds us earlier in the *sūrah*: "Allah always prevails in His affairs, but most people do not know."[5]

'I KNOW A GUY'

Allah ﷻ says: "Do not think of those who are delighted with what they did and love to be praised for what they never did—do not think they are secure from the punishment."[6] When Allah ﷻ cast into his heart the remembrance of Yūsuf ﷺ,[7] the freed inmate said, "I will inform you of its interpretation!" He did not say, "There is a righteous man in prison whom I met many years ago who can interpret this vision."

5 *Yūsuf*, 21.

6 *Āl ʿImrān*, 188.

7 This bolsters the position that it was indeed the freed man who forgot Yūsuf's mention, not Yūsuf ﷺ who forgot his Lord's mention (Q 12:42). Allah ﷻ knows best.

DID YOU KNOW?

Allah 🕮 says about the freed man remembering Yūsuf 🕮: *Wa iddakara ba'da ummah*—'He recalled after a long time.' The word *ummah* is used in four senses in the Qur'an:

- A period of time. This is the meaning in this *āyah*.

- A group of people, as in Q 35:24.

- A way of life and *dīn* (religion), as in Q 21:92.

- A leader, as in Q 16:120.

Yūsuf 🕮 had spoken to him with kindness, called him to Allah 🕮 with wisdom, and interpreted his dream when asked to do so. He 🕮 sought no recompense for his services, and simply bade him that he mention him before his master, such that perhaps his plea for innocence is heard. Yet, he forgot. When he finally remembered many years later, he did not fulfil this bygone favour, nor even mention that Yūsuf 🕮 was a dream interpreter. He simply said to the king's guard, "Send me forth and I will return with the dream's interpretation." After all these years, and despite neglecting his case for all this time, the first thing that we are told he said to Yūsuf 🕮 was, "Yūsuf! You good, honest man! Interpret this dream for me!" Not a single apology in sight. Not even an embarrassed explanation of what ensued following his release. Just another blunt, unabashed request, albeit with buttering up beforehand.

What would you do in such a scenario? What would your reaction be? How would you respond to this person had it been you instead of Yūsuf ﷺ? Perhaps expletives would be in order? Not Yūsuf ﷺ. His response was a lesson in supreme forbearance and lofty moral excellence. Allah ﷻ says:

قَالَ تَزْرَعُونَ سَبْعَ سِنِينَ دَأَبًا فَمَا حَصَدْتُمْ فَذَرُوهُ فِي سُنْبُلِهِ إِلَّا قَلِيلًا مِمَّا تَأْكُلُونَ ﴿٤٧﴾

ثُمَّ يَأْتِي مِنْ بَعْدِ ذَٰلِكَ سَبْعٌ شِدَادٌ يَأْكُلْنَ مَا قَدَّمْتُمْ لَهُنَّ إِلَّا قَلِيلًا مِمَّا تُحْصِنُونَ ﴿٤٨﴾

ثُمَّ يَأْتِي مِنْ بَعْدِ ذَٰلِكَ عَامٌ فِيهِ يُغَاثُ النَّاسُ وَفِيهِ يَعْصِرُونَ ﴿٤٩﴾

❝ He said, "You shall plant for seven consecutive years; but whatever you harvest, leave it in its ear, except for a little from which you eat. Then after that will come seven hard ones consuming what you have forwarded to them, except for a little of what you have stored. Then after that will come a year in which people shall have rains and in which they will press. ❞[8]

Yūsuf ﷺ overlooked the crass opportunism of his former fellow prisoner. Instead of reminding him of his favour upon him, or putting some conditions in place for his release, he once again fulfils his asker's request. In fact, there would have been no blame upon him had he pursued some arrangement for his exoneration. It would have been a very human and even reasonable thing to do. But he ﷺ

8 *Yūsuf*, 47-49.

portrayed solemn and uncompromising trust in Allah ﷻ—only He ﷻ controlled his destiny. He had taken the means once, and that sufficed in his eyes. Doing so again was unbecoming in his estimation. When Allah decrees it is time for his release, he will be released.

TRANSFORMATIVE WISDOM

Complete *tawḥīd* entails reliance on Allah ﷻ alone. Yūsuf ﷺ does not associate with Allah *min shayʾ*—'anything in the slightest' [Q 12:38]. Having taking the means, he entrusted his release to Allah ﷻ and no one else. *Tawḥīd* is not mere theory or a checklist of doctrinal points that guarantees you salvation. It is a lived state with the Divine ﷻ.

Not only did Yūsuf ﷺ interpret the dream, but he prescribed appropriate measures that ought to be taken to mitigate the potential harms. He could have just said, "There will be seven years of good harvest, followed by seven of severe drought, then finally one year of rainfall." Instead, he advised as to the suitable course of action at each stage: "Store grain during the first seven years, because the seven after them will not yield harvest. Remain patient, as there will finally be relief with a year of abundant rainfall—you will once again press fruits for oil and juice."

Subḥān Allah! What clemency, altruism, and magnanimity Yūsuf ﷺ possessed! What faith and devotion to his Lord he unfailingly portrayed! May Allah's peace and blessings be upon him and upon all His noble prophets.

DID YOU KNOW?

The Arabs used similar linguistic terms for 'rainclouds' or 'heavy rain' and 'relief' or 'deliverance': both meanings come from *ghayth* and *ghawth*. After extreme drought, heavy rains came as a means for rejuvenation and revival, hence the etymological link.

The phrase in the *āyah* here is: *yughāthu al-nās*. It means both: "The people will be given respite." And: "The people will be given rain." In other words: they will be given the relief of rainfall following drought.

HARDSHIP AND EASE

Allah ﷻ says: "Every soul will taste death. We test you with evil and with good as trial; and to Us you will be returned."[9] Life is a roller-coaster. There will be good times, and there will be bad times. There will be times of health, wealth, and good livelihood, and there will be times of sickness, poverty, and loss of life. The underlying baseline for both states, however, is that they are a test. Our problem is in thinking that ease is an indication of Allah's pleasure, while hardship is an indication of His displeasure. Allah ﷻ addresses this misconception and highlights man's weakness and lack of sound judgement. He ﷻ says: "As for man, whenever his Lord tries him through honouring and blessing him, he says, 'My Lord has honoured me.' But whenever He tries him through restricting his provision, he says,

9 *al-Anbiyā'*, 35.

'My Lord has humiliated me.'"[10]

Allah ﷻ has no need for us. Whoever is grateful during ease and patient through hardship, that is for their own benefit and it increases Allah in nothing. Whoever is ungrateful in luxury and scornful during adversity has truly transgressed against themselves—it decreases Allah in nothing. Allah ﷻ says: "Whoever is grateful is in fact grateful for his own benefit, and whoever is ungrateful, then Allah is free of all need, worthy of all praise."[11]

REFLECT...

When Allah ﷻ commands us to do good, be grateful, and be patient, it is for the benefit that it will give us as His slaves. It does not affect Him in the slightest. Yet, when we do obey Him, He is appreciative of our efforts and rewards us for our worship. Truly, He is most kind and most generous!

Nonetheless, Allah ﷻ has ordained that ease supersedes hardship. Divine mercy and compassion is always present, even during the most difficult circumstances! Allah ﷻ says: "Allah wants ease for you and does not want hardship for you."[12] He ﷻ also says: "Allah wishes to lighten your burden; man was created weak."[13] He ﷻ says: "Allah shall bring ease after hardship."[14]

In fact, for every one difficulty, there are two eases! Allah ﷻ says: "So, indeed, along with the hardship (*al-ʿusr*) there is ease (*yusrā*).

10 *al-Fajr*, 15-16.

11 *Luqmān*, 12.

12 *al-Baqarah*, 185.

13 *al-Nisāʾ*, 28.

14 *al-Ṭalāq*, 7.

Undoubtedly, along with the hardship (*al-ʿusr*) there is ease (*yusrā*)."[15] One benefit scholars have extrapolated from this passage is that hardship is mentioned with the definite article twice: *al-ʿusr*—'the hardship.' However, ease is mentioned indefinitely twice: *yusr*—'ease.' In other words, it is the same hardship being mentioned on both occasions, but a new ease that is emphasised each time respectively. Such is the subtle mercy of Allah ﷻ and His benevolence!

TRANSFORMATIVE WISDOM

Ease is not always realised through the lack of hardship. Sometimes, ease is achieved through the necessary strength to bear hardship with dignity and patience. This is the way of the prophets. Thus do not just ask Allah for an easy life, rather pray to be a stronger believer.

This constant care from the heavens is palpable at every stage in the life of Yūsuf ﷺ. There is subtle mercy in his elder brother intervening and halting plans for his assassination. There is a subtle mercy in him being sold to the ʿAzīz and the latter taking care of him. There is even a subtle mercy in his imprisonment, for it is through that ordeal that he interprets the dream of the king and is brought before him.

There is another opportunity for a micro and macro analysis at this point, all in light of the literary brilliance of the Qur'an and its narrative. The current scene sees Yūsuf ﷺ interpret the dream as two periods of good harvest standing at either side of a period of drought. Likewise, it is at this point where the life of Yūsuf ﷺ is represented as two periods of ease standing at either side of difficulty and trials. He

15 *al-Sharḥ*, 5-6.

is about to pass through the bottleneck of worldly abasement into a state of worldly status and honour.

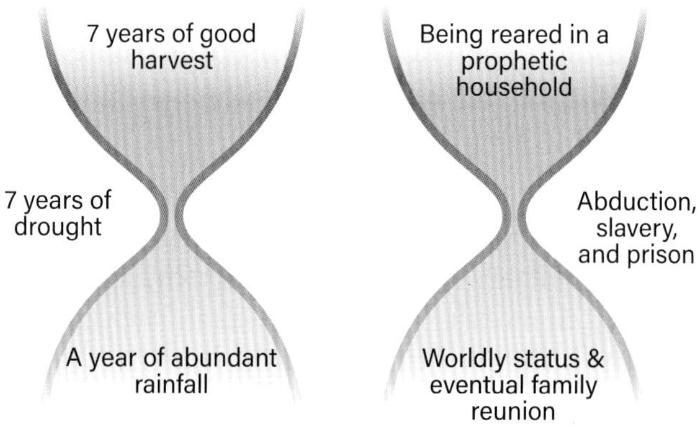

PART

XIV

YŪSUF عليه السلام AND THE KING

Our choice is often between doing what is right or what is easy.

With complete trust in Allah's plan for him, Yūsuf ﵇ interpreted the king's dream and even gave expert economics related advice to avoid impending famine. He did not ask the wine-pourer for anything in return. The king was wise to his contribution, though. He wished to see this dream interpreter in person. The grace and patience Yūsuf ﵇ maintained during hardship was to be portrayed one more time. Allah ﷻ says:

وَقَالَ الْمَلِكُ ائْتُونِي بِهِ فَلَمَّا جَاءَهُ الرَّسُولُ قَالَ ارْجِعْ إِلَى رَبِّكَ فَاسْأَلْهُ مَا بَالُ
النِّسْوَةِ اللاتِي قَطَّعْنَ أَيْدِيَهُنَّ إِنَّ رَبِّي بِكَيْدِهِنَّ عَلِيمٌ ﴿٥٠﴾

قَالَ مَا خَطْبُكُنَّ إِذْ رَاوَدْتُنَّ يُوسُفَ عَنْ نَفْسِهِ قُلْنَ حَاشَ لِلَّهِ مَا عَلِمْنَا
عَلَيْهِ مِنْ سُوءٍ قَالَتِ امْرَأَةُ الْعَزِيزِ الآنَ حَصْحَصَ الْحَقُّ أَنَا رَاوَدْتُهُ
عَنْ نَفْسِهِ وَإِنَّهُ لَمِنَ الصَّادِقِينَ ﴿٥٢﴾

ذَلِكَ لِيَعْلَمَ أَنِّي لَمْ أَخُنْهُ بِالْغَيْبِ وَأَنَّ اللَّهَ لا يَهْدِي كَيْدَ الْخَائِنِينَ ﴿٥٣﴾

وَمَا أُبَرِّئُ نَفْسِي إِنَّ النَّفْسَ لأَمَّارَةٌ بِالسُّوءِ إِلا مَا رَحِمَ
رَبِّي إِنَّ رَبِّي غَفُورٌ رَحِيمٌ ﴿٥٤﴾

“The king said, “Bring him to me.” But when the messenger came to him, he said, “Go back to your lord and ask him, ‘What about the women who cut their hands?’ Surely, my Lord is knowing of their plotting.” He said, “What happened with you when you sought to seduce Yūsuf?” They said, “God forbid! We know of no indecency about him.” The governor's wife said, “Now the truth has come to light. It was I who sought to seduce him, and he is most surely one of the truthful. That is so he may know that I did not betray him in his absence, for surely Allah does not guide the plotting of the betrayers. And I do not acquit myself. Indeed, the soul ever enjoins evil, except those upon whom my Lord has mercy. Indeed, my Lord is forgiving, merciful." ﴿[1]

PATIENCE

Allah ﷻ says: "Be patient. Your patience is through none but Allah."[2] He ﷻ also says: "Indeed, the patient will be given their reward in full without measure."[3] He ﷻ commands us: "O you who believe, seek help through patience and prayer. Surely, Allah is with the patient."[4] He ﷻ also commands us: "O you who believe, be patient,[5] outdo others in patience,[6] be ready, and be mindful of Allah that you may become successful."[7]

Everything is difficult until it becomes easy. There is no virtue except that it may be described in terms of patience. Every religious endeavour is bound to some capacity by being patient for the sake of

1 *Yūsuf*, 50-54.

2 *al-Naḥl*, 127.

3 *al-Zumar*, 10.

4 *al-Baqarah*, 153.

5 The Arabic is *iṣbirū*; from *ṣabara, yaṣbiru, fa-huwa ṣābir*.

6 The Arabic is *ṣābirū*; from *ṣābara, yuṣābiru, fa-huwa muṣābir*. It is a more emphatic form than the previous. In the context of the *āyah*, it refers to outperforming the enemy in endurance and enjoining one another towards steadfastness and perseverance.

7 *Āl ʿImrān*, 200.

Allah 🕮. To be specific, there are three types of patience that we are commanded to nurture in ourselves and others:

1. Patience in maintaining the obligatory.
2. Patience in abstaining from the impermissible.
3. Patience over divine decree.

An example of the first is upkeeping the five daily prayers, regardless of how tired or busy one may be. An example of the second is not engaging in illicit relations, regardless how alluring the setup is and how inclined towards it one may feel. An example of the third is when a student's test results come back but they are not good enough for that college or university they were hoping for, despite their best efforts. Allah knows best what is best for His slaves.

However, there is another taxonomy for patience which is highlighted in this part of the narrative. Yūsuf 🕮 gladly gave the dream's interpretation, and even delivered further advice as to how to handle Egypt's store-houses given said interpretation. The king was clearly impressed and wished to meet him. He sent for him, and it was a figurative red carpet from the prison gates all the way to the king's palace. All Yūsuf 🕮 had to do was accept this get-out-of-jail card and immediately be freed. But he 🕮 deemed this unbecoming of a prophet of Allah. Yūsuf 🕮 wilfully chose to remain in prison until his name was unbesmirched and he was absolved of all false allegations. Thus, there are two types of patience to consider here:

I. Necessary patience—*al-ṣabr al-iḍṭirārī.*

II. Voluntary patience—*al-ṣabr al-ikhtiyārī.*

Necessary patience is essentially all three previous forms combined.

It is when one chooses to persevere and obey Allah, but that is the most practical course of action regardless. So far, Yūsuf ﷺ had no choice but to remain patient in the unfavourable, unsavoury circumstances he found himself in. Here, however, he was actively choosing patience as opposed to being forced to exercise it—voluntary patience.[8] He was choosing the difficult outcome over the easy one because of a higher goal. It's not that the other choice was unlawful, but he did not wish that aspersions be cast as to the circumstances of his release. The king was doing him no favours. Rather, he was righting a wrong. He ﷺ wanted to make that crystal clear. Allah ﷻ says: "To Allah belongs honour, and to His messenger and the believers."[9]

TRANSFORMATIVE WISDOM

Think carefully about the decisions you make and their overarching implications. Do not immediately jump on an opportunity that seems favourable, for it may have adverse long-term consequences or negative side effects on others who find themselves in a similar position in the future. A united vision for wellbeing under the obedience of Allah is the tool to mitigate unwanted repercussions across the board.

8 The Prophet ﷺ praised previous prophets and their honourable positions. In a tradition narrated on the authority of Abū Hurayrah ﷺ, he ﷺ humbly said: "Had I stayed in prison for as long as Yūsuf did, I would have answered the call of the messenger [and left prison]." Reported by Bukhārī (3372) and Muslim (151). This is said rhetorically to highlight the noble character of Yūsuf ﷺ and his profound propensity for patience. It is also a demonstration of the modesty of the Prophet ﷺ and his self-effacement. It is not to be understood literally.

9 *al-Munāfiqūn*, 8.

The Arabs say: "For each context there is an appropriate statement."[10] Wisdom is saying the right thing in the right way at the right time. Choosing the right words is critical for effective communication.[11] Yūsuf ﷺ employed beautiful language in his directive to the king's emissary. "Go back to your master[12] and ask him about the women who cut their hands", he ﷺ told him. He did not say, "The ladies in the city are indecent women who continuously tried to seduce me!" He did not even mention the wife of the ʿAzīz, the underlying cause of his imprisonment.[13] He simply guided the king to explore the right avenues, and trusted Allah ﷻ that the truth was going to come to light. The hand cutting incident was a sufficient hint as to his innocence. Sometimes, you have to lose the battle to win the war.

Yūsuf ﷺ continued, "My Lord[14] is knowing (*ʿalīm*)[15] of their schem-

10 The popular adage reads: *li-kulli maqāmin maqāl* (لكل مقام مقال).

11 See Part IX and Part XI for more on the value of words and how Yūsuf ﷺ was a brilliant speaker.

12 The word in Arabic is *rabbik*—'your lord'—and is referring to the king. It is possible that the ʿAzīz had passed away by that point or had been at least removed from his post. Hence why Yūsuf ﷺ referenced the ladies as opposed to the ʿAzīz and was directly dealing with the king now instead of his old master. In his commentary on Q 12:50, Qurṭubī ﷺ said: "The king sent to the womenfolk and the wife of the ʿAzīz. The ʿAzīz had passed away."

13 In his commentary on Q 12:50, Qurṭubī ﷺ said: "He (Yūsuf ﷺ) mentioned the women altogether such that the wife of the ʿAzīz is included indirectly without explicit mention. This is an appreciation of the time he spent in her care (*ḥusn ʿishrah*) and a manifestation of his propriety (*adab*)."

14 The word in Arabic is: *inna Rabbī*—'verily, my Lord.' This is referring to Allah ﷻ. It may possibly be referring to the ʿAzīz as well, since he was aware of the situation surrounding Yūsuf ﷺ and the womenfolk. Though it seems he was out of the picture by that point (see footnote 12 above regarding his possible passing).

15 This is one of the two Divine Names which Yaʿqūb taught Yūsuf ﷺ many decades ago. Throughout his trials and tribulations, the *īmān* inculcated within him by his father was a continuous source of solace and strength: Allah is knowing of all, wise to all.

ing." He constantly refers to Allah ﷻ in all situations and all circumstances. It is a demonstration of his godliness and orientation to the Divine ﷻ. Additionally, Yūsuf ﷺ is giving further allusions as to the women's immorality without publicly shaming them. In the science of rhetoric (*balāghah*), this is referred to as *taʿrīḍ* as opposed to *taṣrīḥ*: the use of the implicit as opposed to the explicit in expressing an idea. He is not wholly outing them, as it were, though still firmly communicating his innocence and their guilt. It is another example of his graciousness, dignity, and moral excellence.

DID YOU KNOW?

Egypt is referenced many times in the Qur'an, especially its ruler. Allah ﷻ does not use the same word in *Sūrah Yūsuf* as He ﷻ does in the story of Mūsā ﷺ. In the former, the word used is *malik*—'king.' In the latter, it is *firʿawn*—'pharaoh.' Contrastingly, the Bible uses the word 'pharaoh' indiscriminately for all rulers of Egypt.

Modern ancient Egyptian scholarship reveals that the title 'pharaoh' was used in Egypt during the 18th Dynasty in the second half of the second millennium BCE, aligning with the time of Mūsā ﷺ and the Exodus. However, earlier rulers during the time of the Israelite patriarchs were referred to as 'kings.' This is proof that the Qur'an could not have been from the Prophet ﷺ: neither could he have known the civilisational nuance by himself, nor was he blindly regurgitating previous scriptures.

THE NAFS

Allah ﷻ says: "By the self and Him who fashioned it—He inspired it with its [knowledge of] wickedness and piety. Successful is he who purifies it, and doomed is he who corrupts it."[16] The word in Arabic for 'self', used plentifully in the Qur'an and the Sunnah, is *nafs*. An entity's *nafs* is its being and essence. The Arabs say: *nafs al-shay'* to mean 'the same thing.' Literally, *nafs al-shay'* is 'the essence of the thing.' This is why the word has many connotations with regards to selfhood, some positive and others negative. The *nafs* is one's inner self—the conscience. It is one's holistic being in the life of this world. It may also refer to the ego—the lower self. There are three states or stages to the *nafs* that have been highlighted in the Qur'an.

16 *al-Shams*, 7-10.

They are summarised in the table below:

TYPE OF *NAFS*	QUR'ANIC REFERENCE	DESCRIPTION
النَّفس الأَمَّارَة بِالسُّوء *al-nafs al-ammārah bil-sū'* The self which incites and enjoins towards evil.	"Indeed, the soul ever enjoins evil, except those upon whom my Lord has mercy." Q 12:53	The wrongfully disposed spirit is one easily enticed to wrongdoing. It is not inherently evil, but unrestrained and self-indulgent.
النَّفس اللَّوَّامَة *al-nafs al-lawwāmah* The self-reproaching, regretful self	"No! I swear by the Day of Resurrection. And no! I swear by the reproaching conscience." Q 75:1-2	The self-reproaching spirit is one that has moral inhibition. It is morally aware and feels guilt upon wrongdoing. Its moral conscience has the potential to hold its base desires in check.
النَّفس المُطْمَئِنَّة *al-nafs al-muṭma'innah* The well-pleased, tranquil self	"O you soul at peace! Return to your Lord, content in His good pleasure. So enter among My servants, and enter My Garden." Q 89:27-30	The morally contented spirit is at peace and in harmony with its moral existence. There is no conflict between its inner desires and motivations and the dictates of its moral conscience.

When confronted with the potential of an impending exposure, the wife of the ʿAzīz admitted to her faults. All the other women said that Yūsuf ﷺ had committed no indecency.[17] The logical follow-up

17 A remarkable piece of story-telling is the fact the women were asked: "What happened when you tried to seduce Yūsuf?" [Q 12:51] As discussed, Yūsuf ﷺ did not mention any attempted seduction, but clearly his message was understood by the king. This is part of

question would be: what then caused him to be incarcerated? There was no way out, and it was time for the truth to manifest. "It was I who seduced him, and he is truthful!", she proclaimed.[18] "That is so that he may know that I did not betray him in his absence, and that Allah does not guide the plot of the betrayers", she continued.[19] "I

---

the miraculous compendiousness of the qur'anic rhetoric. See 'Brevity' in Part V for more on this point.

18   In his commentary on Q 12:51, Qurṭubī said: "When she (the wife of the ʿAzīz) saw their (the other women) proclamation of Yūsuf's innocence, she feared that they would testify against her if she denies [his innocence], so she concurred [and admitted her sin]. This was subtle divine care (luṭf) that reached Yūsuf."

19   The statements in verses 52 and 53 are disputed over with regards to who said them and consequently the references made therein. In plain English, the passage reads: "That is so that he may know that I did not betray him in his absence, and Allah does not guide the plot of the betrayers. And I do not absolve myself of blame. Indeed, the soul incites towards evil except for whom Allah shows mercy. Indeed, my Lord is forgiving, merciful." There are two main positions:

1.   Yūsuf is the one being quoted. The meaning becomes: "That—sending the messenger back—is so that the ʿAzīz may know that I did not betray him in his absence, for Allah does not guide the plot of the betrayers. And I do not absolve myself of blame—for I inclined towards her when she enticed me. Indeed, the soul incites towards evil except for whom Allah shows mercy. Indeed, my Lord is forgiving, merciful." This is the position of Ṭabarī, Zamakhsharī, Qurṭubī, as well as the vast majority of early exegetes, including Saʿīd ibn Jubayr, Mujāhid, Qatādah, and al-Ḥasan.

2.   The wife of the ʿAzīz is the one being quoted. The meaning becomes: "That—admitting my sin—is so that the ʿAzīz may know that I did not betray him in his absence—I ultimately did not commit adultery—Allah does not guide the plot of the betrayers. I certainly do not absolve myself of blame, for I nonetheless tried to seduce Yūsuf. Indeed, the soul incites towards evil except for whom Allah shows mercy. Indeed, my Lord is forgiving, merciful." This is the position of Māwardī, Ibn Taymiyyah, Ibn Kathīr, Ibn ʿĀshūr, and Saʿdī. It is the most befitting understanding given the narrative, and Allah knows best.

It should be noted that which interpretation is preferred seems to be a direct function of one's understanding of the hamm—inclination—mentioned in Q 12:24. Our understanding there informs our understanding here. If one takes the hamm to be a real and palpable inclination that was almost realised, the former position is most congruent. If it was

do not acquit myself—the soul enjoins one towards evil but for the mercy of my Lord. He is forgiving, merciful." The truth was clear as day. There could no longer be any blemishes on the character of Yūsuf 🙢 and his integrity.

DID YOU KNOW?

It is said that, following her repentance, the king married Yūsuf 🙢 to the ex-wife of the ʿAzīz after the latter passed away and the former assumed his office. Her name was either Rāʿīl or Zulaykhā. The betrothal is relayed by Ibn Abī Ḥātim (7/2161) and Ṭabarī (16/151) in their respective qurʾanic commentaries, and is also mentioned by Suyūṭī in his *al-Durr al-Manthūr* (4/553) and Ibn al-Qayyim in *Rawḍat al-Muḥibbīn*. Though narrated by some of the Successors (*Tābiʿīn*), the account likely goes back to Judeo-Christian narratives.

FROM SLAVE TO MINISTER

Just as suddenly and swiftly as Yūsuf 🙢 was placed into prison, he was now being taken out of it. In an instant, Allah 🙞 can change

solely hypothetical due to the *burhān* (divine proof) Allah 🙞 showed Yūsuf 🙢, then the latter position is most congruent. Finally, Qurṭubī 🙢 mentions that, if the second position is adopted, it may be Yūsuf 🙢 who is the referent in: *li-yaʿlama annī lam akhunhu*—'That **he** may know I did not betray **him**' as opposed to the ʿAzīz. That is, the wife of the ʿAzīz is saying: "I confess to my misdeed so that Yūsuf knows I did not speak ill of him in his absence." He 🙢 also passingly mentions the possibility that it is the ʿAzīz being quoted for the whole passage, though this is not a strong position and he does not give it much attention.

everything. He is the Subtle (*al-Laṭīf*), the Aware (*al-Khabīr*). The king was adamant he was going to meet this judicious, now-exonerated dream interpreter. Allah ﷻ says:

وَقَالَ الْمَلِكُ ائْتُونِي بِهِ أَسْتَخْلِصْهُ لِنَفْسِي فَلَمَّا كَلَّمَهُ
قَالَ إِنَّكَ الْيَوْمَ لَدَيْنَا مَكِينٌ أَمِينٌ ﴿٥٤﴾

قَالَ اجْعَلْنِي عَلَىٰ خَزَائِنِ الْأَرْضِ إِنِّي حَفِيظٌ عَلِيمٌ ﴿٥٥﴾

وَكَذَٰلِكَ مَكَّنَّا لِيُوسُفَ فِي الْأَرْضِ يَتَبَوَّأُ مِنْهَا حَيْثُ يَشَاءُ نُصِيبُ بِرَحْمَتِنَا مَنْ
نَشَاءُ وَلَا نُضِيعُ أَجْرَ الْمُحْسِنِينَ ﴿٥٦﴾

وَلَأَجْرُ الْآخِرَةِ خَيْرٌ لِلَّذِينَ آمَنُوا وَكَانُوا يَتَّقُونَ ﴿٥٧﴾

❝ The king said, "Bring him to me, and I shall employ him purely for myself." So, when he talked to him, he said, "Today you are with us well-placed, fully trusted." He said, "Put me in charge of the storehouses of the land; I am indeed a knowledgeable keeper." And thus We established Yūsuf in the land to live therein wherever he so willed. We reach with Our mercy whomever We will, and We never waste the reward of those who excel in doing good. But the reward of the Hereafter is better for those who believe and are mindful. ❞[20]

Allah ﷻ is the Expansive Reliever (*al-Bāsiṭ*) just as He is the Severe Constrictor (*al-Qābiḍ*). For the first time in this prophetic epic, we breathe a sigh of relief. At the edge of our seats throughout, we could not help our anxiety as we saw Yūsuf عليه السلام being struck with

20 *Yūsuf*, 54-57.

trial after trial. Now, he was established. He was once owned, now he is an owner. He had nothing, now he has "the earth to dwell in it, wherever he wished". Unbeknownst to him and every human actor involved, everything before that moment of establishment was guiding Yūsuf ﷺ inexorably towards it. Everything is for an ordained, precise purpose. Such is the subtle care of Allah ﷻ.

TRANSFORMATIVE WISDOM

Yūsuf ﷺ did not know what Allah ﷻ had planned for him, but he trusted Him and constantly maintained His faith by doing righteous deeds. We ought to take him as a role model in his impeccable character despite severe hardships. For decades he upheld moral excellence despite his suffering. Trust Allah ﷻ, do your best, and He will take care of everything else.

At every stage of his life, Yūsuf ﷺ was living solely for Allah ﷻ. Nothing mattered to him except what Allah ﷻ thought of him. When he spoke, he knew Allah heard his words. When he acted, he knew Allah saw his deeds. When he thought, he knew Allah knew his thoughts. At every point, the question for him was: is this beloved to Allah? If yes, he proceeded. If not, he desisted. This is the reality of *lā ilāha illā Allāh* at a lived, experienced level: practical *tawḥīd*. Yūsuf ﷺ made his life an endowment for Allah ﷻ.

For the second time, the king called for him. Having had his public honour reinstated in front of the highest of worldly authorities, he ﷺ obliged. The king was already aware that this is no ordinary person. For starters, he was a dream-interpreter. Furthermore, he foresaw more than the vision directly implied—the concluding year of abundant rain was a prophecy beyond the symbolism in the dream.[21] Finally, he had given expert agricultural advice that only a learned, sagacious man could have provided. He helped avert a transgeographical catastrophe without asking for a penny in return.

And so they spoke. One can only imagine the nature of that conversation. Yūsuf would have had no nerves or desperation whatsoever—he had chosen to remain in prison shortly before their meeting. His stances have always been for the truth and in servitude to Allah . He must have been assertive and confident. He knew himself and what he could offer. The king was already impressed, but, after beholding the physical and spiritual awe of Yūsuf before him, he was now dead set on acquiring his services. He said, "Today, you are well-established and completely trusted with us." Just like that, Yūsuf's jail time was expunged, his records shredded, and all hindrances lifted. Allah says: "Whatever mercy Allah opens up for people, none can withhold it. And whatever He withholds, none but Him can release it. For He is the Almighty, the Wise."[22]

Allah says: "Say, 'O Allah, Owner of Dominion, You grant dominion to whomever You will and You strip dominion from whomever You

---

21 The dream had seven cows, both skinny and fat, as well as seven ears of grain, both green and dry. It did not contain any symbols indicating the year of abundant rain. Therefore, this knowledge is either borne of direct divine revelation to Yūsuf or an appreciation that he had of Allah's *sunan*—patterns of being—in His creation. Adopting the former view, Ṭabarī said: "It (the year of abundant rain) is from the knowledge of the Unseen which Allah gave him (Yūsuf) as evidence for his prophethood and proof for his truthfulness." Adopting the latter view, Ibn ʿĀshūr said: "It (the year of abundant rain) is a logical entailment of the intense period concluding, and one of the *sunan* of Allah in realising ease after hardship." This is found in their respective commentaries on Q 12:49.
22 *Fāṭir*, 2.

will, and You honour whomever You will and You humiliate whomever You will; in Your hand is all goodness. You are indeed powerful over all things.'"[23] Allah ﷻ is the one who honours and disgraces, and He is the one who raises and abases. He is the King of Kings, the Master of Sovereignty. Accordingly, He ﷻ has dissuaded His slaves from actively seeking positions of rulership and authority. The Prophet ﷺ advised one of his companions: "Do not ask for rulership. If you are given it having asked for it, it will be given authority over you. If you are given it without asking for it, you will be aided in its fulfilment."[24] He ﷺ also said: "Surely you shall covet rulership, but it will be a source of regret on the Day of Resurrection!"[25] The exception to this is where corruption would ensue if one did not step up to an occasion.[26]

TRANSFORMATIVE WISDOM

Never seek out positions of authority. It is an immense burden that one will be answerable for before Allah. However, appreciate that if Allah ﷻ has endowed you with certain blessings, part of being grateful for them is employing them for His pleasure alone.

---

23 *Āl 'Imrān*, 26.

24 Reported by Bukhārī (7146) and Muslim (1652).

25 Reported by Bukhārī (7148).

26 For example, among a congregation that is about to pray without an appointed imam, it is possible that the majority cannot recite the Qur'an properly. If one is reasonably confident that this is indeed the case, and one has had formal lessons where his qur'anic recitation has been approved by qualified teachers, one would need to step up and lead for the sake of the validity of everyone's prayer. An even clearer example is presented by Prophet Yūsuf ﷺ in this point of the story.

Thus, Yūsuf ﷺ responded to the king's offer: "Grant me authority to supervise Egypt's storehouses, for I am responsible and knowledgeable." He ﷺ was a man of substance. He did not invoke his lineage. If anyone has the right to cite their ancestry to boost their credibility, then surely it would have been him: he was Yūsuf, the son of Yaʿqūb, the son of Isḥāq, the son of Ibrāhīm ﷺ. Instead, he ﷺ said he is both skilled and trustworthy.

The Prophet ﷺ said: "The strong believer is better and more beloved to Allah than the weak believer, though there is goodness in both."[27] Among the supplications of righteous leaders and activists is their calling upon Allah ﷻ: "O Allah, I seek refuge in you from the impotence of the trustworthy and the competence of the wicked."[28] Piety, when restricted to the ritualistic acts of worship, is insufficient for the reform of a people. Likewise, prowess and adeptness that is misguided will never yield blessed fruits. It is the combination mentioned by Yūsuf ﷺ that is necessary for *iṣlāḥ*—divinely guided activism and rectification. He ﷺ was *ḥafīẓ* and *ʿalīm*. He had the integrity and God-consciousness to make moral decisions and favour the common good over personal gain. But he also possessed the necessary skillset to navigate tumultuous terrains and execute with precision. He was *ḥafīẓ*—responsible and trustworthy—as well as *ʿalīm*—knowledgeable and intelligent.

27 Reported by Muslim (2664) on the authority of Abū Hurayrah ؓ.

28 The prayer is commonly attributed to ʿUmar ibn al-Khaṭṭāb ؓ. Ibn al-Jawzī ؒ ascribes it to him in his *Manāqib*.

REFLECT...

There's a difference between information and knowledge. The latter is the former processed. There are those who conflate the two and think themselves knowledgeable due to accumulating information. They quote figures and passages, boasting how well-read they are, but it's only noise. Put a loud exhaust on a basic car and it may sound like a sportscar, but it will not be able to drive like one.

THE ETERNAL REWARD

Yūsuf ﷺ was given both worldly and after-worldly eminence. He was a prophet, and a righteous, chaste, truthful man who called to Allah and enjoined goodness wherever he was. He always sought Allah's pleasure and the reward of the Hereafter (*ākhirah*). He was also given sovereignty in this worldly life (*dunyā*). However, at least at an individual level, the latter is not a necessary entailment of the former. In fact, Yūsuf ﷺ was among a minority of prophets to enjoy such administrative control. The generic pattern is that the prophets ﷺ resided with the weak and down-trodden, stood up to authority, and, when denied and ridiculed, were given divine deliverance whilst their enemies perished. Other than Dāwūd and Sulaymān ﷺ—and indeed the Seal of Messengers ﷺ—this is what we come across throughout the prophetic stories in the Qur'an.

This leads us to the understanding that there is nothing inherently evil about wealth and worldly status, otherwise Allah ﷻ would not have granted it to some of his virtuous slaves. What it does mean, however, is that having power is a test that all too many fail. Those granted the *dunyā* must always keep it in their hands, but never in their hearts. The moment love of the *dunyā* penetrates one's heart is the moment where love of the *ākhirah* wanes therein.[29]

Appropriately therefore, Allah ﷻ concludes this passage by reminding us of the only thing that matters. Regardless of what one's station in this world may be: "The reward of the Hereafter is better for those who believe and are conscious of Allah." For them is bliss beyond anything comprehensible in this worldly life.[30] Bliss which "no eye has ever seen, no ear has ever heard, and no heart can ever imagine."[31] Allah ﷻ says: "No soul knows what is kept hidden for them of joy as a reward for what they used to do."[32]

DID YOU KNOW?

The word *dunyā* literally means 'lowest.' So, *al-samā' al-dunyā* is 'the lowest heaven,' and *al-ḥayāt al-dunyā* is literally 'the lowest life,' even if effectively translated to 'the worldly life.' That is to say: the lives we live now are but a fraction of the full, opulent, unimaginably blissful lives we will enjoy in Paradise, *in shā' Allāh*!

29 In an eschatological prophecy, the Messenger of Allah ﷺ told us of a time where we will be many yet like the froth of the sea, and that our enemies will gather against us as diners gather around their food. The fundamental root cause of all this will be *wahn*—weakness—in our hearts. Asked about the nature of this weakness, the Prophet ﷺ said: "Love of the *dunyā* and a dislike of death." Reported authentically by Abū Dāwūd (4297).

30 The last man to be entered into the Garden—the man with the lowest level of enjoyment—will be given tenfold the kingship and bliss of the greatest kings of the *dunyā*, and then some. See the narration reported by Muslim (189).

31 An excerpt from a narration reported by Bukhārī (4779) and Muslim (2824).

32 *al-Sajdah*, 17.

PART

XV

FAMINE IN PALESTINE

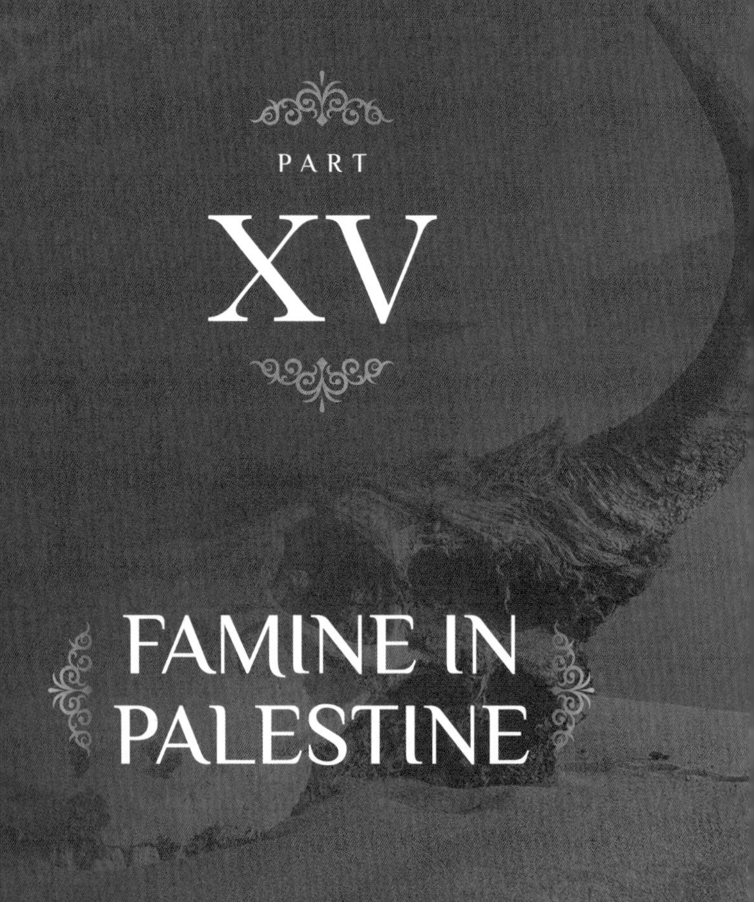

You are your patience when you have nothing, and your attitude when you have everything.

Yūsuf عليه السلام was a true *muḥsin*. He had taken Egypt's agricultural output to unprecedented success. The country's economy was flourishing under his wise governance. The boom was such that neighbouring regions now relied on Egypt for trade and support. The surplus Egypt enjoyed was being exchanged in quotas with travelling Canaanites afflicted by famine. By Allah's grace and His guiding hand, Yūsuf's brothers now stood before him as one of the most powerful men on earth. Allah تبارك وتعالى says:

وَجَاءَ إِخْوَةُ يُوسُفَ فَدَخَلُوا عَلَيْهِ فَعَرَفَهُمْ وَهُمْ لَهُ مُنْكِرُونَ ﴿٥٨﴾

وَلَمَّا جَهَّزَهُمْ بِجَهَازِهِمْ قَالَ ائْتُونِي بِأَخٍ لَكُمْ مِنْ أَبِيكُمْ أَلَا تَرَوْنَ
أَنِّي أُوفِي الْكَيْلَ وَأَنَا خَيْرُ الْمُنْزِلِينَ ﴿٥٩﴾

فَإِنْ لَمْ تَأْتُونِي بِهِ فَلَا كَيْلَ لَكُمْ عِنْدِي وَلَا تَقْرَبُونِ ﴿٦٠﴾

قَالُوا سَنُرَاوِدُ عَنْهُ أَبَاهُ وَإِنَّا لَفَاعِلُونَ ﴿٦١﴾

وَقَالَ لِفِتْيَانِهِ اجْعَلُوا بِضَاعَتَهُمْ فِي رِحَالِهِمْ لَعَلَّهُمْ يَعْرِفُونَهَا
إِذَا انْقَلَبُوا إِلَىٰ أَهْلِهِمْ لَعَلَّهُمْ يَرْجِعُونَ ﴿٦٢﴾

❝ Yūsuf's brethren came and presented themselves before him, and he knew them but they knew him not. Then, when he had supplied them with their supplies, he said, "Bring me a brother of yours from your father. Do you not see that I fill up the measure, and I am the best of hosts? If you do not bring him to me, you will have no measure with me, and you will not come near me again." They said, "We will try to win him from his father: that we will surely do." He said to his servants, "Place their merchandise in their saddlebags so that they may know it when they go back to their folk, and so will come again." ﴾[1]

PROFICIENCY PRESENTS OPPORTUNITY

The Prophet ﷺ said: "Allah has prescribed excellence in all matters. So if you sacrifice, then do so with proficiency. Let each of you sharpen his blade and have mercy on his slaughter-animal."[2] Yūsuf ﷺ was such an adept agricultural minister that Egypt witnessed economic prosperity it had never known before him. Wherever he expended effort and applied his skillset, he did so with precision, diligence, and proficiency—a *muḥsin* par excellence.[3]

TRANSFORMATIVE WISDOM

We each have our unique God-given qualities and abilities. Recognise your strengths, appreciate where they will be most useful, and employ them for the service of Allah ﷻ.

There was a surplus of produce, and the possibility for regional trade presented itself. Journeying traders were given a quota based on

1 *Yūsuf*, 58-62.

2 Reported by Muslim (1955) on the authority of Shaddād ibn Aws ﷺ.

3 See Part XI for more on the virtue of *iḥsān* and the excellence of Yūsuf ﷺ.

their respective offerings and the number of their family members.[4] Enter a band of brothers, ten men of striking appearance, standing out from the crowd, and eerily familiar to Yūsuf ﷺ. Could it be? Surely not. As they drew nearer and nearer, their features got clearer and clearer. It was unmistakably them: his half-brothers, travelling from Canaan to seek sustenance for their families.

Only Allah knows the emotions that overcame Yūsuf ﷺ when he recognised them.[5] He once again chose the path of patience, as he did in prison when the king's messenger came to him. There they were, his own flesh and blood who betrayed him and plotted his demise, entering upon him where he had everything, and they had nothing. Retribution was within arm's reach, but it is not the way of Allah's chosen ones. Exercising immense self-control, he remained composed. He did not show his cards, and instead ensured the wellness of his father and his younger brother, Binyāmīn.

We can imagine the conversation. Maintaining his poise, Yūsuf ﷺ wished to save his brother from harm's way. What befell him could very well befall his younger brother—their father's new and now sole 'favourite.'[6] But how to draw him away? He clearly wasn't with the

---

4 This may be understood from the wording of the passage: *jahāz* (supplies), *biḍāʿah* (merchandise or goods), *riḥāl* (saddlebags or camel packs), and even *ḥimlu baʿīr* (a camelback's worth) mentioned later in the *sūrah*.

5 There are many potential reasons why he ﷺ was able to recognise his brothers while they failed to recognise him. Most notably among those: he was a child when they last saw him, and is now a full-grown man. On the other hand, they were already men when he last saw them, so would have changed less in comparison. Additionally, in their minds, the likelihood that the powerful governor before them, surrounded by guards and servants, was the same shirtless boy they put in the well and sold into slavery would have understandably been negligible.

6 When they were plotting against Yūsuf ﷺ, his half-brothers are quoted to have said: "Yūsuf and his brother (Binyāmīn) are more beloved to our father than we are" Q 12:8.

rest of his brothers. Thinking on the spot, Yūsuf ﷺ devised a plan. He was to ensure Binyāmīn is present next time his brothers come, then keep him under his care. He said to them, "Bring me a brother of yours from your father."[7] It is possible that they came with a camel to carry Binyāmīn's share and requested it from Yūsuf ﷺ, to which he responded by asking about the reason for his absence. A conceivable interchange, at least in terms of content, may have been as follows:

Furthermore, when he ﷺ executed his plan and is successfully reunited with his brother, he tells him: "I am your brother, so do not be saddened over what they used to do" Q 12:69.

7 A question which begs itself is how Yūsuf ﷺ asked about Binyāmīn whilst withholding his true identity. In his commentary on Q 12:59, Qurṭubī ﷺ quotes Suddī ﷺ and Ibn ʿAbbās ﷺ offering their respective explanations as to how the conversation went between Yūsuf ﷺ and his brothers:

Suddī ﷺ said: "The brothers of Yūsuf had eleven camels with them, though they were only ten. They said to Yūsuf, 'We have a brother who stayed behind, and his camel is with us.' He asked them, 'Why did he stay behind?' They replied, 'His father's love for him.' They also mentioned that he (Binyāmīn) had an older brother who went out in the wilderness and died. He (Yūsuf ﷺ) said to them, 'I wish to see this brother of yours so that I may appreciate the reason his father loves him so, and so that I may confirm the truth of what you say.'"

Ibn ʿAbbās ﷺ said: "He (Yūsuf ﷺ) said to the translator, 'Tell them: Your language is different from ours, and your raiment is different from ours, so perhaps you are spies.' They said, 'By Allah, we are not spies! Rather, we are the sons of a single man (i.e. half-brothers), and he is a righteous old sage.' He said, 'How many are you?' They replied, 'We were twelve, but a brother of ours went out in the wilderness and perished.' He said, 'Where's the other one (i.e. the eleventh, Binyāmīn)?' They said, 'He's with his father.' He asked, 'Who can attest to your truthfulness?' They replied, 'No one knows us here. We told you of our lineage; so where does your heart rest in our regard?' Thus, he said, '**Bring me a brother of yours from your father if you are indeed truthful** [Q 12:60], for that will suffice me. **Do you not see that I give the measure in full** [Q 12:59]'—meaning give it its due without decrease—'and I shall increase you another camel-load for your brother? **If you do not bring him to me, you shall have no measure with me!** [Q 12:59]' He threatened them that he will not sell them the food if they do not bring him (Binyāmīn)."

- The brothers: "We came to trade for eleven camelback worths."

o Yūsuf : "I see you are only ten."

- "The eleventh among us stayed behind."

o "Why?"

- "His father loves him dearly and is protective over him."

o "Why is your father not the same with you?"

- "He is actually our half-brother, and his full sibling went out into the wilderness as a young boy and tragically died."

o "Do you have any proof as to the veracity of this tale? I'm sure you appreciate how easily a story like yours can be fabricated for the purposes of more food."

- "We are travellers from Palestine, and this land is not one where we have relatives or friends."

o "Bring me this half-brother of yours. Do you not see that I give the measure in full and am the best of Egypt's hosts? If you do not bring him, there is no deal, and you shan't come here again."

- "We will try to win him from his father—that we will surely do!"[8]

---

8   See previous footnote. The two accounts are non-contradictory. Though we cannot know any details for certain other than those explicitly given in the Qur'an, this account is essentially that given by classical exegetes rendered for a modern audience. The last interaction from Yusuf ﷺ and his brothers respectively—a rough translation of Q 12:59-60—is what we know for sure took place. See 'Brevity' as well as the four P's of qur'anic reflection found in Part V for more on this.

There is a noteworthy rhetorical device that is employed by Yūsuf 🕮 at the end. So far, there have been multiple examples of appropriate wording and effective communication used in the story.[9] Here, Yūsuf 🕮 exercises a tool known as *targhīb* and *tarhīb*: enticement and repulsion. *Targhīb* is to rhetorically lure one's addressee into a course of action via desirable outcomes. *Tarhīb* is to rhetorically deter them from pursuing it via undesirable outcomes. It is a literary push and pull: the proverbial carrot and stick.[10] Yūsuf 🕮 pointed out to his brothers, "Do you not see that I give the measure in full and that I am the best of hosts?" That is: "You would be foolish not to take this opportunity with so much to gain." He also warned them, "If you do not bring your brother to me, you will have no measure nor will you approach me again." That is: "You would be unwise to disobey my command with so much to lose."

TRANSFORMATIVE WISDOM

Targhīb and *tarhīb* are a classical form of effective communication in managerial positions. Know when to use which and with whom, clarifying the favourable results if directives are followed properly and the unfavourable ones if they are not.

---

9   These include how Yūsuf 🕮 communicated the dream to his father, how Yaʿqūb 🕮 responded, how the latter addressed his sons when they came to him with their lies about Yūsuf 🕮, how Yūsuf 🕮 addressed the ʿAzīz when his wife accused him of indecency, how he 🕮 spoke to his inmates and invited them to truth, how he 🕮 spoke to the king's messenger and eventually the king, and now how he is addressing his brothers.

10   The word *targhīb* comes from *raghbah*—desire, and the word *tarhīb* comes from *rahbah*—awe and horror. They are both of the *tafʿīl* morphological setup of their respective roots; i.e. to incite desire (*targhīb*) and to cause horror (*tarhīb*). In the Qurʾan, passages pertaining to Allah's mercy and the Garden are a form of *targhīb*, whereas passages pertaining to His wrath and the Fire are a form of *tarhīb*.

The brothers' response was telling: "We shall persuade (*nurāwidu*) his father in his regard—that we will surely do." There are two indications as to the psychological barrier they placed between themselves and their father and Binyāmīn—an 'us and them' mentality. The first is the verb *nurāwidu*—to entice, lure, and tempt via appealing and charged language: what is termed today emotional blackmail.[11] The second is their saying "**his** father" as opposed to "**our** father". Evidently, when it came to Yūsuf and Binyāmin, Ya`qūb was 'theirs', not 'ours'.

Yūsuf was not going to take any chances with his plan for Binyāmīn. Their giving their word in the heat of the moment and while under pressure was insufficient in his eyes—they may later get dissuaded or end up forgetting about the matter during their long journey home. Thus, he took extra measures to ensure their return. While they were unaware, he instructed his servants[12] to place their goods back in their saddlebags. That way, when they return home, they will be further incentivised to come back for more.[13]

---

11 See Part VI for more on how the brothers used emotional blackmail with their father before. Also, note that the term *murāwadah* is what is used when referring to what the wife of the ʿAzīz tried to do with Yūsuf (as in Q 12:30). See 'Smear Campaign' in Part X for more on this term.

12 The word in Arabic is *fityah* or *fityān*. Note how he himself was once a *fatā* (e.g. Q 12:30), but now has his own *fityah*. Allah is the best of planners!

13 It is possible that, on top of this, Yūsuf also recognised their dire need and so wanted to give them more without making his intentions apparent. Undoubtedly, he greatly cared for his father's wellness and the family overall. This is mentioned by Ṭabarī and Qurṭubī among others.

FOOL ME ONCE

The brothers returned back to their families. Now, they had to face their father and, once again, ask him for who is purportedly his most beloved son—to take him away from his loving care to a faraway land. It was an all too familiar scene for Yaʿqūb ﷺ. Allah ﷻ says:

فَلَمَّا رَجَعُوا إِلَىٰ أَبِيهِمْ قَالُوا يَا أَبَانَا مُنِعَ مِنَّا الْكَيْلُ فَأَرْسِلْ مَعَنَا أَخَانَا نَكْتَلْ وَإِنَّا لَهُ لَحَافِظُونَ ﴿٦٣﴾

قَالَ هَلْ آمَنُكُمْ عَلَيْهِ إِلَّا كَمَا أَمِنتُكُمْ عَلَىٰ أَخِيهِ مِن قَبْلُ فَاللَّهُ خَيْرٌ حَافِظًا وَهُوَ أَرْحَمُ الرَّاحِمِينَ ﴿٦٤﴾

وَلَمَّا فَتَحُوا مَتَاعَهُمْ وَجَدُوا بِضَاعَتَهُمْ رُدَّتْ إِلَيْهِمْ قَالُوا يَا أَبَانَا مَا نَبْغِي هَٰذِهِ بِضَاعَتُنَا رُدَّتْ إِلَيْنَا وَنَمِيرُ أَهْلَنَا وَنَحْفَظُ أَخَانَا وَنَزْدَادُ كَيْلَ بَعِيرٍ ذَٰلِكَ كَيْلٌ يَسِيرٌ ﴿٦٥﴾

قَالَ لَنْ أُرْسِلَهُ مَعَكُمْ حَتَّىٰ تُؤْتُونِ مَوْثِقًا مِّنَ اللَّهِ لَتَأْتُنَّنِي بِهِ إِلَّا أَن يُحَاطَ بِكُمْ فَلَمَّا آتَوْهُ مَوْثِقَهُمْ قَالَ اللَّهُ عَلَىٰ مَا نَقُولُ وَكِيلٌ ﴿٦٦﴾

❝ When they returned to their father, they said, "O our father, we were denied measure, so send our brother with us so that we can obtain measure, and we shall most surely be his preservers." He said, "Am I to entrust him to you as I entrusted his brother to you before? Allah is a better preserver, and He is the most merciful of the merciful ones." And when they opened their baggage they found that their goods had been returned to them. They said, "O father, what more could we want? Here are our goods, returned to us; we will provide for our family and preserve

our brother and have an additional camel-load; that is an easy measure."
He said, "I will not send him with you unless you give me a binding pledge before Allah that you will most surely bring him back to me, unless you get trapped." So when they gave him their binding pledge, he said, "Allah is over what we say a trustee." [14]

The Prophet ﷺ said: "The believer is not stung from the same hole twice."[15] For the first time since his moving display of beautiful patience, we once again hear the voice of Yaʿqūb. The brothers created a scene. The language is melodramatic and ostentatious. The way their response is relayed by Allah makes it seem as if they said, "Woe betide us! How we tried, but oh how tragically we failed! We were denied, father! Denied after a long and arduous travel from what we so eagerly sought out, for your and our families' sake! Send our brother with us, and we will surely take good care of him!"[16] This time, Yaʿqūb was not moved by their theatrics. He exclaimed back at his sons' request, "Should I entrust him to you as I did his brother before him?!" Yaʿqūb was not a credulous, naïve man. Though many decades ago, he had experienced that which justifiably made him wary of his sons' intentions. He has learnt from that ordeal. This a feature of the wakeful and prudent believer.

14 *Yūsuf*, 63-66.

15 Reported by Bukhārī (6133) on the authority of Abū Hurayrah.

16 The last statement: *wa innā lahū la-ḥāfiẓūn*—'we will most surely take good care of him', is the exact promise the brothers gave their father when they asked him to take Yūsuf with them all those years ago (Q 12:12). They were now making the same request with the very same wording for Binyāmīn (Q 12:63). Allah is emphasising the apparent similarity between the two instances.

TRANSFORMATIVE WISDOM

Though anyone can be deceived, it is not a sign of strong faith in Allah that one repeatedly fall for the same old trick. Once a person has shown you their true colours, it is not kindness to pretend like it never happened, rather foolishness. Unless amends have been appropriately made, one cannot deal with such a person in the same way again nor trust them without contingencies. Fool me once, shame on you; fool me twice, shame on me.

Yaʿqūb ﷺ was upon knowledge and guidance from Allah ﷻ.[17] He always related all matters back to his Lord and entrusted his affairs to Him ﷻ. He caveated the rebuke to his sons by saying, "Allah is best as a protector, and He is the most merciful of those who show mercy." It is as if he was saying, "Yes, I've lost a beloved son, but Allah is nonetheless the best of protectors and the most merciful of the merciful—He has a better plan for him. Yes, I'm taking care of my youngest lest he is met by a similar fate, but it is Allah who is the best of protectors and He is the most merciful of the merciful—He is the one who safeguards us and encompasses us in His mercy."

Furthermore, this is another subtle acknowledgement from Yaʿqūb ﷺ that it was through his sons' doing that Yūsuf ﷺ was lost. The first was his saying, "Your souls have prompted you to do an evil deed."[18] Now, he was implicitly incriminating them by telling them that, "You

17 This is explicitly mentioned later (Q 12:68), as discussed in the next subheading.

18 *Yūsuf*, 18.

really 'took care' of Yūsuf before such that I may let you 'take care' of Binyāmīn in the same way, right?"[19]

Dejected, the sons went to their luggage and opened their bags, and were surprised to find their goods therein. Yūsuf's prompt had the desired effect. Now, with further ammunition as to their benign intention, they said to Yaʿqūb 🌸, "Father, we are not here to create problems![20] Look, this is our merchandise—it has been returned to us. Let us then provide for our families, preserve our brother, and increase in a camel-load—what an easy measure!" Their case was certainly stronger now. As the patriarch, Yaʿqūb 🌸 knew best the needs of his wider family: each one of his sons had at least one wife, and each wife was likely to have borne many children. He may have even been a great-grandfather at this point. This Egyptian governor was clearly generous and seemed like he was going to be true to his word. Then again, Binyāmin... what was he to do?

As always, he brought things back to Allah 🌸. He said to his sons, "I will not send him with you unless you give me an oath in Allah's

---

19   There are more hints to come in the story that Yaʿqūb 🌸 did not believe his sons' account with regards to Yūsuf 🌸. For example, he later tells them, "Go and seek out Yūsuf and his brother" Q 12:87. He was confident he was still out there somewhere, and was not eaten by a wolf.

20   The Arabic states: *mā nabghī*. The particle *mā* has many possible usages in the Arabic language. The preferred understanding is that it is used for *istifhām*—to pose a question. That is: "What could we possibly want?" See the translation of the Qur'an passage quoted at the beginning of this sub-heading. In the current retelling of the story, the possibility is given for *nafy*—negation. That is: "We are not looking for any trouble." Naturally, the original conversation between Yaʿqūb 🌸 and his sons may have included both sentiments. The Qur'an narrates accounts—which often took place in languages other than Arabic—in a compendious, beautiful, pithy manner, with a perfect balance between giving the necessary information and withholding the irrelevant, allowing the recipient to contemplate the nature of the latter and its modality.

name that you will bring him back to me, unless you are overcome by unforeseen circumstances." Though he 🕮 capitulated to their demands, he did so with caution. He exercised additional protocols to ensure the return of his sons; and what better protocol than to have them swear by Allah that they will do their utmost best to return him. Notice the qualification at the end. He 🕮 said: *illā an yuḥāṭa bikum*—unless you are surrounded; i.e. by what you cannot resist: some unforeseen force majeure.

TRANSFORMATIVE WISDOM

Set people up for success, not failure. Do not set them unreasonable standards that they are sure to fall short of. Instead, give them a way out and clauses in case of the unforeseeable. The books of *fiqh* (jurisprudence) and *uṣūl al-fiqh* (legal theory) are replete with such stipulations and exceptions: "If this... then that... but if not... then this... and if that... then this..." That is how one nurtures a healthy environment for his subordinates to thrive and achieve.

Yaʿqūb 🕮 concluded just as he started: with a reminder of Allah 🕮 and His sovereignty. He said to his sons, "Allah is a trustee over our agreement. He is witness over what we say and is knowing of our intentions." Despite everything, these were men raised in a godly house, and appreciated what severe blasphemy it would be to take such a stringent oath in the name of Allah then break it. Allah 🕮 says about the pledge of allegiance to the Prophet 🕮: "Indeed, those who pledge allegiance to you are actually pledging allegiance to Allah: the hand of Allah is over their hands. So whoever reneges in fact reneges to his own detriment. And whoever fulfils what he has covenanted with Allah, then He will grant him a great reward."[21]

EVIL EYE

Yaʿqūb ﵇ acquiesced to his sons' request once they complied with his condition. It was a binding pledge in the Name of Allah ﷻ, witnessed by Him from above seven heavens—a heavy, stringent oath upon their shoulders. But he ﵇ was not yet finished. He had further dictates to delineate, founded upon intimate knowledge of Allah ﷻ and His commandments. Allah ﷻ says:

وَقَالَ يَا بَنِيَّ لَا تَدْخُلُوا مِنْ بَابٍ وَاحِدٍ وَادْخُلُوا مِنْ أَبْوَابٍ مُتَفَرِّقَةٍ
وَمَا أُغْنِي عَنْكُمْ مِنَ اللَّهِ مِنْ شَيْءٍ إِنِ الْحُكْمُ إِلَّا لِلَّهِ عَلَيْهِ
تَوَكَّلْتُ وَعَلَيْهِ فَلْيَتَوَكَّلِ الْمُتَوَكِّلُونَ ﴿٦٧﴾

وَلَمَّا دَخَلُوا مِنْ حَيْثُ أَمَرَهُمْ أَبُوهُمْ مَا كَانَ يُغْنِي عَنْهُمْ مِنَ اللَّهِ مِنْ
شَيْءٍ إِلَّا حَاجَةً فِي نَفْسِ يَعْقُوبَ قَضَاهَا وَإِنَّهُ لَذُو عِلْمٍ لِمَا
عَلَّمْنَاهُ وَلَٰكِنَّ أَكْثَرَ النَّاسِ لَا يَعْلَمُونَ ﴿٦٨﴾

❝ And he said, "O my sons! Go not in by one gate; go in by different gates. I can avail you naught against Allah. Judgement rests with Allah alone. In Him do I put my trust, and in Him let all the trusting put their trust." And when they entered in the manner which their father had enjoined, it would have availed them naught against Allah; it was but a

21 *al-Fatḥ*, 18.

need of Yaʿqūb's soul which he thus satisfied. He is most surely a person of knowledge inasmuch as We have taught him, but most of mankind know not. ❞[22]

The Prophet ﷺ said: "The evil eye (ʿ*ayn*) is true."[23] Allah ﷻ says: "Those who disbelieve would gladly strike you down with their eyes when they hear the Reminder and say, 'He is indeed a madman!'"[24] Ibn ʿAbbās, Mujāhid, and others said: "*layuzliqūnaka bi-abṣārihim*—'strike you down with their eyes' means: they will afflict you with evil eye... This *āyah* is evidence that the effect and impact of evil eye is real, but only happens by Allah's will."[25]

Thus, the believer is cognisant of evil eye and takes the appropriate measures to safeguard himself and his family from its harms. It certainly isn't the case that all problems go back to evil eye, as some among the masses would have us believe. But, contrary to what many modernists espouse, evil eye is undoubtedly true and has tangible repercussions. It would serve us well to act with balanced and moderate caution.

A part of this is to attribute all goodness to Allah ﷻ. Narrating a conversation between a God-fearing man and his misguided friend, Allah ﷻ quotes the former as saying: "If only, when you entered your garden, you had said, 'This is Allah's will; there is no power except

22 *Yūsuf*, 67-68.

23 Reported by Muslim (2188) on the authority of Ibn ʿAbbās ﷺ.

24 *al-Qalam*, 51.

25 Quoted by Ibn Kathīr ﷺ in his *Tafsīr* (4/408), commenting on the *āyah*.

through Allah (*mā shā'a Allāhu lā quwwata illā billāh*).'"[26] Another is to upkeep the morning and evening words of remembrance.[27] Additionally, there are certain regiments with regards to ritualistic bathing one should adhere to if they believe they have been afflicted with evil eye and they know its source.[28]

---

26 *al-Kahf*, 39. There are also many prophetic traditions to this effect. One should pray for another person with whom they see blessings, supplicating Allah: *Allāhumma bārik lahū*—'O Allah, bless him'; or: *Bāraka Allāhu lak*—'May Allah bless you.'

27 See 'Satanic Dreams' in Part XII for some examples. The well-known text *Ḥiṣn al-Muslim* (The Fortress of the Muslim) is a booklet with examples of these invocations as well as much more in terms of divine remembrance, all appropriated for space and time.

28 The full narration reported by Muslim (2188) reads: "The evil eye is real, and if anything were to overtake divine decree it would be the evil eye. If one of you is asked to wash [in order to provide water for its removal], let him do so." Thus, in a vessel of water, the one who is the cause of the evil eye should:

a. rinse out his mouth;
b. wash his face;
c. pour water over his right hand;
d. pour water over his left hand;
e. pour water over his right forearm;
f. pour water over his left forearm;
g. pour water over his right foot;
h. pour water over his left foot;
i. pour water over his right knee;
j. pour water over his left knee;

Note: All the above will be done above the vessel of water.

k. Place the waistband of his trousers in the vessel of water.

Once this procedure is completed, the water should be immediately poured over the affected individual's head from behind him. [*Sunan al-Bayhaqī* (9/252)]

DID YOU KNOW?

There is a difference between envy (*ḥasad*) and evil eye (*ʿayn*). Envy is accompanied by resentment, such that the envious one wishes that the blessing is removed from the envied. By contrast, the one who puts the evil eye on another merely admires something but does not remember Allah in that moment. Hence, the evil eye can come from a righteous person, and one can put the evil eye on one's own wealth, child, or family without realising it.

The sons of Yaʿqūb ☙ did not possess the beauty of Yūsuf ☙, but they were sure to have been handsome men. Now, they were going to return back to Egypt, to engage in more trade, within a short space of time, and with an additional younger brother.[29] It was an amalgam that was sure to draw bystanders' eyes—an unwelcome form of attention. Thus, after they gave him their word in a binding pact, and before they set off once again to Egypt, Yaʿqūb ☙ instructed his sons, "Do not enter altogether through a single gate. Rather, enter from various, separate gates." He continued, "I cannot avail you in the slightest from Allah: all judgement belongs to Him alone. I entrust my affairs unto Him, and so do all His trusting slaves." He ☙ makes it clear to his sons: Allah alone is in control of everything. While these are means to avoid potential harm, one can take all the means they possibly can yet still be afflicted if Allah so wills, or one may take none of the means yet be saved if He ☙ so wills.

29　Having a large number of sons has always been praiseworthy in traditional societies.

We take the means, but we do not rely on them. Instead, we rely on Allah to make the means effective.[30]

Allah ﷻ affirmed that this was a need of His slave which he fulfilled, and that this is an acceptable form of 'letting things out.' He ﷻ praised the knowledge of Yaʿqūb ﷺ, and that he adhered to that which his Lord had taught him.

REFLECT...

Especially as they get older, our parents may sometimes tell us to do things that they have already told us to do many times before, or things that may not manifestly make sense to us. Cherish their voice and their presence, for they will be dearly missed once they are absent from our lives.

30 See 'Tie Your Camel' in Part XI for more on the virtue of *tawakkul*.

PART

XVI

OPERATION BINYĀMĪN

Good fortune is when planning meets opportunity.

The brothers returned to Egypt, and this time with one extra sibling to add to their personnel. Yūsuf ﷺ had a plan, and he was going to masterfully execute it. He first drew his brother Binyāmīn to his private quarters and told him of his true identity, and that everything was going to be alright by the grace and mercy of Allah ﷻ. Allah ﷻ says:

وَلَمَّا دَخَلُوا عَلَىٰ يُوسُفَ آوَىٰ إِلَيْهِ أَخَاهُ قَالَ إِنِّي أَنَا أَخُوكَ فَلَا تَبْتَئِسْ بِمَا كَانُوا يَعْمَلُونَ ﴿٦٩﴾

فَلَمَّا جَهَّزَهُم بِجَهَازِهِمْ جَعَلَ السِّقَايَةَ فِي رَحْلِ أَخِيهِ ثُمَّ أَذَّنَ مُؤَذِّنٌ أَيَّتُهَا الْعِيرُ إِنَّكُمْ لَسَارِقُونَ ﴿٧٠﴾

قَالُوا وَأَقْبَلُوا عَلَيْهِم مَّاذَا تَفْقِدُونَ ﴿٧١﴾

قَالُوا نَفْقِدُ صُوَاعَ الْمَلِكِ وَلِمَن جَاءَ بِهِ حِمْلُ بَعِيرٍ وَأَنَا بِهِ زَعِيمٌ ﴿٧٢﴾

❝ When they presented themselves before Yūsuf, he drew his brother close to him. He said, "Indeed it is I—I am your brother, so do not be saddened by what they used to do." And when he provided them with their provision, he put the drinking-cup in his brother's saddlebag, and then a crier cried, "O camel-riders! You are surely thieves!" They said, coming toward them, "What is it that you have lost?" They said, "We have lost the king's cup, and he who brings it shall have a camel-load, and I am answerable for it." ❞[1]

1 *Yūsuf*, 69-72.

BROTHERS REUNITE

Once his brothers returned with Binyāmīn, the first thing Yūsuf 🕮 did was draw him close away from everyone else, tell him who he was, and give him solace, comfort, and affection. One's eyes well up contemplating this brotherly reunion and how moving it must have been. Binyāmīn would have been very young when his brother disappeared from his life. They weren't too far from one another in age, and were from the same mother. Throughout his life, Binyāmīn would have constantly felt the physical, intellectual, and spiritual hole Yūsuf 🕮 left behind in his absence. The rest of his brothers were much older than he was, and were somewhat cold towards him and sometimes even hostile. He missed the warmth and stability provided by a loving older brother. Now, there they were, Yūsuf 🕮 and Binyāmīn, brought back together through Allah's gentle decree.

> ## TRANSFORMATIVE WISDOM
>
> It is from the love and mercy that Allah 🕮 has placed in the hearts of man that we are naturally drawn in affection towards our brothers, especially our blood-brothers. We must honour and serve our siblings at every available opportunity.

After many difficulties, unrelenting, one after the other, Allah 🕮 was now giving Yūsuf 🕮 ease after ease, opening after opening, and manifest[2] mercy after manifest mercy. He was kidnapped, abducted, thrown into the depths of a well, sold into slavery, seduced by his

---

2   Allah 🕮 was, is, and always will be merciful, even at times of constriction and hardship. The difference is between mercy that is made manifest, and mercy that is hidden.

mistress, unjustly thrown into prison, and forgotten about for many years by a man whom he helped. Then, his innocence was publicly declared, he was brought before the king of Egypt, appointed as his minister, became the source of unprecedented regional prosperity, had his brothers returned to stand before him, and was finally re-united with his dearest sibling. Allah ﷻ is the master planner, and nothing can delay or avert His final decree. "Allah always prevails in His affairs, though most people do not know."[3] Everything was coming back full circle.[4]

Allah ﷻ says: "He is the one who created death and life to test you who is best in deed."[5] We are only ever accountable for what we do—our actions and the intentions behind them. The Prophet ﷺ said: "Actions are in accordance with their intentions, and each person will be given what they intended."[6] Where we place our concerted effort and what we seek out in our lives is what Allah ﷻ will question us about. Outcomes are not in our hands. It is our deeds which we will witness before us on the Last Day, not whether or not some goal was accomplished.

Allah ﷻ says: "They found what they had done present before them; your Lord does not wrong anyone."[7] He ﷻ also says: "Say, 'Act! For Allah will behold your actions; and so will His Messenger and the believers. Then, you will be returned to the knower of the unseen and the witnessed, and He will tell you what you used to do.'"[8] Everyone

3 *Yūsuf*, 21.

4 See 'Timeless Perfection' (the coherent structure of the story) in Part IV for more on this.

5 *al-Mulk*, 2.

6 Reported by Bukhārī (54) and Muslim (1907).

7 *al-Kahf*, 49.

8 *al-Tawbah*, 105.

will witness the deeds that everyone else did. May that day be one where we are all proud of what we put forth, jovially receiving our record of deeds with our right, happily rejoicing to all, "Here! Read my book!"[9] May it not be a day where we receive it with our left, hiding it behind our backs, ashamed of what it contains, biting our tongues in regret saying, "Oh would that I had not been given my book!"[10]

REFLECT...

We should view tests and tribulations as a means to prove ourselves to Allah ﷻ and earn His love. The choicest of Allah's slaves are the most tested, and our share of love is proportional to our share of righteous deeds and perseverance during testing times. Thereafter, the *sunnah* (way and nature) of Allah ﷻ is to bring about ease after hardship.

The first words we are told Yūsuf ﷺ said to Binyāmīn were, "It is me, your brother, so do not grieve over what they used to do." Every opportunity Yūsuf ﷺ is presented with is one where he orients all matters to Allah ﷻ. He tells his brother, "Do not be sad about what they did to me, what they did to our father, and what they undoubtedly also did to you. Allah is the best of planners, and He shall set everything aright, just as He brought us back together."

As mentioned in the previous chapter, this constant realignment with divine principles is a feature of Yaʿqūb ﷺ and his speech. Allah ﷻ says: "With this (*islām*[11]), Ibrāhīm frequently enjoined his children,

9 *al-Ḥāqqah*, 19.

10 *al-Ḥāqqah*, 25.

11 The transliteration is deliberate. 'Islam' is the final revelatory dispensation to humanity:

and so did Yaʿqūb,[12] 'O my children, Allah has indeed chosen for you the religion, so do not die except as men who have surrendered to Him (*muslimūn*[13]).' Or were you witnesses when death approached Yaʿqūb, and he said to his children, 'What will you worship after me?' They said, 'We will worship your God and the God of your fathers, Ibrāhīm, Ismāʿīl, and Isḥāq: One God, and to Him we submit ourselves in devotion (*muslimūn*).'"[14] In the short years he was reared under his care and tutelage, Yūsuf ﷺ gained a great deal of foundational knowledge from his father, Yaʿqūb ﷺ. As they say, like father like son.[15]

As promised, Yūsuf ﷺ gave his brothers what they came for. However, he ensured that an important artefact was slid into Binyāmīn's luggage: the king's goblet,[16] a measuring as well as a drinking uten-

---

the Prophet ﷺ and the Qur'an. However, *islām* is what all believers, prophets, and messengers are upon, from the time of Ādam ﷺ until the Trumpet is blown and the Last Day is established. This latter rendition—*islām*—is submission and devotion to the one true God, regardless of the particular legislative specifics relative to space and time.

12 A valid, alternate *qirāʾah* renders the meaning: "With this Ibrāhīm frequently enjoined his children and Yaʿqūb." That is: Ibrāhīm ﷺ reminded his direct children (Ismāʿīl and Isḥāq ﷺ) as well as his grandson (Yaʿqūb ﷺ) about the centrality of the Divine ﷻ in all our lives. The main body translation renders the meaning: Ibrāhīm frequently enjoined his children towards *islām*, and Yaʿqūb also frequently enjoined his children towards *islām*. Naturally, the two variant recitations are complimentary and non-contradictory, enriching the meaning and diversifying it. This is especially obvious since the next *āyah* quotes Yaʿqūb ﷺ reminding his children of Allah ﷻ.

13 Similarly to the earlier footnote, a 'Muslim' is a follower of the Prophet ﷺ and an adherent to Islam. A *muslim* (fem: *muslimah*; pl: *muslimūn*) is someone who has surrendered, submitted, and devoted themselves to the Supreme Creator and Sustainer; regardless of their time and place.

14 *al-Baqarah*, 132-133.

15 For more on their intimate relationship prior to the abduction of Yūsuf ﷺ, see Part V.

16 In his commentary on Q 12:70, Ṭabarī ﷺ said: "The *siqāyah* is a drinking utensil. It is the goblet whence the king would drink and measure his food."

sil. By the time the caravan was setting off back to Canaan, the fact it was missing had been noticed and word immediately spread: who else was in the palace other than these wayfaring Canaanites? It must have been them![17] They were called out to: "Camel-riders! You are surely thieves!" Bewildered, they turned back in the caller's direction and asked, "What are you missing?" Notice that a thief, when found, usually shoots off away from the one he stole from. On this occasion, they were wholly truthful. The brothers are willingly going back without hesitation: they know they are in the clear.

Once they had turned back and the guards had reached them, Yūsuf ﷺ himself[18] said, "We are missing the king's goblet. Whoever comes forth with it will have a camelback's worth of goods, and I am here to guarantee it."[19] Once again, no one stepped forward since they were being completely honest. This is the first of two occasions where the brothers interact with transparency and truthfulness without a

---

17 Ṭabarī ﷺ offers the following scenario: "He (Yūsuf ﷺ) supplied them with their supplies, honoured them, gave them their due and more. He prepared camel after camel for them, and prepared a camel for his brother (Binyāmīn) specifically just as he did for them. He then asked for the king's goblet (*siqāyah*)—it is the same as the *ṣuwāʿ* (chalice)—and placed it in Binyāmīn's saddlebag. He waited until they had set off and gained a fair distance from the township, then ordered that they be stopped, and so they were halted. A caller then called out, **'O caravan, you are thieves indeed!** [Q 12:70] Stop!' His (Yūsuf's ﷺ) emissary reached them and said, 'Did we not nobly host you, grant you your measures in full, honour your stay, treat you like we have never treated others like you, and even entered you into our homes?!' Or the like. They (the brothers) replied, 'You did indeed. What's the matter?' He replied, 'The king's goblet: it's missing! We do not know anyone who could've taken it but you.' They said, **'By Allah, you know we have not come to do corruption in the land and we are not thieves!'** [Q 12:73]"

18 What makes it likely that it was Yūsuf that replied here is the fact that he gives himself as a guarantor for another camel-load for the one who finds the goblet. A messenger wouldn't usually have such authority.

19 Jurisprudential fields like *jaʿālah* (advertising a reward for some desired deed), *wakālah* (trusteeship), and *kafālah* (employing guarantors) all benefit greatly from this passage.

secondary agenda.[20] Compare their rhetoric and mannerisms here to when they abducted Yūsuf and sold him into slavery then returned to their father with crocodile tears and a concocted narrative. The contrast is even clearer when they are forced to return to their father without their youngest sibling for the second time, but this time due to no fault of their own.[21] It is a direct case-for-case comparison with fascinating psychological implications.

MISSION ACCOMPLISHED

The brothers were confident in their occupying the moral high ground. They were innocent after all, and had nothing to hide. As far as they were concerned, the governor—Yūsuf —was free to check whatever and whomever he wanted. Little did they know that the orchestration was about to reach its crescendo. Allah says:

قَالُوا تَاللَّهِ لَقَدْ عَلِمْتُم مَّا جِئْنَا لِنُفْسِدَ فِي الْأَرْضِ وَمَا كُنَّا سَارِقِينَ ﴿٧٣﴾

قَالُوا فَمَا جَزَاؤُهُ إِن كُنتُمْ كَاذِبِينَ ﴿٧٤﴾

قَالُوا جَزَاؤُهُ مَن وُجِدَ فِي رَحْلِهِ فَهُوَ جَزَاؤُهُ كَذَٰلِكَ نَجْزِي الظَّالِمِينَ ﴿٧٥﴾

فَبَدَأَ بِأَوْعِيَتِهِمْ قَبْلَ وِعَاءِ أَخِيهِ ثُمَّ اسْتَخْرَجَهَا مِن وِعَاءِ أَخِيهِ كَذَٰلِكَ كِدْنَا
لِيُوسُفَ مَا كَانَ لِيَأْخُذَ أَخَاهُ فِي دِينِ الْمَلِكِ إِلَّا أَن يَشَاءَ اللَّهُ نَرْفَعُ دَرَجَاتٍ مَّن
نَّشَاءُ وَفَوْقَ كُلِّ ذِي عِلْمٍ عَلِيمٌ ﴿٧٦﴾

20 The second is when they go back to their father without Binyāmīn.

21 See the next chapter, Part XVII, for more on this.

“ They said, “By Allah, you know well we came not to do evil in the land and are no thieves.” They said, “So what shall be the penalty for it, if you prove liars?” They said, “The penalty for it! He in whose bag it is found, he is the penalty for it. Thus we requite the wrong-doers.” Then he began with their bags before his brother’s bag, then he produced it from his brother’s bag. Thus did We plan for Yūsuf. He could not have taken his brother according to the king’s law unless Allah willed. We raise in stations whom We will, and over every possessor of knowledge there is one more knowing. ”[22]

Confused at the callers’ behest, the brothers retorted: "You know us. We’ve come here before, and you have just graciously hosted us. Why would we ruin such a fantastic means of economic recourse for petty gain? We know not how long this famine will last, and we hope to maintain our trade in Egypt. We are not here to spread corruption and we are not thieves!" Straightforward, logical, and transparent discourse. Such is the power of being truthful.

REFLECT...

There is an immense empowerment to adhering to truth. Speaking firmly about what you know and remaining silent about what you don’t will never fail you. On the other hand, those who dance around the truth will eventually slip and fall on it. When a person makes one lie, they will often have to make a dozen others to ensure the first one sticks, and will inevitably trip up when they later have to recall them.

22 *Yūsuf*, 73-76.

The question was now posed to the band of brothers: "What then is the recompense for this misdeed if you turn out to be lying?" Boldly, the brothers replied, "The recompense? It is the thief himself! They become the recompense if they have stolen—the one from whom they stole takes them as a slave! That is how we punish the wrong-doer in our land."[23] Yūsuf ﵇ heard exactly what he needed to hear. Unknowingly, the brothers had perfectly set themselves up for Yūsuf ﵇ to take Binyāmīn away from them. Yūsuf ﵇ started searching their supplies first, then finally withdrew the lost goblet from his brother's bag. Had he done otherwise, it would have potentially roused the suspicion of those present, making it appear like a setup.

This is how Allah ﷻ established Yūsuf ﵇ and granted him the ability to win Binyāmīn from the rest of his brothers. The way He ﷻ planned everything was perfect. But for their admission of the thief's punishment according to Canaanite law, Yūsuf ﵇ would not have been able to take his brother. But even then, it is possible if Allah ﷻ wills it! He ﷻ says: "Thus did We plan for Yūsuf. He could not have taken his brother according to the king's law unless Allah willed." Allah ﷻ reminds us that what binds and limits us does not bind and limit Him ﷻ. Where we need proximal causes, He ﷻ is free of need. There is nothing that can resist Him or delay His decree: Allah ﷻ does as He wills, whenever He wills, wherever He wills, to whomever He wills, however He wills. Above each possessor of knowledge is another more knowledgeable, until we reach the source and owner of all knowledge: the Knowing, the Omniscient, exalted be He.

---

23 This is clarified when Allah ﷻ says: "He (Yūsuf ﵇) would not have been able to take his brother by the law of the king (i.e. Egyptian law)" Q 12:76. Canaanite law was ideal to invoke in this specific scenario. And it didn't come from Yūsuf ﵇, but from the horse's mouth, as they say. Such is the subtlety of Allah in His decree.

DID YOU KNOW?

Muslims have formalised an accreditation system for seeking sacred knowledge known as *ijāzah*. It literally means 'permission', and acts as a seal of approval from the teacher to their student that the latter has mastered the science or text in question to a satisfactory level. The teacher dictates the satisfactory level, as it was set for him by his teachers, and their teachers for them, and theirs for them, and so on. This is known as a *sanad*—an unbroken chain of transmission. Depending on the science, the *sanad* may go back all the way to the Prophet ﷺ, to Jibrīl ﷺ, to the Lord of the Worlds ﷻ. Truly: "Above every possessor of knowledge is One Most Knowledgeable." Q 12:76

PLEA

Havoc ensued. The brothers were in utter disarray. Binyāmīn stole?! He was to become a servant to this governor?! They were entrusted with him and took a binding, stringent oath before Allah that they were to take good care of him and bring him back safe and sound to his father. The very real possibility of them having to return to Yaʿqūb ﷺ without his youngest son, and that for the second time, was too much for them to handle. What to do? What to say? In a frenzy, and almost in a state of delirium, they started hurling excuses and pleas at the minister. Allah ﷻ says:

قَالُوا إِنْ يَسْرِقْ فَقَدْ سَرَقَ أَخٌ لَهُ مِنْ قَبْلُ فَأَسَرَّهَا يُوسُفُ فِي نَفْسِهِ وَلَمْ يُبْدِهَا
لَهُمْ قَالَ أَنْتُمْ شَرٌّ مَكَانًا وَاللَّهُ أَعْلَمُ بِمَا تَصِفُونَ ﴿٧٧﴾

قَالُوا يَا أَيُّهَا الْعَزِيزُ إِنَّ لَهُ أَبًا شَيْخًا كَبِيرًا فَخُذْ أَحَدَنَا مَكَانَهُ
إِنَّا نَرَاكَ مِنَ الْمُحْسِنِينَ ﴿٧٨﴾

قَالَ مَعَاذَ اللَّهِ أَنْ نَأْخُذَ إِلَّا مَنْ وَجَدْنَا مَتَاعَنَا عِنْدَهُ إِنَّا إِذًا لَظَالِمُونَ ﴿٧٩﴾

❝ They said, "If he steals, well, a brother of his has stolen before." But Yūsuf kept it secret within himself and did not reveal it to them: he said, "You are in a worse situation, and Allah knows best what you describe." They said, "O mighty governor, he has a father—a very old man, so take one of us in his place; we see that you are of the good-doers." He said, "Allah forbid that we should seize except him with whom we found our property; then truly we should be wrong-doers." ❞[24]

"His brother also stole from before!"[25] In a moment of madness, the brothers tried to excuse Binyāmīn's theft by the fact that, supposedly, he had this older brother—the aforementioned deceased full-sibling—who did the same before, and Binyāmīn was just following in

24 *Yūsuf*, 77-79.

25 There are various accounts mentioned by exegetes as to what prompted the brothers to make such an accusation, none of which are authentic, nor is this information critical to the narrative. What seems to be clear, though, is that they wished to clear their own names from such a heinous deed. They had proudly proclaimed before in self-defense, "You know well we are not here to do evil and we are not thieves!" Q 12:73. Caught red-handed, they wished to avert the blame away from themselves and their lineage and onto Binyāmīn and Yūsuf's mother's side.

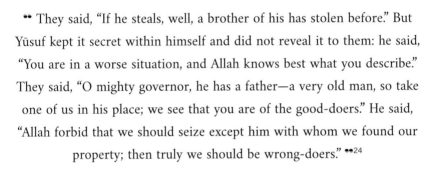

his footsteps: it's in his blood from his mother's side, and he didn't know any better. It was a knee-jerk reaction.

To behold another unprovoked slander to his name, said directly to his face, from his own blood-brothers and once-abductors, after he had fulfilled their trade in full, and said only so that they may clear their own reputations... there are levels to moral excellence, and that of Yūsuf ﷺ can only be described as prophetic! He maintained decorum despite his brothers' brazen accusation. He withheld from externalising his discontent and disappointment, saying within himself,[26] "Oh how low you have stooped—Allah knows best the falsity that you describe!"[27]

Once they came to their senses, they changed tactics, and tried to give the governor any reasonable alternative. They couldn't possibly face their father without Binyāmīn. "O minister, his father is an old man, and we have told you about the intense love he has for him. Please, take any one of us in his stead! We see that you are among the good-doers." The latter statement reads: *Innā narāka min al-muḥsinīn*. Where have we heard Yūsuf ﷺ being recognised as a *muḥsin* before? In the dark, desolate depths of his dungeon all those years ago, Yūsuf ﷺ was acknowledged by all around him as a *muḥsin*. This very statement was uttered by his then-inmates when

26 Zajjāj and Zamakhsharī ﷺ—among other qur'anic commentators—consider this statement to have been said internally; i.e. Yūsuf ﷺ to himself. This is supported by the statement right before: "Yūsuf concealed it within himself and did not reveal it to them, saying..."

27 As the poet said:

إِنَّ الْكَلَامَ لَفِي الْفُؤَادِ وَإِنَّمَا ∴ جُعِلَ اللِّسَانُ عَلَى الْفُؤَادِ دَلِيلاً

"Verily, speech is found in the heart; and
The tongue is made for the heart as its outlet."

they approached him for their dreams to be interpreted.[28] It is his *iḥsān*—excellence and beneficence—which the brothers chose to cite when imploring Yūsuf ﷺ to change his mind.

REFLECT...

The complete believer is he who strikes and defines moments, not him who allows the moment to strike and define him.

Yūsuf ﷺ replied with *istiʿādhah*[29]: "Allah forbid! I seek refuge in Him. We shan't take anyone other than him whose bag carried the chalice,[30] otherwise we would be wrong-doers!" He turned the tables against them: if he were to remain a good-doer, he would have to adhere to justice, and justice dictates that the thief—and only the thief—be punished.

28 See Q 12:36.

29 Another reference to his father's lesson to him as a child: "Indeed, the devil is a clear enemy to man" Q 12:5.

30 The wording is interesting here. Yūsuf ﷺ said: "We will not take anyone except the one with whom we found our property." He did not explicitly accuse anyone of stealing and so was able to maintain truthfulness despite the circumstances. Earlier, it was his workers—not him—who called out to the brothers and told them, "Surely you are thieves" Q 12:70. Exegetes offer further possibilities as to how Yūsuf ﷺ avoided lying, but this seems a clean and smooth explanation befitting of a prophet of Allah.

PART

XVII

THE GREAT REVEAL

Good things may come to those who wait; but great things come to those who persevere.

The brothers were in utter despair. Beg as they might, the minister—Yūsuf ﷺ—was not going to budge. They had spelled out the penalty for theft to him themselves, and their brother, the one whom their father entrusted them with, had been caught red-handed. They exhausted all options, but no expiations nor substitutions were going to be accepted. Having finally given up, they convened among themselves. Allah ﷻ says:

فَلَمَّا اسْتَيْأَسُوا مِنْهُ خَلَصُوا نَجِيًّا قَالَ كَبِيرُهُمْ أَلَمْ تَعْلَمُوا أَنَّ أَبَاكُمْ قَدْ أَخَذَ عَلَيْكُمْ مَوْثِقًا مِنَ اللَّهِ وَمِنْ قَبْلُ مَا فَرَّطْتُمْ فِي يُوسُفَ فَلَنْ أَبْرَحَ الْأَرْضَ حَتَّى يَأْذَنَ لِي أَبِي أَوْ يَحْكُمَ اللَّهُ لِي وَهُوَ خَيْرُ الْحَاكِمِينَ ﴿٨٠﴾

ارْجِعُوا إِلَى أَبِيكُمْ فَقُولُوا يَا أَبَانَا إِنَّ ابْنَكَ سَرَقَ وَمَا شَهِدْنَا إِلَّا بِمَا عَلِمْنَا وَمَا كُنَّا لِلْغَيْبِ حَافِظِينَ ﴿٨١﴾

وَاسْأَلِ الْقَرْيَةَ الَّتِي كُنَّا فِيهَا وَالْعِيرَ الَّتِي أَقْبَلْنَا فِيهَا وَإِنَّا لَصَادِقُونَ ﴿٨٢﴾

قَالَ بَلْ سَوَّلَتْ لَكُمْ أَنْفُسُكُمْ أَمْرًا فَصَبْرٌ جَمِيلٌ عَسَى اللَّهُ أَنْ يَأْتِيَنِي بِهِمْ جَمِيعًا إِنَّهُ هُوَ الْعَلِيمُ الْحَكِيمُ ﴿٨٣﴾

❝ So when they completely despaired of him, they conferred privately. Their eldest said, "Do you not know that your father took a binding pledge from you before Allah, and in the past you failed with regard to Yūsuf? Therefore, I will not leave this land until my father permits me or Allah judges for me, for He is the best of judges. Go back to your father and say, "Our father, your son has committed theft, and we do not testify except what we know, and we could not guard against the unseen. Ask the town where we were and the caravan in which we came, for indeed, we are truthful." He said, "Rather, your souls have tempted you to do something. So, a comely patience! It may be that Allah will bring them all unto me. Indeed, He—only He—is the Knowing, the Wise. ﴾[1]

DÉJÀ VU

The daunting reality of their circumstances had dawned on the band of brothers. Discussing the magnitude of the situation they found themselves in, the eldest[2] among them announced: "Do you not realise that your father has taken a covenant from Allah binding you to bring Binyāmīn back to him?! And, before this, you failed him and broke his heart with regards to Yūsuf. He will never believe us! I will not leave Egypt until my father permits me or Allah ordains a matter for me,[3] He is the most judicious of judges." To uphold the oath he

1 *Yūsuf*, 80-83.

2 Notice how the identity of the speaker is highlighted here compared to when the brothers plotted against Yūsuf ﷺ. As per many commentators' view, it is the same person on both occasions—the eldest brother. However, when they were scheming, Allah hid his identity to conceal his sin, but made it known when he was advising his brothers and heeding the promise he made to his father. Allah ﷻ loves to conceal the ugly and manifest the beautiful. The Prophet ﷺ said: "Whoever covers up [the weakness and unintentional shortcomings of] a Muslim, Allah will cover up for him on the Day of Resurrection." Reported by Bukhārī (2442). See 'Unseen Protection' in Part VI for more on this.

3 Exegetes differ regarding what is being referred to here: either it is that Allah decrees events such that the eldest brother is allowed to return without Binyāmīn, or that He leg-

made with his father, the oldest[4] among the brothers was not returning with the rest of the clan. He was to remain behind as a token of
their truthfulness. The rest were to go back to their father not one,
but two brothers short.

"Go back to your father", Ra'ūbīn continued his counsel to his brothers, "And say, 'Dear father, your son stole, and we can only testify to
that which we know, and we cannot guarantee the unseen! Ask the
town we were in and the caravan we came in to ascertain our claim.
We are telling the truth!'" The tone which they strike with Ya'qūb ✽
on this occasion is markedly different from the one they adopted
when giving their excuses for losing Yūsuf ✽. Here, it is candid truth
claims with an open invitation to prove them via impartial testimony.
There,[5] it was a projection of their father's insecurities back onto
him and a clumsy—though telling—shirking of responsibility: "You
wouldn't believe us even if we were telling the truth." On this occa-

---

islates fighting for him until he is either overwhelmed or successful in taking his brother
away from the minister. Ṭabarī ✽ says: "Aw yaḥkuma Allāhu lī—'Or Allah judges for me':
i.e. that Allah ordains I leave it (Egypt) and leave Binyāmīn behind." He then quotes a
view that it refers to taking up arms. Qurṭubī ✽ offers an incredibly lengthy and vivid
account regarding how the brothers were going to fight for Binyāmīn but were ultimately
subdued by Yūsuf ✽.

4   This is the most accurate understanding. Some exegetes understand kabīruhum—literally, 'the biggest'—in a figurative sense, referring to the wisest among the brothers—
Sham'ūn—as opposed to the oldest—Ra'ūbīn. It is the latter who addressed the brothers
as opposed to the former. Ṭabarī ✽ says in this regard: "The best claim to veracity made
on this discussion is by those who opined that kabīruhum refers to Rūbīl (an alternative
spelling of 'Ra'ūbīn', 'Reuben' in English). By consensus, he was the oldest. The Arabs do
not know from the usage of kabīr al-qawm—the senior of a people—anything save two
understandings: the chieftain of a people or the greatest in age among them. As for reason and sagacity, they would add it explicitly as a qualification: kabīruhum fī al-'aql—the
most senior in intellect."

5   See Q 12:16-18.

sion, they offered their father an objective and verifiable description of events. Before, they offered him a fanciful tale which he had unwittingly served them on a silver platter, and a stone-cold double bluff of the highest order. The qur'anic storytelling is impeccable in its subtlety and precision!

Notwithstanding their truthfulness, Yaʿqūb ﷺ was traumatised. For him, it was another inexcusable breaking of trust. He is perfectly justified for not believing them. He had been stung from this hole before, and, given their history, had no reason to accept their narrative at face value. "No! Rather, your lower selves have enticed you to do something!" He lambasted them. It is as if he was telling them, "Again I trusted you, and yet again you fail me!" Despite his unimaginable hurt, Yaʿqūb ﷺ concluded with *ṣabr* (patience) and *ḥusn al-ẓann* (thinking well) of Allah ﷻ. He said, "Most fitting for me is a beautiful patience, then. Perhaps Allah will bring them all back to me. Indeed, He and He alone is the Knowing, the Wise."

TRANSFORMATIVE WISDOM

If you've failed someone before, you must excuse them if they are unable to immediately offer you the same trust again. It takes time to heal, and, having been hurt before, it is wise on their behalf to be wary. It is not to say you will fail them again, but it is human nature to exercise caution.

MERCY IN GRIEF

Yaʿqūb 🌿 had heard enough. As far as he was concerned, his sons were entrusted with the youngest among them—of whom they were jealous—and have returned without him, and this for the second time in their lives. Even the most stringent oaths of his safety were insufficient to ensure his return. Not only that, his eldest son also stayed behind. Three of his sons were now missing. It was all too much to bear. Allah 🌿 says:

وَتَوَلَّىٰ عَنْهُمْ وَقَالَ يَا أَسَفَىٰ عَلَىٰ يُوسُفَ وَابْيَضَّتْ عَيْنَاهُ مِنَ الْحُزْنِ فَهُوَ كَظِيمٌ ﴿٨٤﴾

قَالُوا تَاللَّهِ تَفْتَأُ تَذْكُرُ يُوسُفَ حَتَّىٰ تَكُونَ حَرَضًا أَوْ تَكُونَ مِنَ الْهَالِكِينَ ﴿٨٥﴾

قَالَ إِنَّمَا أَشْكُو بَثِّي وَحُزْنِي إِلَى اللَّهِ وَأَعْلَمُ مِنَ اللَّهِ مَا لَا تَعْلَمُونَ ﴿٨٦﴾

يَا بَنِيَّ اذْهَبُوا فَتَحَسَّسُوا مِنْ يُوسُفَ وَأَخِيهِ وَلَا تَيْأَسُوا مِنْ رَوْحِ اللَّهِ إِنَّهُ لَا يَيْأَسُ مِنْ رَوْحِ اللَّهِ إِلَّا الْقَوْمُ الْكَافِرُونَ ﴿٨٧﴾

⁜ He turned away from them and said, "Alas, my grief for Yūsuf!" And his eyes turned white with sorrow that he was suppressing. They said, "By Allah, You will not cease remembering Yūsuf till your health is ruined or you become of those who perish!" He said, "I do not complain of my anguish and sorrow to anyone but Allah, and I know from Allah what you do not know. O my sons, go and find out about Yūsuf and his brother and despair not of relief from Allah. Indeed, no one despairs of relief from Allah except the disbelieving people. ⁜"[6]

6 *Yūsuf*, 84-87.

One of the greatest mercies within prophecy is that the prophets ﷺ were human. Allah ﷻ says: "Allah has been truly gracious to the believers in sending them a messenger from among their own."[7] He ﷻ also says: "There has come to you a messenger from among yourselves. Grievous to him is what you suffer, full of concern for you, for the believers full of pity, merciful."[8] Had Allah ﷻ sent angels as moral exemplars for us fallible beings, there would be no hope for emulation. That the unbelievers of each community were unimpressed at the humanity of their prophet is a sign of their spiritual blindness. After listing some of the ludicrous demands the spiritually blind made to the Messenger of Allah ﷺ, Allah ﷻ says: "Say, 'My Lord be glorified! Am I anything but a mortal messenger?' And nothing prevented mankind from believing when the guidance came unto them except that they said, 'Has Allah sent a mortal as messenger?' Say, 'If there were angels on earth walking around in peace, We would have bestowed upon them from heaven an angel messenger.'"[9]

Sadness, grief, and sorrow do not contravene patience, so long as they are expressed within a framework of reliance upon Allah ﷻ and trust in His plan. At the passing of his son Ibrāhīm, the eyes of the Prophet ﷺ welled up and he said: "Surely do the eyes tear, and does the heart sadden, and we say naught save what pleases our Lord. By Allah, Ibrāhīm, we are saddened at your parting."[10]

To this day, Yaʿqūb ﷺ remains a paragon of patience. Nonetheless, he was deeply grief-stricken at the loss of not one, but three of his children: Yūsuf ﷺ, Binyāmin, and Raʾūbīn. He turned away from his

7 *Āl ʿImrān*, 164.

8 *al-Tawbah*, 128.

9 *al-Isrāʾ*, 93-95.

10 Reported by Bukhārī (1303) and Muslim (2315).

sons, tears flowing unabated, overtaken by the heartache of severance. So much did he 🕮 weep that his eyes went white and he could no longer see. "Alas! Oh my Yūsuf... how sorrowful I am for your loss!" The scenario took him back to his first tragedy when he lost young Yūsuf all those decades ago. His hurt was compounded, and it was a heavy load to bear.

His sons, wishing to console him in any way, said to him, "Father! You are destroying your health in your grief! Please, father, for your own wellbeing, rest easy!" He responded, "You do not understand. I complain of my sorrow only to Allah, and outpour my sadness unto Him alone—I know from Him what you know not!" In his distress, Ya'qūb 🕮 sought none other than Allah 🕮 as his emotional outlet and source of solace. Furthermore, he said to them, "My sons, go forth and look for any traces of Yūsuf and his brother and never despair of relief from Allah. Surely, only the disbelieving people despair of relief from Allah." Despite incomprehensible loss and overwhelming sadness, Ya'qūb 🕮 reminded his sons of Allah's mercy.

REFLECT...

The mercy of Allah ﷻ is incomprehensibly vast. Every manifestation of compassion we witness in this world is but 1 of 100 divine mercies—99 are reserved for the Hereafter! (Bukhārī 6000) When it comes to sinning, Allah's mercy is such that thinking we would not be forgiven for our sin is a greater sin than the sin itself—regardless of what it was! Allah ﷻ quotes Ibrāhīm ﷺ in the Qur'an as saying: "Who despairs of his Lord's mercy except those astray?!" [Q 15:56] In an immensely optimistic passage, Allah ﷻ says: "Say, 'O My servants who have gone to extremes against themselves: despair not of Allah's mercy, for indeed Allah forgives all misdeeds; indeed, He is the Forgiving, the Merciful.'" Q 39:53

Islam is a holistic and complete way of life which caters for every component of the human composite. Our religion is *islām*, *īmān*, and *iḥsān*; respectively adhering to the needs of the body, mind, and spirit.[11] Our physical, intellectual, and spiritual powers are all interlinked. A bashful person blushes when shy, an angry person's veins show as they hyperventilate, and a depressed, broken soul renders the body of its possessor weak and frail. Highlighting the inseparability of mental poise and proper conduct, the Prophet ﷺ said: "Let no judge rule between two people while he is angry."[12] A judge who

11 See Bukhārī (50) and Muslim (9) for what has become known as *Ḥadīth Jibrīl*—The Narration of Gabriel ﷺ. At its conclusion, the Prophet ﷺ says: "It was Jibrīl, he came to teach you your religion."

12 Bukhārī (7158) and Muslim (1717).

is internally in a state of upheaval and turmoil cannot reason as effectively as one whose soul is steady and tranquil.

Ya'qūb ☙ was emotionally distressed to a severe degree. It is perhaps this, not just his tears, that led to his physical blindness.[13] By the same token, it was likely the emotional relief of knowing Yūsuf ☙ is well and awaiting him that helped in recovering his sight.[14] Allah knows best.

ENDGAME

The brothers heeded their father's advice. For the third time, they packed and set off for Egypt. On this occasion, though, a despondent mood was in the air as only nine of them went on their way. To add insult to injury, the brothers were returning to the minister with meagre goods. They had nothing of value to trade. Impoverished, and with a distant hope of their brother's retrieval, they presented themselves to the governor. Allah ☙ says:

فَلَمَّا دَخَلُوا عَلَيْهِ قَالُوا يَا أَيُّهَا الْعَزِيزُ مَسَّنَا وَأَهْلَنَا الضُّرُّ وَجِئْنَا بِبِضَاعَةٍ مُزْجَاةٍ فَأَوْفِ لَنَا الْكَيْلَ وَتَصَدَّقْ عَلَيْنَا إِنَّ اللَّهَ يَجْزِي الْمُتَصَدِّقِينَ ﴿٨٨﴾

قَالَ هَلْ عَلِمْتُم مَّا فَعَلْتُم بِيُوسُفَ وَأَخِيهِ إِذْ أَنتُمْ جَاهِلُونَ ﴿٨٩﴾

---

13 Allah ☙ says: "His eyes went white from sadness", citing the emotional state as the underlying cause.

14 See the following chapter and our commentary on Q 12:96. Allah ☙ first describes how the wind carried the fragrance of Yūsuf ☙ to his father—hope and the anticipation of relief. Then, the "bearer of glad tidings" confirmed that Yūsuf ☙ was alive and well, casting his shirt on his father's face. It was then that the sight of Ya'qūb ☙ returned.

قَالُوا أَإِنَّكَ لَأَنْتَ يُوسُفُ قَالَ أَنَا يُوسُفُ وَهَذَا أَخِي قَدْ مَنَّ اللَّهُ عَلَيْنَا
إِنَّهُ مَنْ يَتَّقِ وَيَصْبِرْ فَإِنَّ اللَّهَ لَا يُضِيعُ أَجْرَ الْمُحْسِنِينَ ﴿٩٠﴾
قَالُوا تَاللَّهِ لَقَدْ آثَرَكَ اللَّهُ عَلَيْنَا وَإِنْ كُنَّا لَخَاطِئِينَ ﴿٩١﴾
قَالَ لَا تَثْرِيبَ عَلَيْكُمُ الْيَوْمَ يَغْفِرُ اللَّهُ لَكُمْ وَهُوَ أَرْحَمُ الرَّاحِمِينَ ﴿٩٢﴾
اذْهَبُوا بِقَمِيصِي هَذَا فَأَلْقُوهُ عَلَى وَجْهِ أَبِي يَأْتِ بَصِيرًا وَأْتُونِي بِأَهْلِكُمْ أَجْمَعِينَ ﴿٩٣﴾

❝ Then when they entered upon him, they said, "O governor, harm has touched us and our family and we have brought scant merchandise, but give us full measure and be charitable towards us; indeed, Allah rewards the charitable." He said, "Do you know what you did to Yūsuf and his brother when you were ignorant?" They said, "Is it that you are, in fact, Yūsuf?" He said, "I am Yūsuf, and this is my brother. Allah has bestowed favour upon us. Surely, whoever fears Allah and observes patience, Allah does not let the reward of the good-doers to go to waste." They said, "By Allah, Allah has certainly preferred you over us, and we were definitely wrongdoers." He said, "No reproach upon you today! May Allah forgive you, and He is the most merciful of the merciful. Go with this shirt of mine and lay it on my father's face, he will return a seer; and come to me with your family, altogether." ❞[15]

The brothers had nothing worthy to offer. They entered upon Yūsuf ﷺ more abased than ever. They pled him, "O governor, our families grow weaker by the day—harm has touched us all. We come to you

15 *Yūsuf*, 88-93.

with inferior goods. Be charitable to us and give us a full load, surely Allah rewards the charitable." Given their primary motive of searching for Yūsuf and Binyāmīn,[16] their plea to the minister is somewhat peculiar. They are seeking sustenance as opposed to their brother? It is perfectly possible that the famine had taken its toll upon them and their families and was so severe such that their priorities changed—survival before retrieval. Upon reflection, however, the clue is found in their saying, "Be charitable with us, surely Allah rewards the charitable." This is a form of *ta'rīḍ*—a rhetorical device where implicit wording is used to hint at what is truly intended.[17]

In their last conversation with the minister, the brothers had exhausted all means to get Binyāmīn back from him, but to no avail. Regurgitating the same arguments would have likely led them down the same dead end. Instead, they used their dire need for goods as well as the minister's charity to indicate what they were actually after: their youngest sibling. In other words, they invoked his generosity and his prior knowledge of their circumstances to entice him to free Binyāmīn and allow him to return to his father. It is as if they were saying, "Out of your immense magnanimity, mighty governor, give us what we seek and bestow upon us a generous giving—our brother is whom we are truly after! Be kind to us and show us pity, for verily Allah rewards the charitable."[18] The brothers lowered themselves before the governor of Egypt: they admitted to him every right and deferred unto him all power. They were simply begging him, of his

16 Ra'ūbīn was likely with them now. They would have passed by him to join them on their mission of retrieving their siblings, since that was the reason he stayed behind.

17 This is also mentioned in 'Patience' in Part XIV.

18 Ibn 'Āshūr ﷺ says in this regard: "They asked him (the minister) for charity as an indirect request (*ta'rīḍ*) to free their brother, since this would be a favour from him (the minister) given that he owns him (Binyāmīn)."

own goodwill, to pity them and give them back their brother.

Allah's justice had been made manifest. Though he never sought any vengeance, Yūsuf ﷺ had been vindicated in a flawless, picture-perfect way. His once-abductors were proverbially on their knees before him, humbled and dishevelled, begging for his benefaction. Despite all the hurt they had caused him, and despite all the lies and all the malice, he could not help but be moved at his brothers' appeal. He never wished them any harm, nor did he revel in their misfortune. Above all, he missed his father dearly and wished to alleviate any suffering he was going through. The promise Allah ﷻ had inspired him with in the bottom of the well was about to be realised.[19] This was the endgame: the great reveal.

TRANSFORMATIVE WISDOM

In your silent suffering, with all around you oblivious as to what ails you, know that Allah ﷻ knows. He ﷻ is enough. He ﷻ will set things right. Place your trust solely in Him, persevere with faith and honour, and witness His divine care manifest before you. "Is Allah not sufficient for His slave?!" Q 39:36

Yūsuf ﷺ said: "Do you know what you did with Yūsuf and his brother when you were ignorant?" As he subtly revealed his identity, Yūsuf ﷺ hinted at his brothers' previous misdeed. However, he does not fustigate them for it. Rather, he excuses them via ignorance. He did not say, "When you were evil, immoral, arrogant, wicked tyrants." In

19 Allah ﷻ says: "Then, when they led him off and were of one mind that they should place him in the depth of the well, We inspired in him, 'You will tell them of this deed of theirs while they are unaware'" Q 12:15. See 'Hope and Inspiration' in Part VI for more on this.

yet another demonstration of impeccable moral excellence, Yūsuf ﷺ cited ignorance as the reason for his brothers' sins. He is able to make this excuse for them due to how cognisant he is of *shayṭān*'s hand in misguiding the progeny of Adam. A lesson he internalised from his father as a young boy: "Indeed, *shayṭān* is a clear enemy to man."[20]

Ignorance—*jahl*—was the very thing Yūsuf ﷺ feared when the town's womenfolk were seeking to seduce him. It is ultimately *jahl* which leads one to sin, and *ʿilm* which—if internalised and not rendered purely theoretical—directs one to proper moral conduct and piety. Good and evil can be summarised in terms of knowledge and ignorance of Allah ﷻ.[21]

The brothers were bewildered. Other than Allah and those present during the ordeal, no one else knew of what they did to Yūsuf ﷺ. How could the minister know about him? The most they told him was that Binyāmīn had an older full-brother who perished. Could it be? Surely not... Was this man before them, this mighty governor of Egypt, their brother whom they put in the well and sold into slavery? Could this really be Yūsuf?! "Is that you, Yūsuf?" they asked the minister, almost in disbelief. "I am Yūsuf and this is my brother", replied the minister. The identity of his brother was never in question, but Yūsuf ﷺ was never going to separate himself from his beloved sibling again. "Allah has conferred favour upon us", he ﷺ continued,

20 *Yūsuf*, 5.

21 Highlighting the state of ignorance that even the believers unwittingly indulge in during heedless sin, the Prophet ﷺ said: "The fornicator—while fornicating—does not fornicate as a believer. The thief—while stealing—does not steal as a believer. The one who drinks alcohol—while drinking—does not do so as a believer." Reported by Bukhārī (2475) and Muslim (57).

"Indeed, whoever is conscious of Allah and is patient—Allah does not allow the reward of the good-doers to go to waste." Yūsuf ﷺ was always acutely aware of the divine nature of good deeds—his *iḥsān* throughout his life was for Allah, and Allah ﷻ is the Appreciative (*al-Shakūr*).

TRANSFORMATIVE WISDOM

We do righteous work as a servant does for his master, and ours is the Master and the Lord of the Worlds ﷻ. Though we do not rely on our deeds, we know that Allah ﷻ is appreciative and loves to reward goodness with its like and more! We are certain that the consequences of good deeds will undoubtedly be witnessed in the next life, if not for this one as well. Allah ﷻ says: "Is the reward for excellence anything other than excellence?" Q 55:60

PARDON

Allah ﷻ says: "To pardon is closer to piety."[22] He ﷻ also says: "Let them pardon and forego—do you not love that Allah forgives you?"[23] He ﷻ says: "The Hour is sure to come, so pardon a gracious pardoning."[24] As much as this was a moment of divine justice, it was even more one of divine forbearance, clemency, and forgiveness. Above all, it was a moment of truth: the guilty's guilt, the innocent's innocence, the good-doer's goodness, and the remorseful's remorse—all

22 *al-Baqarah*, 237.

23 *al-Nūr*, 22.

24 *al-Ḥijr*, 85.

was made manifest on that momentous occasion.

The brothers proclaimed, "By Allah, Allah has truly favoured you over us, and we were truly in error!" The response from Yūsuf ﷺ became a timeless adage in pardoning, recorded in the Qur'an to be recited till the end of times. He ﷺ said: *Lā tathrība ʿalaykum al-yawm*—"There is no blame upon you today." *Allāhu Akbar*! No retribution, no rebuke. Simply pure-hearted, good-willed forgiveness. So powerful was this moment that it was echoed in the *sīrah* of the Beloved ﷺ. At the Conquest of Makkah, the Quraysh feared the vengeance that the Messenger of Allah ﷺ could return with, especially given the torment they subjected him and his companions to for more than two decades.[25] Yet, the Prophet ﷺ did not return to avenge himself and his followers. He returned a merciful victor—the Mercy to the Worlds ﷺ. He ﷺ recalled his brother in prophethood, Yūsuf ﷺ. He ﷺ asked the Makkans—the source of his persecution for more than twenty years: "O people of Makkah! What do you think? What do you say?" They replied: "We think good and we say good—a gracious cousin[26]." He ﷺ then proclaimed: "I say to you as my brother Yūsuf said, 'There is no reproach upon you today! May Allah forgive you. He is the most merciful of the merciful.'"[27] Allah's peace and blessings be upon our role models Yūsuf ibn Yaʿqūb and Muḥammad ibn ʿAbdillāh!

25 The Conquest of Makkah was in the eighth year after the Hijrah, and the Prophet ﷺ had called to Islam in Makkah for thirteen years prior to migrating.

26 The Arabic is: *Ibn ʿamm*—the son of our paternal uncle. The Arabs honour their paternal relations especially, so this is a term of endearment to soften him ﷺ.

27 Reported by Suyūṭī in *al-Durr al-Manthūr* (8/323) on the authority of Ibn ʿAbbās ؓ. There are many accounts as to the exact wording of this report, all with this essential message of forgiveness.

REFLECT...

Mercy is only mercy if expressed from a position of power. A prerequisite of compassion is strength. Mercy expressed in a state of lower-handedness isn't mercy, but weakness and cowardice.

The latter part of the response from Yūsuf ﷺ holds within it an important lesson. Yūsuf ﷺ declared forgiveness for his brothers first, and only afterwards did he pray that Allah forgives them. There are two types of sin we will be answerable for on the Day of Judgement: sins we committed against Allah and ourselves, and sins we committed against others. Allah's immense propensity for mercy aside, we will not be admitted into the Garden without first settling all wrongs between one another. The Prophet ﷺ said: "When the believers escape the Fire, they are trapped at a bridge (*qanṭarah*) between the Garden and the Fire. They are granted retribution from one another over wrongs they incurred in the worldly life. Then, when they have been cleansed and chastened, they are permitted to enter the Garden."[28]

28 Reported by Aḥmad (11110), and Bukhārī in *al-Adab al-Mufrad* (486).

DID YOU KNOW?

There are two bridges we will have to cross on the Day of Resurrection: *al-Ṣirāṭ* and *al-Qanṭarah*. The former is also referred to as *al-Jisr*. The first is a bridge over the breadth of Hellfire, and every person will have to cross it. The speed and ease with which they cross it is proportional to the good they have done and evil they kept away from. The second—*al-Qanṭarah*—is as described in the forementioned report: a bridge between the Garden and the Fire which will only be crossed after all debts between the creation are settled.

One can imagine the scene. It was an emotional spectacle—all twelve brothers reunited, safe and sound, without rancour or ill-intent for one another. They exchanged anecdotes and shared memories, catching up on decades of separation. The conversation shifted to their father and his wellness. Wishing to complete the reunion, Yūsuf ﷺ said to them, "Go with this shirt of mine: cast it upon my father's face and his sight will return, and come back to me with all your family."

PART XVIII

AN EPIC JOURNEY

Dreams come true for those who wake up and chase them.

Between a day and its night, Allah ﷻ changes His slaves' circumstances. The band of brothers had gone to Egypt downtrodden and despondent, but they never lost hope in Allah's mercy. By the grace of Allah, they were now returning with their greatest hope realised, and in a manner that was beyond their wildest dreams! Not only were they able to retrieve Binyāmīn from Egypt's mighty governor, but that very governor was none other than their Yūsuf, the brother they had placed in the pit of a well all those decades ago. United and reconciled, the brothers returned to their father to tell him the amazing news. Allah ﷻ says:

وَلَمَّا فَصَلَتِ الْعِيرُ قَالَ أَبُوهُمْ إِنِّي لَأَجِدُ رِيحَ يُوسُفَ لَوْلَا أَن تُفَنِّدُونِ ﴿٩٤﴾

قَالُوا تَاللَّهِ إِنَّكَ لَفِي ضَلَالِكَ الْقَدِيمِ ﴿٩٥﴾

فَلَمَّا أَن جَاءَ الْبَشِيرُ أَلْقَاهُ عَلَىٰ وَجْهِهِ فَارْتَدَّ بَصِيرًا قَالَ أَلَمْ أَقُل لَّكُمْ إِنِّي أَعْلَمُ مِنَ اللَّهِ مَا لَا تَعْلَمُونَ ﴿٩٦﴾

قَالُوا يَا أَبَانَا اسْتَغْفِرْ لَنَا ذُنُوبَنَا إِنَّا كُنَّا خَاطِئِينَ ﴿٩٧﴾

قَالَ سَوْفَ أَسْتَغْفِرُ لَكُمْ رَبِّي إِنَّهُ هُوَ الْغَفُورُ الرَّحِيمُ ﴿٩٨﴾

❝ When the caravan departed, their father said, "I sense the scent of Yūsuf, though you may deem me senile." They said, "By God, you are still in your old fallacy!" So when the bearer of glad tidings arrived, he cast it over his face and he regained his sight. He said, "Did I not tell you that I know from Allah what you know not?" They said, "O father, pray for the forgiveness of our misdeeds; we were indeed wrongdoers." He said, "I will ask forgiveness for you from my Lord. Indeed, it is He who is the Forgiving, the Merciful." ﴾[1]

WINDS OF CHANGE

Abū Hurayrah ﵁ told us about the Messenger of Allah ﷺ: "He loved beautiful optimism and hated superstition."[2] As the brothers were setting off from Egypt back to their father in Palestine, the good news they were bearing beat them to him. Yaʿqūb ﵇ sensed the smell of his dear son Yūsuf and was immediately uplifted.[3] Knowing that those around him would chastise him for what he for sure experienced, he hesitantly said, "I find the scent of Yūsuf, though you would deem me senile."

1 *Yūsuf*, 94-98.

2 Reported by Ibn Mājah (3536) and Aḥmad (8393), classified as *ḥasan*—good—by Ibn Ḥajar ﵀.

3 Ṭabarī ﵀ said: "It is mentioned that the wind sought permission from its Lord to carry the fragrance of Yūsuf to his father before the bearer of glad tidings, so He allowed her, and she did." Qurṭubī ﵀ quotes Mujāhid ﵀ as having said: "A wind blew and it struck Yūsuf's shirt, then the fragrance of Paradise went into the world and reached Yaʿqūb. He realised that there can be no fragrance from Paradise in this world except that which was from the shirt of Yūsuf. At that point he said: 'I sense the fragrance of Yūsuf.'" Ibn ʿĀshūr ﵀ said: "Yaʿqūb sensing the fragrance of Yūsuf ﵇ is borne of supernatural inspiration. [...] It is a form of revelation without the speech of an angel messenger, and it is encompassed in the statement of Allah ﷻ: 'It is not for a mortal that Allah speaks to him except via revelation' Q 42:51."

TRANSFORMATIVE WISDOM

It is such a deep pain when one has to censure oneself in fear of what others might think of them, and an even worse pain when it's one's own family whose judgement is being averted. As our parents and seniors grow old, never dismiss their words and actions out of hand. We may not fully understand them or properly appreciate their needs, but the absolute least we can do is reciprocate the patience and grace they showed us in our youth, and pray: "Lord, show them mercy as they raised me when I was young!" Q 17:24

Those around him haughtily replied, almost rolling their eyes as they did, "By Allah, it is the same old tale over and over with you! You've gone frail-minded in your old age." According to a possible interpretation, it was the grandchildren of Yaʿqūb 👤 who responded so rudely to their grandfather since their fathers had been away. [4] Upon reflection, there is a poignant lesson to be drawn from this understanding. It was due to them witnessing their own fathers interact with their grandfather—Yaʿqūb 👤—with crass impropriety and a lack of decorum over the years that they consequently dealt with him in kind. Children do as they see, not as they are told. They are sponges, and instinctively emulate the behaviour of those around them, especially their parents. Accordingly, the best *tarbiyah* is for one to actively and manifestly seek closeness to Allah 👤. Without

---

4   Ibn ʿĀshūr 👤 says: "Those who said, "By Allah, you are in your old error", were those present among his family at the time. It was not his sons since they were still journeying back to him."

rote didactic instruction to do the same, children will immediately follow suite, *in shā' Allāh*! Allah ﷻ says: "Let those who, were they to leave behind them weak offspring would be afraid for them, fear [Allah's punishment]. So let them be mindful of Allah and let them speak for justice."[5] As the Arabic wisdom goes: *Kamā tudīnu tudān*—"You reap what you sow."[6]

TRANSFORMATIVE WISDOM

While guidance is ultimately in the hands of Allah ﷻ, a child surrounded by *dhikr*, *du'ā'*, *tilāwah*, and *'ibādah* will not be the same as one surrounded by cursing, backbiting, cheating, and lying. Fathers ought to be the men they want their sons to be, and mothers the women they want their daughters to be. That way, children will likely even surpass their parents in virtue, picking up where they left off. That is how—by the grace of Allah—continuous generational and communal ascension towards God-consciousness can be realised.

TOLD YOU SO

Finally, the brothers returned. They gave their father the good news,[7]

5 *al-Nisā'*, 9.

6 This is incorrectly attributed to the Prophet ﷺ as a *ḥadīth*. Allah knows best.

7 According to qur'anic commentators, it was Yahūdhā who told his father the good news and cast the shirt on his face. When they received it from Yūsuf ﷺ, it is relayed that he said: "I shall take the shirt today to bring my father happiness as I took it to him smeared in blood before and brought him sadness." This is mentioned by Qurṭubī ﷺ where he attributes the account to Ibn 'Abbās ﷺ, as well as by Ṭabarī ﷺ who attributes it to Suddī

and Yaʿqūb ⚜ was overjoyed! Just as his sadness took an immense toll on him, he was imbued with jubilance at realising Allah ⚜ had preserved his dear son. Yūsuf's shirt was cast on his face, and his sight returned. It wasn't just the wind carrying the scent of his once-lost boy anymore, but his very garment directly upon his countenance. The relief was as sweet as the suffering that led to it was bitter—or even sweeter! Truly, Allah ⚜ is as He told us, "I am as My slave expects Me to be."[8] Yaʿqūb ⚜ had an incredibly lofty opinion of his Lord, and, despite all the hurt, he never lost sight of that.

In a most noble, righteous, and deserving 'I told you so', Yaʿqūb ⚜ addressed his sons, "Did I not tell you? Did I not assure you Allah has a greater plan which you have no knowledge of? Did I not tell you that I know from Him that which you know not?"[9] Immediately, and as they had with Yūsuf ⚜, the brothers displayed humble remorse and admitted their guilt before their father. No more ploys; no more lies. They said, "Our father, seek forgiveness for us for our misdeeds; surely we have been wrongdoers!" Yaʿqūb ⚜ responded, "I shall seek forgiveness for you from my Lord. Indeed, He—He alone—is the Forgiving, the Merciful."

⚜ with a similar wording.

8   Reported by Bukhārī (7405) and Muslim (2675). The full, beautiful *ḥadīth qudsī* states: "I am to My slave as he thinks of Me, and I am with Him whenever He remembers Me. If he remembers Me in himself, I will remember him in Myself. If he remembers (also: mentions) Me in a congregation, I will remember (also: mention) him in one that is even better. If he draws near to Me a handspan, I draw near to him a cubit. If he draws near to Me a cubit, I draw near to him a wingspan. If he comes to Me walking, I go to him running."

9   This is a reference to Q 12:86 where Yaʿqūb ⚜ says this to his children when they rebuke him for his grief. In Q 12:68, Allah ⚜ Himself affirms a lofty station for his noble slave and messenger Yaʿqūb ⚜: "Verily, he is upon sound knowledge due to what We taught him."

As can be immediately understood from the translation, the original qur'anic Arabic implies futurity—*sawfa astaghfiru*. The use of the particle *sawfa* before the verb *astaghfiru* indicates there is no immediacy with regards to the action at hand, and that it will instead be realised at a later time. Many exegetes understand this as Yaʿqūb ﷺ waiting for the last third of the night (*saḥar*) to pray for his sons due to the incredible virtue associated with it.[10] Some understand it to be specifically referring to the night of Friday due to a narration[11] reported on the authority of Ibn ʿAbbās ﷺ where the Prophet ﷺ tells ʿAlī ﷺ to remedy a problem of his by specifically praying at that time. The narration quotes the Prophet ﷺ as saying, "My brother Yaʿqūb said to his children, 'I will seek forgiveness for you from my Lord,' and he waited until the night of Friday."[12]

Yaʿqūb ﷺ forgave his sons' transgressions, and it is very much likely that he sought out a blessed time for prayer to ask Allah to forgive them. However, another subtle implication of *sawfa* here is that it is a father disciplining his sons: he wished them to truly appreciate the magnitude of their error and consequently perfect their repentance.[13] Unlike their brother—Yūsuf ﷺ—who immediately said:

10 The Prophet ﷺ said: "Every night, our Lord descends to the lowest heaven in the last third and says, 'Who calls upon Me that I may answer him? Who asks Me that I may give him? Who seeks My forgiveness that I may forgive him?'" Reported by Bukhārī (1145) and Muslim (758). This virtue would have been known to previous messengers and prophets.

11 It is classified as weak, and Allah knows best.

12 It is a very lengthy report of which this is the relevant section. Ṭabarī and Qurṭubī ﷺ quote this or a similar excerpt in their respective commentaries. Ibn Kathīr ﷺ questions its status a *marfūʿ* (a statement of the Prophet ﷺ. The alternative in Hadith science is for the report to be *mawqūf*: a statement of a companion).

13 Ibn ʿĀshūr ﷺ said: "He (Yaʿqūb ﷺ) promised to seek forgiveness for them (his sons) in the future—saying: *sawfa astaghfiru lakum*—to indicate that he will continuously do so moving forward. From the context, it is evident that he nonetheless did so at the time.

Yaghfiru Allāhu lakum—"May Allah forgive you"; their father—Yaʿqūb ﵇—said: *sawfa astaghfiru lakum Rabbī*—"I will ask my Lord to forgive you." While both relationships are founded on love, a brother with his siblings is not the same as a father with his sons. There is a hierarchy of authority in the latter that can never be surmounted.

A DREAM COME TRUE

There was no more bad blood. Having repented and directly asked for their father's forgiveness, it was time for a family reunion of monumental proportions. Yaʿqūb ﵇, the head of the family, with his wives,[14] his sons,[15] his sons' wives and children, and likely many grandchildren—all of them were heading to Egypt to be with Yūsuf ﵇. It was a scene to behold. Allah ﷻ says:

فَلَمَّا دَخَلُوا عَلَىٰ يُوسُفَ آوَىٰ إِلَيْهِ أَبَوَيْهِ وَقَالَ ادْخُلُوا مِصْرَ إِن شَاءَ اللَّهُ آمِنِينَ ﴿٩٩﴾
وَرَفَعَ أَبَوَيْهِ عَلَى الْعَرْشِ وَخَرُّوا لَهُ سُجَّدًا وَقَالَ يَا أَبَتِ هَٰذَا تَأْوِيلُ رُؤْيَايَ مِن قَبْلُ

However, he wished to accentuate the gravity of their sin and the greatness of Allah ﷻ, and that he will continue to pray for their forgiveness on future occasions. It has also been said that he delayed seeking forgiveness for them in a time where supplications are hoped to be accepted. On the authority of Ibn ʿAbbās, a *marfūʿ* report states that he delayed it till the night of Friday. This is reported by Ṭabarī. Ibn Kathīr deemed its grading as *marfūʿ* questionable."

14 While Yaʿqūb ﵇ had four wives, we do not know how many were still alive at the time. What is clear is that Yūsuf raised his *abawayn*—literally, 'parents'—on the throne. The identity of the lady who was with Yaʿqūb in that instance is discussed later in this subheading.

15 Though we do not know for sure, it is likely that Binyāmīn stayed with Yūsuf ﵇. Therefore, it would have been ten brothers who returned from Egypt to their father and returned back with him to Yūsuf ﵇.

قَدْ جَعَلَهَا رَبِّي حَقًّا وَقَدْ أَحْسَنَ بِي إِذْ أَخْرَجَنِي مِنَ السِّجْنِ وَجَاءَ بِكُمْ مِنَ الْبَدْوِ مِنْ بَعْدِ أَنْ نَزَغَ الشَّيْطَانُ بَيْنِي وَبَيْنَ إِخْوَتِي إِنَّ رَبِّي لَطِيفٌ لِمَا يَشَاءُ إِنَّهُ هُوَ الْعَلِيمُ الْحَكِيمُ ﴿١٠٠﴾

رَبِّ قَدْ آتَيْتَنِي مِنَ الْمُلْكِ وَعَلَّمْتَنِي مِنْ تَأْوِيلِ الأَحَادِيثِ فَاطِرَ السَّمَاوَاتِ وَالأَرْضِ أَنْتَ وَلِيِّي فِي الدُّنْيَا وَالآخِرَةِ تَوَفَّنِي مُسْلِمًا وَأَلْحِقْنِي بِالصَّالِحِينَ ﴿١٠١﴾

❝ When they entered upon Yūsuf, he drew his parents close to himself and said, "Enter Egypt, Allah willing, safe and secure." And he raised his parents up on the throne, and they all fell before him in prostration. He said, "My father, here is the fulfilment of my dream from before. My Lord has made it come true. He showed me favour when he released me from the prison and brought you from the desert after the devil had caused a rift between me and my brothers. Surely, my Lord is subtle in what He wills. Surely, it is He who is the Knowing, the Wise." "My Lord, You have given me power to rule and the knowledge of interpreting events. Creator of the heavens and the earth, You are my guardian in this world and the Hereafter. Make me die a muslim and make me join the righteous." ❞[16]

What a magnificent spectacle it must have been.[17] Ya'qūb 🙵 and

---

16   *Yūsuf*, 99-101.

17   -   Ṭabarī 🙵 narrates an account from Farqad al-Sabakhī 🙵 where the latter says: "Yūsuf was informed [by his emissaries] when Ya'qūb had neared Egypt, so he went out to receive him. The Egyptians went out with him since they venerated him. They (Ya'qūb and Yūsuf 🙵) started approaching one another [from a distance]. Ya'qūb was walking whilst leaning on one of his sons called Yahūdhā. Ya'qūb looked at all the people and the horses and asked, 'Yahūdhā, is this the king of Egypt?' He replied, 'No, that's your son!' When they drew near to one another, Yūsuf was going to greet him first, but was stopped (to give his father the honour and pleasure of doing so). Ya'qūb had more right to greet him first. He (Ya'qūb 🙵) said: *al-salāmu 'alayka yā dhāhiba al-aḥzāni 'annī*—'Peace be

dozens from his progeny[18] all approaching the borders of Egypt. Yūsuf ﷺ was there to graciously receive them.[19] He drew his parents[20] close to him and embraced them. Ya'qūb and Yūsuf ﷺ were finally reunited, holding one another in a hug that had been decades in the making. All that longing, the pain of severance; the worry, grief, and strife—all of it dissipated as a loving father held his dear, long-lost son. Though the minister of Egypt and the second most powerful man on earth, Yūsuf ﷺ was still that little dreamer to his father, boyishly running and playing around in their home. It wasn't the

---

upon you, alleviator of my grief!'" Ṭabarī ﷺ also quotes a report that Yūsuf ﷺ went out with the king along with four-thousand Egyptians to greet Ya'qūb ﷺ and his sons.

- Ibn Kathīr ﷺ says: "When Yūsuf ﷺ was alerted as to their impending arrival, he went out to greet them. The king ordered his ministers and the eminent among his people to go out [with Yūsuf ﷺ] to receive Prophet Ya'qūb ﷺ. It is said that the king himself also went out, and this was most likely the case."

18 It was this group of people who went on to populate Egypt with Israelites: the Banū Isrā'īl—literally the Descendants of Israel, Ya'qūb ﷺ. Decades or centuries later, it will be the members of this extended lineage and its branches who will be persecuted by Pharaoh and consequently follow Mūsā ﷺ out of Egypt in the Exodus. One possible understanding is that the twelve sons of Ya'qūb ﷺ were the heads of the twelve tribes of Israel mentioned in the Qur'an and previous scriptures.

19 This is the understanding offered by Ṭabarī and Ibn Kathīr ﷺ. Ṭabarī ﷺ says: "Yūsuf ﷺ met his father before entering Egypt in order to honour him. He embraced him, then told him and those with him, 'Enter Egypt, Allah willing, in peace.'" It doesn't make obvious sense to greet them like this if they had already entered and were with him at his palace.

20 There is a difference opinion whether the wife of Ya'qūb ﷺ referred to in *abawayh*—'his parents'—was the mother of Yūsuf ﷺ or his father's wife and his maternal aunt. It is said that his mother, Rāḥīl, passed away giving birth to his full-brother Binyāmīn, and Lī'ah, his aunt, raised him until his abduction. This is the position adopted by Ibn 'Āshūr ﷺ as well as many early exegetes. Ṭabarī ﷺ cites both views then gives preference to the position that the lady was his own biological mother. He says: "The opinion with the best claim to veracity is that of Ibn Isḥāq (i.e. that it was his biological mother), since this is the most prevalent usage of the word *abawayn* (parents). This is unless what has been said is proven to be true—that his mother passed away before—with undeniable proof; then we would submit to that view." Ibn Kathīr ﷺ echoes these sentiments.

wind carrying his scent. It wasn't his shirt atop his head. It was his boy, standing before him as a beautiful, majestic man, enveloping him with love and compassion. "Indeed, the patient are given their reward in full without measure."[21]

"Come into Egypt—Allah willing—safe and sound!" Yūsuf ﷺ announced to his extended family. They will be secure and taken care of in Egypt. They shall encounter no fear and no hunger in his quarters. As scholars have reflected, the greatest needs of man are two: security from harm and sustenance for nourishment. Allah ﷻ says, reminding the Quraysh of his favour and bounty over them: "He is the one who fed them against hunger and has made them secure from fear."[22] The family of Yūsuf ﷺ will not go hungry anymore, in his care. Thank Allah, the famine which struck the region has been mitigated by his wise governance. Furthermore, they will fear no harm so long as he ensures their protection.

Yūsuf ﷺ returned with his family to his palace. In venerating and honouring his parents, he raised them on his throne. Immediately, they reciprocated this reverence by falling prostrate before him. His father, mother, and eleven brothers were bowing down before him in respectful gratitude.[23] This was it! The manifestation of his

21 *al-Zumar*, 10.

22 *Quraysh*, 4.

23 Commentators differed over the exact nature of this prostration—whether it was a lowering of the head, a bowing, or a complete falling to the ground as per the term's common inference (*sujūd* denotes 'prostration'). What they did not differ over is its significance. By consensus, it is a greeting of respect undertaken to honour the one it is done to. Naturally, it is not borne of worship, just as the angels' prostration to Ādam ﷺ was not one of worship. In the final, perfected revelatory dispensation to mankind, *sujūd* may only be to Allah ﷻ, and the people's greeting among themselves is that of the people of Paradise: *Salām*—'Peace!'

dream that he confided in his father about when he was a boy. The vision had come true! He ﵇ said to his father, "Dear father, this is the interpretation of my dream from long ago. Allah made it true!" The first moment of this epic narrative has come to its perfect close.[24] The story began with Yūsuf ﵇ as a young boy telling his father about a magnificent dream he had. The story is now concluding with Yūsuf ﵇ telling his father about that dream coming true. Just as he addressed him then with the endearing *abati*—'dear, beloved father'—so did he here.[25]

24 See the following figure as well as the table at the end of the chapter.

25 See Part V for more on this.

SYMMETRY OF SŪRAH YŪSUF

1. Yūsuf ﵇ has a dream
2. The brothers plot against Yūsuf ﵇
3. The wife of the ʿAzīz tries to seduce Yūsuf ﵇
4. The ladies of the town join the temptation
5. Yūsuf ﵇ goes to jail
6. The king has a dream
7. The king's dream is interpreted
8. Yūsuf ﵇ gets released from prison
9. The ladies testify to the innocence of Yūsuf ﵇
10. The wife of the ʿAzīz confesses
11. The brothers learn from their lesson
12. The dream of Yūsuf ﵇ comes true

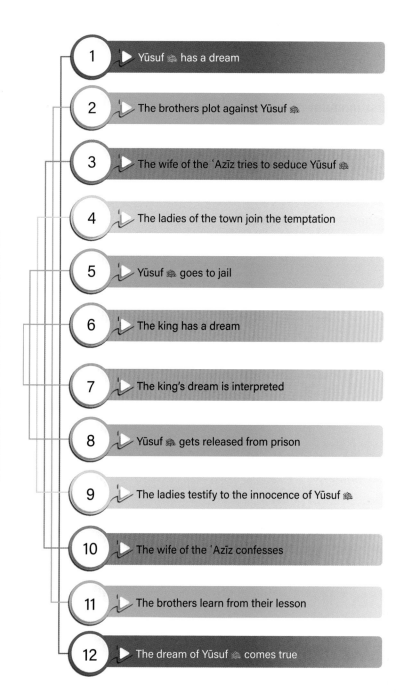

DID YOU KNOW?

There is deep and subtle significance behind the symbolism in the dream of Yūsuf ﷺ. According to some exegetes, the sun represents the father, the moon the mother, and the stars the children. The sun provides light, warmth, and vitality. It is the symbol of providence. Likewise, the father is the provider and the safekeeper of his household. The moon is enigmatic and serene. It is the symbol of beauty. Likewise, the mother is the source of her home's adornment and tranquillity. The stars are seen at night with the moon, not as much with the sun—children's primary reliance is on their mother. The moon gets its light from the sun: the stronger the sun shines, the more sublime the moon's reflection. Likewise, the stronger the father figure, the more the mother is able to reside in her femininity and excel in her role.

However, if ever there is a proverbial clash between the two majestic celestial bodies—a 'reversal' as it were—there is a complete eclipse, and only darkness is felt without visible stars in the sky. Likewise, an inversion of roles between husband and wife leads to a social eclipse where neither parental role is felt and, tragically, the children suffer most.

Yūsuf ﷺ continued: "Allah truly showed me favour and grace when He took me out of prison and brought you to me from the desert after the devil had sewn discord between me and my brothers." As always, He attributed all goodness to Allah ﷻ. There are those among the faithless who would recall difficult times and bemoan them, and even—God forbid—curse the circumstances that led to them.[26] Instead, Yūsuf 🕮 praises Allah for their happening! He appreciates that without the well, the slavery, the temptation, and the prison, he would not have experienced this profound and moving moment of happiness with his father. The magnitude and sweetness of relief is proportional to the severity of the suffering which preceded it.

Notice how he 🕮 only explicitly mentioned imprisonment instead of being enslaved or cast into the well. This is because the latter ordeals were caused by his brothers, and he had already forgiven them. Mentioning the well in their presence would not only be ignoble, but would also serve to reignite old tensions and act as an indirect reprimand for them, one which they no longer needed.[27] Allah 🕮 says: "You who believe, do not nullify your charity with reminders thereof and subsequent harm."[28] Notice also how he blames *shayṭān* for their wrongs. It is a lesson he had learned from his father the last time they were together: *shayṭān* is a clear enemy to man, and his hand in misguiding the creation should never be understated. This is also a manifestation of moral excellence. Yūsuf 🕮 is waiving all blame from his brothers, completely absolving them of their heinous crimes, and instead ascribing evil to the forsaken, accursed devil.

---

26 The Prophet 🕮 said: "Allah 🕮 says, 'The son of Adam insults Me; he says: "How awful are the misfortunes of time!" Let none of you say: "How awful are the misfortunes of time", for indeed, I—yes I—am time. I alternate its night and day, and when I will, I shall grasp them.'" Reported by Muslim (2246) on the authority of Abū Hurayrah 🕮. Inveighing time is equivalent to bemoaning the decree of Allah 🕮.

27 Qurṭubī 🕮 said: "He (Yūsuf 🕮) did not say, '[... whcn He took me out of] the well', out of nobility. He did not wish to remind his brothers of their misdeed having pardoned them for it when he said, 'There is no blame upon you today' [Q 12:92]. This is the normative principle among the mystic sages: *Dhikru al-jafā fī waqti al-ṣafā jafā*—'The mention of past enmity at the time of affability is a form of enmity.'"

28 *al-Baqarah*, 264.

He 🕮 did not say, 'My brothers did this and that', rather, he said, 'It was *shayṭān* who caused a rift between us.'

"Indeed, my Lord is *laṭīf* in what He wills", Yūsuf 🕮 proclaimed, "Indeed, He, and He alone, is the Knowing, the Wise." The word *luṭf* has connotations of fineness and subtlety as well as gentleness and kindness. Thus: *Inna Rabbī laṭīfun limā yashā'*—translates to, "Verily, my Lord is subtle and tender in what He wills." Allah 🕮 is *al-Laṭīf*. There is subtle kindness in what He decrees. It may be difficult to see at times because of how fine it is, but it is certainly there and can be witnessed by those whom Allah endowed with vision. The story began with Yaʿqūb 🕮 teaching his young son two beautiful names of Allah 🕮 and the fundamental principles behind them, and we now hear Yūsuf 🕮 quote these two names again to his father:

$$ إِنَّهُ هُوَ الْعَلِيمُ الْحَكِيمُ $$

•• Indeed, He—only He—is the Knowing, the Wise... ••

Yūsuf 🕮 never forgot. Regardless of where he was and what he was doing, and regardless of the challenges, trials, and tribulations he was facing, his father's counsel was always at the fore of his mind and soul:

•• *Allah is my Rabb! He is my protector and guardian.*

He knows full well my state, and is wise as to why I am there.••

The final time Yūsuf 🕮 is quoted in the story is in address to the Divine 🕮. He supplicates Allah 🕮, saying: "My Lord, You have given me some sovereignty and taught me something of the interpretation of dreams. Originator of the heavens and the earth, You are my protecting guardian in this life and the next. Cause me to die in complete devotion to You, and allow me to join the righteous." Yaʿqūb ﷺ told young Yūsuf that Allah ﷻ will choose him and take him on the path of his forefathers before him, and that He ﷻ will teach him the interpretation of dreams and events. Indeed, Yaʿqūb ﷺ spoke the truth. Yūsuf ﷺ acknowledged Allah's bounty upon him, and that all dominion belongs ultimately to Him—He gives it to whom He pleases and seizes it from whom He pleases. In humble invocation, he concludes his prayer by asking his Lord to allow him to return to Him a *muslim*, and to allow him to reach the stations of the righteous.

And we ask Allah ﷻ to cause us to return to Him as *muslimīn*, and to allow us to reach the station of Yūsuf ﷺ and his like. In trials, he was patient and faithful. In temptation, he was chaste and honourable. In power, he was just and sagacious. In judgement, he was fair and merciful. May Allah confer blessings of peace upon Prophet Yūsuf, his father, his grandfather, and his great grandfather. May Allah confer blessings of peace upon the Final Messenger, the Mercy to the Worlds, Muḥammad the son of ʿAbdullāh.

Praise be to Allah, the Lord of the Worlds.

SUBJECT OF SYMMETRY	OPENING SCENE	CLOSING SCENE
Dream	My dear father, I saw eleven stars, the sun, and the moon—I saw them fall prostrate before me. [Q 12:4]	My dear father, this is the interpretation of my dream from long ago. [Q 12:100]
Shayṭān	Indeed, the devil is a clear enemy to man. [Q 12:5]	The devil had caused a rift between me and my brothers. [Q 12:100]
Interpretation	As such your Lord shall favour you and teach you of the interpretation of events. [Q 12:6]	My Lord, You have given me some sovereignty and taught me of the interpretation of events. [Q 12:101]
ʿIlm* and *Ḥikmah	Indeed, your Lord is knowing, wise. [Q 12:6]	Indeed, He—He alone—is the Knowing, the Wise. [Q 12:100]

PART

XIX

CONCLUDING COUNSEL

He who has Allah has everything, and he who has all but Him has nothing.

The address returns back to the Chosen One ﷺ—the one upon whom this Heavy Word was cast.[1] The story of Yūsuf ﷺ is a timeless tale for all mankind. Specifically, however, it was revealed at a time when the early Muslims were in severe need of counsel and spiritual solace. None more so than the one who bore the most suffering among them:[2] Allah's Messenger ﷺ.[3] The last time he ﷺ was addressed in the *sūrah* was in its opening verses where Allah ﷻ said: "We relate to you the best of stories."[4] Here, at the conclusion of the *sūrah*, Allah ﷻ says:

ذَٰلِكَ مِنْ أَنبَاءِ الْغَيْبِ نُوحِيهِ إِلَيْكَ وَمَا كُنتَ
لَدَيْهِمْ إِذْ أَجْمَعُوا أَمْرَهُمْ وَهُمْ يَمْكُرُونَ ﴿١٠٢﴾

وَمَا أَكْثَرُ النَّاسِ وَلَوْ حَرَصْتَ بِمُؤْمِنِينَ ﴿١٠٣﴾

وَمَا تَسْأَلُهُمْ عَلَيْهِ مِنْ أَجْرٍ إِنْ هُوَ إِلَّا ذِكْرٌ لِّلْعَالَمِينَ ﴿١٠٤﴾

وَكَأَيِّن مِّنْ آيَةٍ فِي السَّمَاوَاتِ وَالْأَرْضِ يَمُرُّونَ عَلَيْهَا وَهُمْ عَنْهَا مُعْرِضُونَ ﴿١٠٥﴾

---

1 *al-Muzzammil*, 5.

2 As the poet said:

لَمْ يُبْقِ فِي قَلْبِهِ صَبْراً وَلَا جَلَداً ∴ تَلقِينُهُ الْمُؤْمِنِينَ الصَّبْرَ وَالْجَلَدَا

"It left no resolve nor mettle in his heart,
His dictating to the believers resolve and mettle."

3 See Part II for more on this, especially the section under the subheading 'Sūrah Yūsuf.' The Context of Revelation—known in Arabic as *Asbāb al-Nuzūl*—is one of the sciences of the Qur'an. There is a specific context and historical reason wherein a given qur'anic passage is revealed, then there is the universal benefits that scholars derive therefrom till the Last Day.

4 *Yūsuf*, 3.

وَمَا يُؤْمِنُ أَكْثَرُهُم بِاللَّهِ إِلَّا وَهُم مُّشْرِكُونَ ﴿١٠٦﴾

“ This is of the tidings of the Unseen which We reveal unto you. You were not present with them when they fixed their plan as they were scheming. And most of mankind will not believe, no matter how keen you are. Yet you do not ask of them for it any payment; it is not except a reminder to the worlds. How many a sign in the heavens and the earth do they pass by while they disregard them? And most of them believe not in Allah except while they associate others with Him. ”[5]

THE GIFT OF FAITH

One of the many proofs of the truthfulness of the Prophet ﷺ is, indeed, his access to the *ghayb*—the Unseen. He ﷺ was not there when Yūsuf's brothers were of one mind in their scheming against him. The intricate details and startling beauty with which Allah ﷻ relayed this story is irrevocable evidence that he ﷺ was "not speaking of his own whim—it is but a revelation revealed!"[6]

5 *Yūsuf*, 102-106.

6 *al-Najm*, 3-4.

DID YOU KNOW?

There is significant, broad-stroke overlap between the accounts of the prophets ﷺ found in previous scripture and the Qur'an. The story of the flood, for example, is practically universal, transcending culture and language. The Judeo-Christian narratives in the Old and New Testaments respectively agree with much of what was revealed in the Final Testament. However, there are also notable omissions as well as fundamental, unassailable contradictions between the biblical and qur'anic accounts of prophetic stories. Had the Prophet ﷺ been simply regurgitating previous peoples' folklore—a lazy, unacademic claim—there would be no discrepancies. Yet, the Qur'an is very particular in its telling of these timeless tales.

It is not the sun's fault that the blind cannot attest to its brilliance. That one receives an objective, unadulterated, and unbiased dose of the prophetic message—via the Qur'an or the Sunnah or both—yet still wholeheartedly chooses to reject it is naught but an indication of one's own spiritual ailment. *Īmān*—faith—is purely a gift from Allah ﷻ. He is the Bestower, the Giver of Gifts—*al-Wahhāb*.[7]

On His ability to unite mankind upon faith if He so willed, Allah ﷻ says:

7 Alluding to this, Allah ﷻ teaches us a supplication to preserve our faith: "Our Lord, do not cause our hearts to deviate after You have guided us and grant us from Yourself mercy; indeed, You—truly You—are the Bestower" Q 3:8. The Prophet ﷺ also taught us a similar *du'ā'*: "O Turner of Hearts, keep my heart firm upon Your religion." The two prayers are coupled together in an account reported by Tirmidhī (2140).

- "Had your Lord willed, everyone on earth would have believed, all of them together. Will you compel mankind to become believers? And never could a single soul believe except by Allah's leave. He lays abomination upon those who do not reason."[8]

- "Had your Lord willed, He could have made mankind one community; but they will continue to differ, except those upon whom your Lord has bestowed mercy—and for that reason He created them."[9]

On the wilful blindness of the spiritually blind and it never being about 'proof', Allah ﷻ says:

- "Even if We sent the angels down to them, and the dead spoke to them, and We gathered all things right in front of them, they still would not believe unless Allah so willed, but most of them are ignorant."[10]

- "They denied them (Allah's signs), in their wickedness and their pride, even though their souls acknowledged them as true. See, then, how those who spread corruption met their end!"[11]

- "Even if We opened unto them a gate of heaven and they kept mounting through it, they would say, 'Surely our sight has been stupefied; rather, we are a people bewitched.'"[12]

---

8 *Yūnus*, 99-100.

9 *Hūd*, 118-119.

10 *al-An'ām*, 111.

11 *al-Naml*, 14.

12 *al-Ḥijr*, 14-15.

On the indefatigability with which the Prophet ﷺ called to truth and his sole responsibility being delivery of the message, Allah ﷻ says:

- "Perhaps you would decimate yourself, sorrowing after them, if they do not believe in this discourse."[13]
- "Whether We let you see some of what We have threatened them with or cause you to die [before that], your only duty is conveyance: Ours is the Reckoning."[14]

Despite the best efforts of the best of mankind, people disbelieved. And they will continue to do so until the Hour is established. This is the Qur'an manifesting as its title *al-Furqān*—the differentiator. That is: the differentiator between right and wrong, virtue and vice, good and evil, and truth and falsehood. Each will choose their camp, and Allah's word will always reign supreme.

Allah ﷻ is consoling the Prophet ﷺ through this discourse, especially given the magnificent story which preceded it. The Prophet ﷺ was denied and rejected by his own kith and kin—his tribe, the Quraysh. Yūsuf ﷺ was betrayed by his brothers. The Prophet ﷺ and his companions ﷺ were suffering at the hands of the idolaters for more than a decade. Yūsuf ﷺ suffered for many more until Allah ﷻ altered his circumstances. It is as if Allah ﷻ is telling His messenger ﷺ through this story: "Fret not, Muḥammad, for Allah is with the patient, and His relief is ever near to the good-doers!" And indeed, almost a millennium and a half later, some two billion people celebrate the Messenger of Allah ﷺ and his legacy of pure monotheism, and follow his way.

13 *al-Kahf*, 6.

14 *al-Ra'd*, 40.

REFLECT...

Disbelievers will inevitably exist. In fact, the minority of mankind will truly believe. However, these divine promises have no bearing on our calling to Islam. We are not morally responsible for realising Allah's cosmological will. We are taken into account for our adherence to His legislative will. In other words, we do not know who will die in what state. Thus, we ask Allah ﷻ for guidance and steadfastness, and we call to His way with wisdom and good counsel.

Another sign of the truthfulness of the messengers and prophets ﷷ is that they never asked their people for material compensation in return for their ministry. The chosen among Allah's servants simply wish goodness for mankind. Thus, they altruistically sacrifice their own wellbeing for that of others. Yet, and despite their admirable selflessness, even some of those who do believe in God among mankind only do so while committing *shirk*—polytheism. Multiplicity and plurality dazzles them such that they mistake the pointers for whom they are pointing to: the One, the Only—*al-Wāḥid al-Aḥad*. The creation is truly stunning, but it is still the creation. Allah alone is the Creator, the Originator, the Fashioner—*al-Khāliq al-Bāri' al-Muṣawwir*. Allah ﷻ is the Innovator of the Heavens and the Earth—*Badīʿ al-Samāwāt wa al-Arḍ*. Everything relies on Him, and nothing may be without Him.[15] Allah is the Eternal Refuge—*Allāh al-Ṣamad*![16]

15 The truest line of poetry said was:

أَلَا كُلُّ شَيْءٍ ما خَلا اللَّهَ باطِلٌ

"Verily, all other than Allah is false!"

This is the testimony of the Prophet ﷺ as reported by Bukhārī (3841) and Muslim (2256).

16 *al-Ikhlāṣ*, 2.

TRANSFORMATIVE WISDOM

Knowing Allah ﷻ through His sublime names and lofty attributes is the noblest endeavour anyone can undertake. Allah ﷾ says: "To Allah belong the beautiful names, so call Him by them" Q 7:180. The Prophet ﷺ said: "Indeed, to Allah belong ninety-nine names. Whoever encompasses them will enter the Garden." Reported by Bukhārī (2736) and Muslim (2677).

MORAL OF THE STORY

Concluding the *sūrah*, Allah ﷾ says:

أَفَأَمِنُوا أَنْ تَأْتِيَهُمْ غَاشِيَةٌ مِنْ عَذَابِ اللَّهِ أَوْ تَأْتِيَهُمُ
السَّاعَةُ بَغْتَةً وَهُمْ لَا يَشْعُرُونَ ﴿١٠٧﴾

قُلْ هَٰذِهِ سَبِيلِي أَدْعُو إِلَى اللَّهِ عَلَىٰ بَصِيرَةٍ أَنَا وَمَنِ
اتَّبَعَنِي وَسُبْحَانَ اللَّهِ وَمَا أَنَا مِنَ الْمُشْرِكِينَ ﴿١٠٨﴾

وَمَا أَرْسَلْنَا مِنْ قَبْلِكَ إِلَّا رِجَالًا نُوحِي إِلَيْهِمْ مِنْ أَهْلِ الْقُرَىٰ أَفَلَمْ يَسِيرُوا فِي
الْأَرْضِ فَيَنْظُرُوا كَيْفَ كَانَ عَاقِبَةُ الَّذِينَ مِنْ قَبْلِهِمْ وَلَدَارُ الْآخِرَةِ خَيْرٌ لِلَّذِينَ
اتَّقَوْا أَفَلَا تَعْقِلُونَ ﴿١٠٩﴾

حَتَّىٰ إِذَا اسْتَيْأَسَ الرُّسُلُ وَظَنُّوا أَنَّهُمْ قَدْ كُذِبُوا جَاءَهُمْ نَصْرُنَا فَنُجِّيَ مَنْ نَشَاءُ
وَلَا يُرَدُّ بَأْسُنَا عَنِ الْقَوْمِ الْمُجْرِمِينَ ﴿١١٠﴾

لَقَدْ كَانَ فِي قَصَصِهِمْ عِبْرَةٌ لِّأُولِي الْأَلْبَابِ مَا كَانَ حَدِيثًا يُفْتَرَىٰ وَلَٰكِن تَصْدِيقَ
الَّذِي بَيْنَ يَدَيْهِ وَتَفْصِيلَ كُلِّ شَيْءٍ وَهُدًى وَرَحْمَةً لِّقَوْمٍ يُؤْمِنُونَ ﴿١١١﴾

" Do they feel secure that an overwhelming event of Allah's punishment will not come upon them, or that the Hour will not come upon them suddenly while they are unaware? Say, "This is my way; I call to Allah with insight—I and whoever has followed me. Glorified be Allah, and I am not of those who associate." And We sent not before you except men to whom We revealed from among the people of the townships. So have they not travelled through the earth and observed how was the end of those before them? The home of the Hereafter is best for those who are mindful of Allah; then will you not reason? Till, when the messengers despaired and thought that they were denied, then came unto them Our help, and whom We would was saved. Our wrath cannot be warded from the guilty. Most surely, in their narrative there has been a lesson for people of understanding. This was not a fabricated tale, but a confirmation of what came before it, a detailed explanation of everything, and guidance and mercy for a people who believe. "[17]

How haughty is the son of Adam! A virus with a crown on its head mocked human civilisation as it brought eight billion people's lives to a halt. Yet, we still dare think ourselves invincible? Will we not heed Allah's warnings? Some humility is in order, and the quicker it settles in all of our hearts the better. Allah ﷻ says: "Calamities have

17 *Yūsuf*, 107-111.

appeared on land and sea because of what the hands of the people earned, so that He makes them taste some of what they did, in order that they may return."[18]

Abundance that is concurrent with decadence is a sign of impending doom, not progress or enlightenment. Allah ﷻ says: "So, when they had forgotten the warning they had received, We opened the gates to everything for them. Then, as they revelled in what they had been given, We struck them suddenly and they were dumbfounded."[19] He ﷻ also says: "Let not those who disbelieve imagine that the rein We give them bodes well for them. We only give them rein that they may grow in sinfulness. And theirs will be a shameful punishment."[20]

Those who are wise to the way Allah dealt with previous nations and civilisations cannot help but be fearful of Allah's wrath. Allah ﷻ says: "How can you know? Perhaps the Hour is near. Those who do not believe in it seek to hasten it, while those who believe are fearful of it and know that it is the truth. Unquestionably, those who argue about the Hour are far, far astray."[21]

Every nation had its warner.[22] Over and over, the devoted were delivered and the deniers were destroyed.[23] The difference for us is that we are not just any nation, rather we are the last of them. Furthermore, prophets of old came for a specific people and time. As such, the punishment for those who rejected them was local. Ours is the

18 *al-Rūm*, 41.

19 *al-Anʿām*, 44.

20 *Āl ʿImrān*, 178.

21 *al-Shūrā*, 17-18.

22 See Q 10:47, 16:36, and 35:24.

23 For example, see the stories of the prophets in *al-Aʿrāf*, *Hūd*, *al-Shuʿarāʾ*, *al-Ṣāffāt*, and *al-Qamar*.

Final Messenger and the Seal of Prophecy ﷺ. He ﷺ was sent to all of mankind.[24] Accordingly, the punishment for those who reject him and his message will not be local, but global—the eschaton. May Allah save us from the cataclysmic calamities of the Last Day!

DID YOU KNOW?

While there will be believers who witness the Major Portents of the Hour (*'Alāmāt al-Sā'āh al-Kubrā*), there will not be any left when Allah seizes the heavens and the earth. The Prophet ﷺ said: "The Hour is only realised upon the worst of mankind." Reported by Muslim (2949).

The trials and tribulations of the worldly life can truly be severe. So much so that they often almost bring us to a breaking point. However, if the story of Yūsuf ﷺ teaches us anything, it is to never give up hope in Allah ﷻ. What we have is but a tiny pixel. Allah ﷻ has woven a splendid tapestry, if only we could see! He ﷻ says: "Do you suppose that you will enter the Garden without first having suffered like those before you? They were afflicted by misfortune and hardship, and they were so shaken that even their messenger and the believers with him cried, 'When will Allah's help arrive?' Truly, Allah's help is near."[25] Indeed, we testify that Allah's help and His victory are near!

On his promise of victory and salvation, Allah ﷻ says:

- "Allah has made a promise to those among you who believe and do good deeds: He will make them successors to the

24 See, for example, Q 34:28.

25 *al-Baqarah*, 214.

land as He did those who came before them, He will empower the religion He has chosen for them, and He will grant them security to replace their fear."[26]

- "Verily we have written in the Scripture, after the Reminder: My righteous slaves will inherit the earth."[27]
- "Our Word has already come to pass in favour of Our servants, the messengers; that they surely will be helped; and that Our host, they surely will be the victors."[28]

On our responsibility to achieve His promise, Allah ﷻ says:

- "You who believe, if you are mindful of Allah, He will bestow unto you profound providence."[29]
- "Do not lose heart and do not grieve, and you are the uppermost if you are [true] believers."[30]
- "You who believe, take care of your own selves. The one who has gone astray cannot harm you if you are on the right path."[31]

TRANSFORMATIVE WISDOM

We do not control the events we encounter. We control only how we react to them. As the Prophet ﷺ advised us all: "Say, 'I believe', then be upright!" Reported by Muslim (38).

26 *al-Nūr*, 55.
27 *al-Anbiyā'*, 105.
28 *al-Ṣāffāt*, 171-173.
29 *al-Anfāl*, 29.
30 *Āl 'Imrān*, 139.
31 *al-Mā'idah*, 105.

This is the immense value of these qur'anic narratives. They inspire within us hope and resilience. They make us appreciate our context in the human story and realise our place in the world we live in. They allow us to perceive matters with the eye of the heart before the eye of the head. Through these stories, we become transformed, divinely-oriented slaves of the Merciful, taking as our models the best of creation, and becoming, as they were, beacons of faith and guidance for all of mankind.

May Allah guide us and guide by us, forgive our shortcomings, and gather us with our role models in eternal bliss: the prophets, the truthful, the martyrs, and the righteous!

Allah ﷻ knows best.

May peace and blessings be upon Prophet Muḥammad,
his family, and his companions.

Praise be to Allah, Lord of the Worlds.